MINOTAUR

MINOTAUR

French Military Justice and the Aernoult-Rousset Affair

John Cerullo

NORTHERN ILLINOIS UNIVERSITY PRESS

DeKalb

Published by the Northern Illinois University Press, DeKalb, Illinois 60115

Design by Shaun Allshouse

Library of Congress Cataloging-in-Publication Data
Cerullo, John J., 1949–
Minotaur : French military justice and the Aernoult-Rousset affair / John Cerullo.
p. cm.
Includes bibliographical references and index.
ISBN 978-0-87580-433-0 (clothbound : alk. paper)
1. Courts-martial and courts of inquiry—France—History—20th century. I. Title.
KJV7568.C47 2010
343.44'0143—dc22
2010019102

TO SHAWN *Simply the best*

Contents

Acknowledgments

Writing this book has been one of the most exciting experiences of my life. Compiling this list of acknowledgments has been one of the most humbling. In recalling just how many people contributed to this project, and how vital those contributions were, I have been reminded of something I thought I had known but apparently had forgotten: there is no such thing as solitary creation.

I'll begin with the invaluable assistance provided me by my university and college. A grant from the University of New Hampshire's Center for the Humanities enabled me to begin writing this book, in the spring of 2008. A sabbatical granted by my own college, UNH–Manchester, enabled me to finish the following fall, just as prior sabbaticals had enabled me to research it. I have spent my entire academic career at UNH–Manchester, and I am enormously grateful for that privilege. It is a place where "collegiality" is more than a word.

At the beginning of this undertaking, I received crucial help with French translations from Ed Dobe, one of the college's language instructors. Later, I received invaluable criticism and feedback on early drafts (*several* drafts, that is) from a number of colleagues and friends at the college: Dan Reagan, Jack Resch, and Terry Savage. "I also received wonderful conversation and counsel from Jeff Haight; and Karla Vogel's patience with a techno-dolt went way beyond the call of duty. And I was supported every step of the way by college administrators Pete Haebler, Karol LaCroix, Dan Reagan, and Kristin Woolever.

I owe special thanks to the faculty and staff of Oudens Library at UNHM. My debt to Ginger Borase and Cindy Tremblay, in particular, is simply incalculable.

Colleagues and friends at UNH's main campus were enormously helpful, as well. I'm deeply grateful for political scientist John Kayser's feedback and ongoing support. I'm grateful, as well, for what faculty and administrators in UNH's Justice Studies program—Ellen Cohn, Charles Putnam, Kevin Souza, Ted Kirkpatrick—gave me, which was more than they themselves may realize. In inviting me to direct the Justice Studies Budapest Program in the fall of 2007, they gave me the opportunity to reflect on the basic themes of this book and to test my ideas in discussion with an absolutely splendid set of students. I will never forget that experience, or what those students did for me.

This study was really motivated by a deep fascination with the nexus of law and politics, a fascination I developed during my year as a visiting scholar at Boston College Law School. If I have thought with anything resembling lucidity on that subject, I owe it to the outstanding teacher/scholars I met there: Charles "Buzzy" Baron, Catharine Welles, Neil Hecht, Dan Kanstroom, and Scott Fitzgibbon. I was also fortunate enough to meet Michel Troper at BC Law, whose encouragement and suggestions were vital as I began entering into the study of French legal thought and practice.

I am grateful, also, to a wonderfully supportive set of friends and mentors in the larger world of historical scholarship, French and other. Wendy Perry provided crucial assistance at a crucial juncture, without which the study would not have proceeded. It would certainly never have been completed without the support and counsel of Bill Irvine, whose encouragement was invaluable. Chris Forth also provided support at particularly important moments, and Paul Miller epitomized the term "gentleman and scholar." Finally, my two oldest and best friends from graduate-school days at the University of Pennsylvania, Dale Light and Dan Sipe, both provided detailed, high-quality feedback on the manuscript. I am deeply grateful to both—for that, and for some thirty-five years of friendship.

I simply cannot say enough about the skill and dedication of the archivists, librarians, and scholars who assisted me in France: at the *Archives Nationales;* the *Bibliothèque Nationale;* the *Préfecture de Police de Paris*; and especially at the *Service Historique de Défense* archives, in Vincennes. It was Madame Claude Ponnou of the *SHD* who located the judicial dossier of Émile Rousset—the key to this entire study. M. Jean-Paul Bodin, Archival Director of the Ministry of Defense, then granted me permission to examine it. I owe a great deal, as well, to Commandant Gérard Croutte, of the *Section justice militaire* at Vincennes, who not only provided me with invaluable secondary sources but gave unstintingly of his time as a sounding board for my ideas. And I benefited enormously from conversation with historian Michel Cordillot, who challenged my thinking at a time when it needed to be challenged.

I want to express special appreciation to personnel at CPEDERF (Paris) for the many varieties of help they provided over the many years this study has extended. This splendid organization offers a range of services to scholars and others with business in France; and I availed myself of nearly all of them, at one time or another. To co-director David Bancroft and to staff members Julia McLaren, Bronwen Pugsley, and Amandine Agic I will simply say: this book would not have happened without you.

Nor would it have happened without the support of two very special French friends. I will not forget Virginia Dae's many kindnesses toward a stranger in Paris, or her encyclopedic knowledge of the city. And what Imelda and Pierre Gaudissart have given me is just impossible to exaggerate. Their hospitality, their conversation, their encouragement—in a word, their friendship—sustained this study more directly and tangibly than they will ever know. It has been a pleasure and a privilege to know them, and their family.

In fact, personal relationships have provided no less vital forms of support in this undertaking than grants, sabbaticals, or any other form of institutional assistance. I will therefore conclude by mentioning the most vital.

There is, always, the memory of my parents, whose gifts were and remain foundational. There is the memory of Jack Reece, of Penn, who introduced me to the drama of French history. There is my brother, Len, and my sister, Carol, and their families, all of whom I cherish. There is the delightful family into which I have been fortunate enough to marry, the Finnegans.

Above all there is my wife, Shawn—who loved me enough to tolerate my long absences in Paris and to see me through the difficult times. I simply do not have the words to express what I feel when I think of what she has given me.

MINOTAUR

Introduction

On the evening of July 2, 1909, an obscure French soldier named Albert Aernoult was found dead in a cell of the military penal camp of Djennan-ed-Dar in Algeria. Earlier that day Aernoult had endured a special punishment detail in a sandy courtyard (the "Court of Miracles") reserved for such things at that camp. According to officers, he had been healthy enough at the conclusion of his punishment, later dying unexpectedly of a stroke. Fellow prisoners, however, told a very different story. By their account, Aernoult had been beaten to death by the officers who had conducted his punishment detail. One of those prisoners, Émile Rousset, would try to amplify that claim by raising it before a court-martial he deliberately provoked.

French antimilitarists would rally behind Rousset, generating that distinctive set of events by which particular incidents (often juridical in origin) are periodically elevated to the status of grand public *aAffaires* in France: impassioned public demonstrations, heated editorial comment, gripping ancillary trials, tense parliamentary exchanges. This particular tumult had more than the usual quota of twists and turns. A particularly dramatic one was Rousset's own indictment for murder in August 1911 at another Algerian camp—whereupon the entire matter took on special urgency for both his defenders and his prosecutors.

The Aernoult and Rousset cases would take very winding paths toward resolution. Yet the basic question they raised was straightforward from the very beginning. They called the theory, structure, and practices of French military justice to public account. That "exceptional jurisdiction" administered by the army had been the subject of intense debate long before these particular cases came to public attention. In fact, the controversy over military justice had reached a boiling point in the aftermath of the Dreyfus Affair: some twenty-one proposals for its reform had been brought before the legislature between 1899 and 1909. This was a quintessentially belle époque controversy, inflected with social and political concerns specific to the time (e.g., the state of the class struggle, the peculiarly exalted status of the French army). But its roots reached back to earlier periods, and its implications extend to our own.

Those roots lay in the history and, especially, the organization of French military justice. The "exceptional jurisdiction" was not some barbaric relic of the *Ancien Régime*, as some critics charged. On the contrary, no unitary, separate military jurisdiction—special laws, courts, and prisons devoted exclusively to regulating the internal order of the military—had existed before the onset of the great revolution in 1789. In fact, the army's "exceptional jurisdiction" was at first deeply imprinted with revolutionaries' new, enlightened juridical standards, which included close monitoring by the civilian political order.

By the time of the system's full and formal instantiation in 1857, however, most of that revolutionary-era heritage had been shed. The officers who actually administered military justice had by then secured an immunity to political intrusions (and public oversight) that was genuinely remarkable in a nation where the idea of judicial independence would be deeply mistrusted well into the twentieth century. That immunity was secured under the general terms of a tacit civil-military compact that had evolved over the course of the nineteenth century, as France embarked on her own long, often violent path to full democracy. Basically, that compact amounted to civilian political authorities' conferral on the army of a privileged role within the state, including a grant of near total autonomy regarding its own internal operations, in return for the army's willingness to defend the regime from domestic insurgents as well as foreign enemies. Not surprisingly, this arrangement grew increasingly problematic as democracy and the principle of state accountability to citizens rooted themselves. With the apparent consolidation of the Third Republic around the end of the nineteenth century, something resembling a paradigm shift in overall civil-military relations seemed to be in the offing. That shift was denoted by the catchphrase "*L'Armée, c'est la Nation*" ("The Army is the Nation"). The essential idea was that the army was to be folded more fully into the nation; its institutions and practices, including those of military justice, were to be reconfigured to mirror more closely modern republican notions of what the nation stood for. To all appearances, the French army's days of isolation and unaccountability were nearing an end—and to fin de siècle French leftists in particular, that was a heartening prospect.

To them, the entire civil-military compact had been an engine of class oppression from the beginning. In light of the army's interventions in the revolutions of 1830, 1848, 1871, and in scores of lesser disturbances since then, they could hardly have thought otherwise. Their animus against military justice, in particular, ran deep. Indeed, when Socialist deputy and journalist Gustave Rouanet described the military jurisdiction as a "judicial minotaur" in early 1907, he didn't need to elaborate the analogy.[1] Most readers, he knew, would understand.

With its human body and bull's head, the mythological minotaur was a freakish admixture of the familiar and the monstrous—quite like the military jurisdiction, in critics' eyes. Its courts might resemble ordinary courts; its judges might speak like ordinary judges; the law they administered might issue from more or less the same sources as ordinary law. But to leftists, the animating spirit of military justice was bestiality itself: unbounded cruelty and capriciousness, specifically designed to break working-class conscripts to the will of the bourgeois state. The minotaur of myth had a savage appetite for the youth of Athens, delivered by city elders to the beast's nominal keeper, King Minos of Crete. And the weird abomination that was French military justice now consumed young French workers just as pitilessly. In fact, argued leftists, working-class French youth were now betrayed by their elders just as unconscionably as Athenian youth had been by theirs, and out of a similarly unholy regard for the beast's master—in this case, the French army itself.

Defenders of the military jurisdiction had an altogether different view. They shared leftists' perception of military justice as a hybrid form; ordinary law and ordinary judicial procedures, defenders recognized, had indeed been reconfigured to serve the extraordinary requirements of military discipline.

But while leftists contended that subordinating legal forms to military purposes debased the very idea of law, many champions of the jurisdiction argued just the opposite. They claimed that military justice represented an elevated brand of justice precisely for having prioritized discipline and authority over and above the rights and liberties around which the civilian code revolved. That taurine head of the minotaur—the specifically military dimension of military justice—was to them its beauty, not its shame.

Military justice, argued its supporters, was structured around duty, not personal license; service to the fatherland, not security of property. Clearly, it was anything but arbitrary. Its procedures were superbly inflexible precisely because the brand of justice they delivered was superbly elemental. If the cleansing and ennobling quality of military discipline was so little appreciated in the civilian world, it was because of the appalling moral decline that had overtaken that world in recent decades. What was absolutely crucial, then, was that the Rouanets of France—the Socialists and their allies, the entire array of political forces now banging at the doors of the military jurisdiction and demanding it be remade in the image of civilian law—be resisted.

But to the oracles of military justice, the challenge was actually much deeper. It wasn't just Socialists, or any particular set of political actors, who must be kept at bay. It was "politics" itself—the activity, the process denoted by the term. The ceaseless partisan strife, the anarchic contest of factions motivated by nothing beyond narrow, material interests, was the surest solvent of military order, discipline, and honor. It must therefore be denied any foothold, any avenue of entry into the military jurisdiction, the integrity of which simply could not survive its encroachments. To preclude those encroachments, to keep the entire world of "politics" at bay, the designers of French military justice had placed a formidable wall between the jurisdiction and the elected branches of government (parliament, cabinet ministries).

The entire Aernoult-Rousset agitation constituted a sustained assault on that wall—and herein lies its relevance for us today. For this Affair was essentially a test of both the practical feasibility and the philosophical viability of a basic and still highly significant juridico-moral proposition: that a particular juridical realm—a particular body of law, and the institutions specially designed to administer it—must be sealed utterly from the corrupting influence of "politics"; that whatever bridges serve to link other components of the legal order to the political universe from which they issued must, in this instance, be burned. For in this particular instance, a moral cornerstone of the entire society is at stake.

This proposition has lost none of its relevance. In fact, the seismic political events of the intervening century have rendered it ever more attractive, while (or perhaps *by*) shifting its general ideological connotations—conservative in the past, "progressive" now. We hear its echoes in certain debates in international law, such as those over the principle of "universal jurisdiction" and the International Criminal Court: champions of each labor tirelessly to construct and sustain jurisdictions that cannot be held hostage to the internal political dynamics of particular nation-states. We hear those echoes in the ongoing controversy over the "rights revolution" that has marked Western jurisprudence in recent decades: its defenders insist strenuously that political considerations be forever extruded from the allocation of rights they deem integral to human dignity itself. We hear the same echoes, in fact, whenever we are told that particular legal codes and/or jurisdictions represent the apex of civic morality and must therefore be more rigorously preserved than other legal quarters from the hard grasp of the *demos.*

Odd as it may seem, in formally juridical terms (i.e., divested of specific political agendas), the progressive position on these issues differs little from that taken by militarists who worked so hard to isolate France's "exceptional jurisdiction" from the political universe in the decades before World War I. This really shouldn't be so surprising. The idea that certain jurisdictions bear a special moral function and must not be made to suffer even light and indirect exposure to exogenous political currents is strong enough to attract adherents on both right and left. It is hardly an ignoble proposition, after all.

Yet it is also hardly an uncontested one. Scholarly debate over the proper relationship between the juridical and political realms, between "law" and "politics," extends back at least to Plato and shows no sign of ending.[2] Establishing clear lines of demarcation between those realms is notoriously difficult; nearly all analysts acknowledge the inevitability of a substantial interface. But whether the interests of "justice" are best served by minimizing that interface or by admitting it in particular circumstances, or even by expanding it, is a question that continues to generate profound reflections on the meaning of law itself. The literature is so rich precisely because the issue is so multivalent—and so vexing.[3] For even as we understand that elisions between these worlds are inevitable and sometimes even salubrious, we also recognize necessary disjunctions, clashes, and even outright antitheses between the fluid, contingent, opportunistic dynamics characterized as "political" and the fixed, routinized, and (hopefully) principled procedures conjured by the term "law." How, when, and where should the boundaries be set? How stringently should they be maintained? The premise of this book is that the Aernoult-Rousset Affair can provide a vehicle for deeper reflection on this fundamentally philosophical question.

To be sure, parts of this story seem germane to more immediate, pragmatic considerations as well, especially for Americans. At this time, any inquiry touching on basic principles and operations of military justice, even those of a distant time and place, appears topical in light of our own, contemporary debates over the role of special military commissions and tribunals in adjudicating certain allegations of terrorism. Here, caution must be exercised. The contemporary American consideration of these questions revolves around very different axes than did the debate over military justice in belle époque France. For us, the most burning issue is how American military justice will treat non-nationals, including civilians and individuals of shadowy, crypto-military status; for the French, the issue was how military justice would treat French citizens, ever vigilant of legal equality and protective of hard-earned republican rights. It would be a mistake to exaggerate what the Aernoult-Rousset Affair can bring to our understanding of the most specific procedural and organizational questions confronting our own military jurisdiction. Yet lessons there definitely are—lessons of a more general order, on things of enduring importance for any and all "special" jurisdictions.

One of them, I submit, involves the perils of legalistic overreach, or a disdain by representatives of a particular jurisdiction for the political realm that is so deep as to become self-defeating in the end. Basically, the argument I wish to make here is that defenders of French military justice clung to an ideal of political insularity that, especially after the Dreyfus Affair, should have been reconsidered; and that the jurisdiction—and, more significantly, France—paid a real, albeit not immediately obvious, price for that intransigence. The system's supporters succeeded in blocking nearly all of the many reform proposals put forward after the Dreyfus Affair by those committed to holding military justice more accountable to the society the army defended. But that reformist element could not be made simply to fade away. Rather, it turned from the parliamentary arena to the streets, and the result was the no-holds-barred public agitation that coalesced around Albert Aernoult and Émile Rousset. The opprobrium and reversals the Aernoult-Rousset Affair brought upon the military jurisdiction were the direct result of its own supporters' stubborn resistance to even the modest, calibrated openings to the civilian juridical and political universe proposed earlier.

Yet it will also become clear by the end of this study that this analysis is not exactly incontestable. In fact, the ultimate meaning of the Aernoult-Rousset Affair cannot be captured in any simple, single political or juridical prescription. For there are surprises aplenty here, and the final outcome of the entire matter was anything but clear-cut. Its deepest lessons, I believe, must be determined by readers themselves. I hope they will follow the many twists and turns of this strange story just as contemporaries did—that is, experiencing the same sensation of assumptions undercut that partisans on both sides must have felt at various points along the way. By the conclusion, I know that readers will have formed their own ideas regarding whether—at least in these particular cases—the intrusion of "politics" in fact illuminated or occluded the truth, and whether it advanced or distorted justice.

For in the end, what the Aernoult-Rousset Affair demonstrates most effectively is that the nexus of law and politics was as maddeningly complex then and there as it is here and now.

"L'Armée, c'est la Nation"

Surveying the state of the French army and its relationship to the nation at the beginning of the twentieth century, General Jules Bourelly did not like what he saw.[1]

The army was an institution Bourelly had known and loved for a long time. Born into a military family in 1853, he was an estimable soldier-scholar who had fought in both the Italian campaign of 1859 and the Franco-Prussian War of 1870–1871, and then written books about each.[2] His study of Abraham de Fabert, France's first plebeian marshal, had been honored with the Thérouanne Prize by the *Académie Française*, and he had gone on to publish specialized works on subjects ranging from comparative military history to contemporary strategy and tactics (while rising to the rank of brigadier general in 1893 while rising to the rank of brigadier general in 1893).[3] By 1902 he was one of the most prolific and respected commentators on military matters in France, with *Le Correspondant de Paris* his preferred vehicle for communicating with the general public.

So when General Bourelly devoted a lengthy article in that journal to the controversial proposition that "*L'Armée, c'est la Nation,*" or the assertion of "an intimate union that must or should reign between the army and the nation," his words carried real weight.[4] Bourelly was convinced the idea was a pernicious one and he argued his case with passion and skill.

To Bourelly France's civilian and military worlds were not only separate but almost ontologically distinct realms. *La Nation* was a political reality, its laws and institutions the arenas where particularistic groupings sought to advance specific, immediate, generally material interests. There was nothing inherently ignoble about that world; it was where human aspirations for material betterment, social status, and personal liberty found their necessary outlets. But *L'Armée* was something else, something higher and finer and all too often misunderstood by outsiders. To Bourelly the army was neither the grand fraternal lodge that some of its champions imagined nor the tribe of brutes excoriated by its critics. To be sure, it was the nation's servant and would kill when the nation required it to kill. But those who knew the institution intimately understood that killing was only its secondary function—even though an acute consciousness of the inescapability of pain and death was integral to its primary one.

The army's real *raison d'être* was the preservation of a certain moral state, a condition that could only exist among those for whom pain and death were omnipresent and viscerally appreciated realities. It was a kind of egoless asceticism that Bourelly, like many others, labeled "the military spirit." The general was careful to distinguish that spirit from both "*esprit de corps*" and "*esprit de guerrier.*"[5] Civilians often reduced the military spirit to the camaraderie of the barracks, or to a sort of swaggering personal belligerence. Actually, the real thing was neither. Men genuinely imbued with the military spirit were men who had made "a pact with honor," a hard and demanding pact. For honor was born of precisely those deprivations, fears, and torments that civilians made every effort to circumvent. In the army ordeals had to be confronted, and honor was the reward men earned by enduring them with a measure of grace. Those who did would never again prize the comforts and liberties of the civilian world quite so highly. Instead, they would prioritize personal courage, and a patriotism unsullied by material interests. Indeed, only men who had fully internalized the military spirit could rise above the pettiness of the civilian world, spurn its cacophony of contending factions and ideologies, and embrace an "absolute devotion to the flag, which is the emblem, not of such or such form of government, but of the common fatherland, of France."[6] They were French in a way that other Frenchmen could never really be.

Bourelly's depiction of the army as a sort of monastery within which the follies and corruptions of the civilian world were kept at bay was hardly new. As early as 1855, General Gaston Gallifet and War Minister Eugène Lamy had described the military spirit in terms that might just as easily have denoted early Christian anchorites. To them, that spirit demanded "the annihilation of all those rebellions which occur in man against the imperatives of suffering and sacrifice . . . the voluntary death of will, in which obedience alone survives."[7] Nor was the idea that military life represented a superior moral model confined to military spokesmen. In the late 1880s the celebrated novelist Anatole France had declared that "if there is anything that is sacred in human society, agreed upon by all, it is the army."[8] A generation later attorney and journalist Gaetan Moisand could still portray the army as "a necessary organization" not because it defended France's frontiers but because it served as "a school of discipline and order," indeed, the only institution where personal honor was "elevated to the level of a cult." In fact, Moisand argued that the point of military service was mainly the inculcation of that quality. He proposed that "*military obligation* has no goal other than giving each citizen a *military education*," and that education "must be complete: moral as well as physical."[9]

But as General Bourelly considered that linkage between the world of soldiers and that of citizens, between monastery and secular society, he was troubled. Their mutual dependence was a simple truism. But sustaining a right and proper relationship with the nation was more difficult for the army now than it had been in, say, Gallifet's and Lamy's day. For by the turn of the twentieth century the nation was riddled by pathogens that had been barely visible in those men's prime, invaded everywhere by the "egoism, the immoderate love of well-being, contempt for authority, and class hatreds" that characterized modernity. That's why Bourelly would have no truck with the notion that either the army's practices or the ethos that animated them should somehow be brought into closer proximity with those that prevailed outside the barracks. Only the ill-informed Bourelly felt, ever described the army as "the nation incarnate." Indeed, to him nothing could have been further from the truth. The army might not even survive an "intimate union" with the nation as it stood in 1902. On the contrary, "The military spirit finds in the army the elements that suit its self-development; it is not communicated from the nation to the army; rather, it is weakened when the nation becomes the army, or even disappears entirely."[10]

Bourelly framed with admirable acuity a problem that a great many military men of his time—and not just in France—had pondered. How could "the school of order, of morality, of discipline, of respect for authority" that was the army serve a nation that was itself increasingly disorderly, divided, and licentious?[11] How could the army place its collective life and honor at the disposal of the nation, while inoculating itself from the toxins the nation now carried? In France the question was particularly complex because the French army was affixed to a state—since 1871, the democratic Third Republic—that, precisely for being more responsive to popular currents than Europe's more authoritarian regimes, tended more than they did to gather, amplify, and transmit to the army all the diseases to which modern society had fallen prey.

To Bourelly one word denoted that penetration of civilian norms and priorities into military settings. "Politics," in the deepest and broadest sense, was the enemy. It had always been the enemy. It was a problem that transcended both party and ideology. Those were carriers, not sources, of the sickness. All parties, all ideologies, all vehicles for the expression of "political" interests were dangerous in their own, varying ways.

Indeed, Bourelly's antipathy to the "politicization" of military culture and organization was not at all reducible to reactionary or reflexively antidemocratic sentiment. Nor, for that matter, was *Le Correspondant de Paris* a reactionary publication (it was directed by Étienne Lamy, son of the former war minister and a Catholic who had chosen to heed the Vatican's recent counsel to bridge the historic divide between the church and republican France). To be sure, Bourelly's commentary in that journal identified the single most objectionable brand of politics as that practiced by democrats who refused to exempt the army from their campaign to render all state institutions fully transparent and accountable. Yet he was also perfectly aware that when authoritarians and conservatives had controlled the state, they too had been dismayingly willing to subordinate the special organizational needs of the army to alien, narrowly political imperatives.

In 1818, Bourelly noted disapprovingly, the restored Bourbon regime had ended universal military service simply out of a desire to secure political acceptance from an exhausted populace. The lottery system they had introduced, with its seven-year term of service for those selected, had seemed adequate when the state's military commitments were minimal (e.g., during the invasion of Spain in 1823). But this prioritization of political exigencies would bear poisoned fruit later in the century, from which France would nearly perish. Fully aware that his own political fortunes were tied to the well-being of the middle classes, Napoleon III had not only retained the lottery system but had eased the way for bourgeois youth to buy their way out of military service. Using those payments to bestow extra pay and benefits on reenlisting veterans, he created an army of "Old Soldiers"—

grizzled veterans to whom the emperor was prepared to entrust the fate of the nation. In fact, those "Old Soldiers" were a kind of glorified praetorian guard drawn from the lower social orders, hardly up to the brand of warfare the Prussian *Landwehr* would visit upon it in 1870.[12]

Indeed, General Bourelly was filled with admiration for the military acumen of the First Republic, which, after constituting itself in 1792, had inaugurated perhaps the most glorious era in French military history. The Third Republic likewise earned a nod of approval from Bourelly for its approach to military organization—at least at its inception. The general noted the willingness of the Third Republic's founders to put "politics" aside, however grudgingly, and lay at least the foundations for an army worthy of the name. That had been no mean feat. It was one thing, amid the disaster of the Franco-Prussian War, to recognize the need for military reorganization. Deciding on its terms was another matter entirely. Left-liberal republicans, impressed by Prussia's military prowess, had urged emulation of her system of compulsory and universal conscription, noting that it had been inspired by France's own "*levée en masse*" under the First Republic. More conservative elements were ill-disposed, after the trauma of the Paris Commune, toward "putting a gun on the shoulder of every socialist," as Thiers put it.[13] They preferred a modified version of the old model, a more professionalized and better led volunteer or lottery-selected force. In the end, the principle of universal service was endorsed—partially, haltingly, but palpably.

In 1872 the new National Assembly agreed after extensive debate on a compromise measure mandating a five-year term of service, with a rather generous set of exemptions (priests, seminarians, and university students; sole supporters of extended families; the physically handicapped). Financial limitations, as well as conservatives' political concerns, would prevent the state from actually holding the entire conscript class under arms for an entire five-year term. So a lottery system reduced the term of service to one year for a fortunate subset of conscripts; and the legal option of buyouts for a portion of whichever term the lottery had devolved remained open to all, and much used. The principle of obligatory and universal service was thus much diluted in practice. Nevertheless, that principle had been broached, as had another that Bourelly found even more vital. This was the idea that the French army must be built in such a way as to advance the day of reckoning with Germany, and not merely to preserve a peace of humiliation—even if that meant taking the political risks that so haunted Thiers. In Bourelly's estimation, the men of 1872 had grasped, at least vaguely, the military spirit (aided, no doubt, by the many officers who served in that particular National Assembly). They knew it could not thrive amid formal, institutional acquiescence in defeat and dishonor.[14]

They knew, as well, the importance of preserving that spirit from the corrosive effects of "politics." In fact, in Bourelly's view what was perhaps most commendable about the men who founded the institutions of the Third Republic was their willingness to dampen the political ardor of military personnel, and to diminish the attractiveness of the army as a source of support to politicians, by denying soldiers the right to vote. Legislators on the left worried about a recurrence of the "Caesarism" that two Bonapartes had inflicted upon France, with support from conservative officers. Those on the right feared the beguilements of socialism for working-class conscripts. By whatever path, all recognized that "politics" was inevitably the solvent of the military spirit they sought to cultivate in the new army they were building. In 1872 the disparate parties and factions that had secured places at the parliamentary table had been willing to subordinate their various political agendas to the nation's military, and therefore its moral, health.

Yet Bourelly knew that 1872 was long gone. Tragically, the Third Republic's founders had been succeeded by a generation of pygmies—legislators who had betrayed the vision of their forebears and visited upon the French army something even more corrosive than the Prussian onslaught which had forced it to its knees in 1870. "After the invasion of the Germans," Bourelly wrote in disgust, "we have had that of politics in our military affairs."[15] In the 1880s and 1890s politicians of the center and moderate center-left, buttressed by parliamentary pluralities, had introduced that plague in particularly virulent form. Soldiers had not gained full voting rights; the barracks were not yet the scene of frenzied electioneering. What had happened had actually been bigger and uglier than that: a multifront, aggressive attempt to reconfigure the entire army, institutionally, along ideological lines—to "republicanize" it, to purge it of any potential for actions other than those deemed properly "republican" by properly republican politicians.

Aware of the shakiness of their new republic, those center/center-left parliamentarians had turned their gaze on the army and decided that the vengeful temperament suffusing it correlated all too easily with disfavored political agendas of varied antirepublican, authoritarian hues. These inclinations they found especially rife within the upper echelons of the officer corps and in the service academies.[16] The connection, in fact, was hardly opaque. Some officers intent on settling accounts with Germany were naturally impatient with the palaver and compromise, the political factionalism and naked self-interest, that seemed inherent features of the new parliamentary system. After surviving the witches' brew of Boulangism in the late 1880s, committed republicans concluded that important sectors of the army would remain hotbeds of reaction unless effectively neutralized. They would act with alarming energy on several fronts to achieve that political goal; and these initiatives, in the aggregate, provided the real content of the catchphrase "*L'Armée, c'est la Nation.*"

There was, for instance, the notion that a new "social role"—specifically, a broader educative function—should devolve onto French officers. This idea had actually emerged from the army itself in the writings of republican officers like General Trochu and, especially, Colonel Lyautey. In the March 15, 1891, issue of the *Revue des Deux Mondes,* then-Captain Lyautey had argued (anonymously) that in this era of universal conscription, when the army was composed of men of hugely varying backgrounds, the formation of a truly unified and effective military would be achieved only if officers helped soldiers see beyond their various social and political divisions by educating them about their common heritage and destiny as Frenchmen. Civilian reformers had seized upon the idea—and subtly inflected it. Yes, they proposed, Lyautey was right: most young Frenchmen knew next to nothing of the nation, its ideals, laws, history. For that matter, they knew little of science, arts and crafts; social solidarity, or modern moral values—even of basic hygiene. Should not officers continue the work begun in the republic's expanding network of elementary schools, helping to transform rough peasants into responsible and productive citizens? And would not a *persona* in which solicitude supplanted bellicosity better suit the modern French officer for life in a progressive, republican order? Might not this transformation serve to "humanize" the military vocation, and narrow the gap between its ideals and those of the democracy it now served?

Bourelly scorned the idea that officers could be pressed into service as facilitators of "social renovation" or reconfigured from steely disciplinarians and models of physical bravery into gentle life mentors. The entire noxious notion was a classic example of the transposition of political concerns onto military organization. It originated in the "egalitarian tendency" of modern democracy itself, which Bourelly found perfectly summarized in the phrase "the soldier is the last of the generals, and the general is the first of the soldiers."[17] The army was not the place for "social solidarism," he insisted. It was the place for hierarchy and the voluntary subordination of weak to strong. It was the place for the willing and personal embrace of pain and physical hardship, not paternalistic ameliorations of them. In Bourelly's view, the Third Republic put an increasingly feeble and decadent citizenry in uniform, then asked the army to adapt itself to that citizenry's limitations rather than requiring citizens to assume a military bearing. He could sympathize with many of those enlisted men's plight; often enough, they were victims of the various social and moral plagues raging throughout modern French society and culture. But one didn't invite plague victims into the monastery to nurse them back to health. Rather, one quarantined the monastery from the plague.

What was involved in this confusion of political with military values, Bourelly argued, was not mere domain error. In his view, what reformers really intended was "to transform the moral education of the soldier into a kind of civic education where the glorification of the political regime of the moment is called to take its place more and more fully alongside, and to the detriment of, professional duty." There was no question in Bourelly's mind that these efforts to forge a more benevolent and intimate bond between soldiers and officers masked reformists' "real design, which is to disarm the military power by enervating it."[18] This, ultimately, was where the politicization of military organization must lead—especially (if not exclusively) when the political values involved were those of the left.

Bourelly understood that the left wing of the political spectrum thought very differently than he did about the "military spirit." In their lexicon it was "militarism," and hardly an elevated moral state. In fact, their lively interest in not only the role of officers but in basic strategic, tactical, and organizational questions as well was driven, quite explicitly, by their desire to terminate what they considered an obscene moral atavism. Paradoxically, Bourelly proposed that Socialists and other leftists were advancing this agenda by working to fully universalize military service in France, and to standardize its terms.

Legislators had endorsed that general direction in 1889, when exemptions were reduced and the term of active service was set at three years for all. In 1902 important elements of the loose coalition of leftists (the "*bloc des gauches*") that had ascended to parliamentary power through victory in the Dreyfus Affair were coalescing around a proposal that would finally pass in 1905, when the term of active service was further reduced to two years and all exemptions were eliminated. This general program was often represented in patriotic terms as a return to the glory days of "*la nation armée*" (the nation in arms) of the 1790s, when the principle of civic equality had entailed equal military obligations and the army, immeasurably strengthened by this commitment to social leveling, had miraculously prevailed over a host of foes.[19] But General Bourelly was not deceived. "It was called 'social evolution,' but in reality it was politics, almost all alone, that drove the transformation," he wrote.[20] 1902, Bourelly understood, was not 1792, and the Third Republic was not the First Republic. He knew perfectly well what full equality of military obligations would mean now.

The plain fact was that France could only afford to train, equip, and sustain an army in which all eligible males served simultaneously if they remained in active service for a much-reduced period of time. There would be more troops on hand, but they would be less well trained, armed, and provisioned. To maintain a serious fighting capability, the shortened period of active service would have to be followed by an extended period of reserve duty.

Just how reliant on reserve forces was France's army to be? If reformists had their way, very reliant indeed. But, Bourelly charged, their interests were anything but military. For one thing, reliance on reserves would mean more regional deployment and recruitment, which Bourelly claimed tended to "enervate the command and weaken the military spirit by rendering soldiers' repeated absences inevitable and favoring the intrusion of politicians in military affairs."[21] The more dire implication of greater reliance on reserves, however, was that it would entail a shift from offensive to defensive strategy and tactics. Here, really, was the reformists' endgame: substantially weakening France's inclination to go to war, now or ever, by deliberately rendering her army less dangerous. Bourelly was hardly alone in this assessment. The Catholic-reformist Count de Mun, among many others, decried the entire "nation in arms" concept, arguing that France might well have a "'nation in arms, but she would no longer have an army.'"[22] After all, argued opponents, no special powers of divination were needed to discern the agenda; it had been all too public for years. Even the rather moderate journalist, academic, and politician Jules Simon had been prepared to announce openly, in 1866:

> When I say that the army we want would be an army of citizens and that it wouldn't have in any degree the military spirit, it's not a concession I'm making, it's a declaration that I'm happy to make . . . *it's so that France won't have any military spirit that we want to have an army of citizens* which will

> be invincible at home and beyond the need to bring war outside it. . . . [I]t's precisely to not have an army in the sense that is attached to that word, that is to say an army having the military spirit, that we ask, without equivocations, *to suppress the permanent army and to arm the entire nation.*[23]

The military spirit was thus to be quite deliberately bleached out of the new, reserve-based army of leftist dreams. Thus had the splendid principle of universal military obligation—broached in 1872 by legislators hoping to restore the *élan* France's armed forces had shown in 1792—been co-opted and redeployed to serve pacifistic ends. But the worst was yet to come.

"Among the attempts to fuse the army with the nation," wrote Bourelly, "one of the most dangerous for the future of the army is unquestionably that whose effect would be to substitute in part civil justice for military justice."[24] For reformers had decided that, just as officers should resemble schoolteachers and soldiers should keep one foot in the civilian world, so too should military justice hew more closely to the civilian model. Here, to Bourelly and all those who shared his views, the politics of "republicanization" threatened to still the beating heart of military life, the crucible of honor and of the military spirit itself: discipline.

Courage, sacrifice, honor—all sprang from discipline. Military discipline had always been, must always be, more demanding than anything in the civilian world. It could be sustained only with a special body of law, a special penal code, and special courts to administer them: a separate military jurisdiction, enforcing a separate and specifically military idea of "justice." It was a justice that explicitly subordinated rights and liberties to discipline and duty, consecrating the latter through an institutional structure carefully designed to be "simple in its forms, prompt in its action, and proportionally more severe in its penalties."[25] Military justice must be swifter and harsher for the simple reason that its "exemplary" quality must always be paramount: in considering the individual cases before them, military courts must always prioritize the impact their resolution would have on the maintenance of discipline. As Gaetan Moisand put it, "The least fault committed by military personnel—be it an offense against common law, be it a purely military offense—is necessarily grave: it implies, if it is renewed, a perverse will, dangerous to the spirit of the soldier."[26] Will, the solvent of discipline, must be detected and repressed quickly and effectively—and 'How could civil justice respond, in all circumstances and in the necessary measure, to that imperious obligation?"[27]

The nation understood that the army had necessarily evolved its "own justice, consequence of its existence, of its organization, of its needs and of its mission."[28] But it must further understand that this justice was not a crueler, debased version of the ordinary variety, to be grudgingly tolerated only out of institutional necessity. On the contrary, just as the military spirit represented a higher moral calling and military discipline a finer moral condition, so too was military justice something not just apart from but, if anything, purer than the civilian variety. Military justice was the brand that was "applied to men disposing of the life and the honor of others . . . organized less to punish the guilty than to bring them around to the path of duty, less to avenge society than to preserve it."[29] In this, Bourelly echoed the core conviction of nearly all defenders of the system. It was a conviction fervently held by, for instance, Lieutenant F.M. Alix, who earned his doctorate in law with a thesis arguing that only the severe discipline enforced by military justice could sustain the higher morality required of soldiers, and insisting on an integral connection between that morality and combat effectiveness. "A troop where immorality reigns," he wrote, "where men don't have confidence in one another, is walking fatally toward indiscipline, failure, and often dissolution; armies that have brought back durable success are honest armies, of rigid morals. . . . [M]oral discipline [is] the only real one, without which the other one is just an illusion."[30]

But Bourelly understood that this special body of law, this jurisdiction apart, was no less assailed than other aspects of military organization in the early years of the twentieth century. In fact, military justice was seen by both the army's defenders and its critics as key to the entire question of civil-military relations, with the former determined to maintain and the latter no less determined to dissolve "the judicial barrier between civil society and the military family."[31] For here—more than in the social role of officers, more even than in questions of recruitment and term of service and strategy—the very essence of republicanism was at stake.

The ideal of the citizen to which the civil code and, indeed, the entire institutional structure of the Third Republic paid at least theoretical homage was an autonomous individual, fully capable of participating in the public arena irrespective of his social or economic rank and endowed with neither more nor fewer rights than anyone else. Indeed, the idea of equality before the law was an absolutely foundational value for republicans.[32] It seemed to be violated no less absolutely by the existence of a separate legal jurisdiction, specifically designed to mete out a swifter and more terrible punishment (i.e., an "exemplary" punishment) than that provided through "ordinary" law. Even worse, Frenchmen in military courts had fewer rights and faced harsher penalties than their civilian counterparts in ordinary courts precisely while—in fact, precisely *because*—they were making the greatest sacrifices on their nation's behalf. In an era of near-universal military service, few Frenchmen could remain indifferent to that glaring inequity, or unaware of its cost. Reformers simply asked how any republic worthy of the name could tolerate that lacuna in a republican legal, even constitutional, order. Military justice must be subsumed within, or at least contoured by, the nation's justice; its procedures and penal code must be brought into closer proximity to those of the civilian world. To the degree that "*L'Armée, c'est la Nation*," the army's "exceptional jurisdiction" must be ended, or at least reduced in scale; and what remained of it, partially civilianized.

On the other side, General Bourelly and many others like him were just as determined to sustain that jurisdiction—precisely for its exceptional qualities. In 1899 he had asked the opponents of military justice whether they could really "imagine that the principle of the universality of civil law and the interests of discipline are safeguarded at the same time?" The answer, to him, was obvious: "Like it or not, we sacrifice the former to the latter" in order to maintain an army worthy of the name. Indeed, argued Bourelly, the stakes for the army were nothing less than survival. "To declare forthwith the incompatibility of the military jurisdiction with the laws that regulate the generality of citizens," he concluded, "is as much as to declare forthwith that the army itself exists only in violation of those laws."[33]

With that comment General Bourelly revealed the heart of the matter. He understood perfectly well that to defend military justice was to defend much more than a jurisdiction. It was to defend the entire institution regulated by that jurisdiction, and the special moral code that animated both. It was to defend that code's integrality to France, alongside that institution's. For that was the basis of the argument that this particular legal order, this "exceptional jurisdiction," was entitled to a form of immunity from public oversight that no other public institution could hope to enjoy in a republican civic culture—that it simply could not be publicly monitored or held publicly accountable in the same way that other organs of government, including other judicial bodies, were in France.[34]

General Bourelly understood that he was contending with a broad and deep political current that, by the early years of the twentieth century, seemed well-nigh irresistible. That current announced itself with the slogan

"L'Armée, c'est la *nation*," but to Bourelly the men carrying this project forward were moved by love for neither. They were politicians, and what they stood for was simply the advancement of partisan agendas. To protect themselves and the narrow interests they represented, they intended to "republicanize" (i.e., politicize) the army, and the "reform" (i.e., termination) of a specifically military jurisdiction was key to that agenda.

Yet to Bourelly the enemy was more than a particular political current. It was "politics" itself. In its eternal elevation of the expedient, the contingent, the ephemeral, "politics" was the inevitable enemy of all that was grounded, firm, and enduring—certainly, of the military spirit. Men like Bourelly saw the army as a tabernacle and the military spirit as a sacred flame kept lit only therein. Military justice was the keeper of that flame. From their perspective, the many-headed hydra of "politics" stood poised to invade that tabernacle, kill that keeper, and extinguish that flame.

They did not intend to let that happen.

The Theory and Practice of French Military Justice

One of the most common charges hurled at French military justice by its left-leaning critics was that this "exceptional jurisdiction" harkened back to the ecclesiastical and *seigneurial* courts of the *ancien régime*, where "justice" meant accommodating the special needs and interests of society's most privileged strata. To suggest that military tribunals dispensed a similar brand of justice was to represent them as radically incompatible with republican civic culture and ultimately doomed to fall before the march of republican progress.[1] But informed defenders of the system yawned at the charge. "It is possible that among the adversaries of military justice, some are found who, in order to have another weapon against it, would have preferred that it descend in a direct line from the old regime," sighed General Bourelly; "but there's nothing to that."[2]

As Bourelly understood, the *ancien régime* had sported no uniform code of military law; no unitary system of military courts with clear and distinct competence; no peacetime military jurisdiction whatsoever. For all practical purposes, there had been no real system of military justice under the *ancien régime*. Military justice, such as it was, had pertained entirely to wartime conditions, when legal authority over military personnel implicated in war-related offenses was parceled out to a welter of provosts and high constabularies, themselves answerable to either the royal court or one or another provincial assembly. Not until 1665 were regiments authorized to assemble their own courts, the *conseils de guerre* (literally, "councils of war"), and deal summarily with offenses specifically denoted "military" (e.g., desertion, treason, trafficking with the enemy, sedition, cowardice, insubordination). "Civil" offenses remained under the jurisdiction of various civilian courts.

Penalties meted out by those early *conseils de guerre* were notoriously severe, especially for indecorous behavior toward officers. Assaulting one commonly merited a severed member, followed by hanging. Assaulting even a corporal could bring a lifetime in the galleys. Religious blasphemy might be discouraged by, for instance, tongue-piercings, and indiscipline of a lesser order by corporal punishments ranging from the strappado to a long stretch on a wooden horse with cannonballs attached to the feet. Irons were a comparatively benign option, as was a forced extension of the term of service. No officers, however, were brought before these regimental tribunals. Officers' internecine disputes and the duels to which they gave rise were the concerns of a special *Tribunal du point d'honneur* (Tribunal of the point of honor).[3]

As General Bourelly and other defenders of *belle époque* military justice never tired of pointing out, most essential features of the system were bequeathed to the nation not by benighted absolutists but by the revolutionaries of the 1790s. Its foundations had actually been laid by progressive men, most of them republicans. In general, it was part of the revolutionary effort to replace the cruelty, arbitrariness, and entrenched privileges of the old order with enlightened, constitutional rule in all areas of national life, including its military. In stressing that provenance, defenders of the military jurisdiction hoped to deflect reformers' claims that, as it stood, it was fundamentally incompatible with the republican ethos, thereby denying them their rationale for intruding on and refashioning it.

Those reformers' designation of military justice as an "exceptional jurisdiction," argued General Bourelly, only revealed the depth of their misunderstanding. Justice "is only exceptional if it departs without necessity from the limits in which it ought to be enclosed," wrote Bourelly, whereupon "it becomes the negation of justice." But France's military tribunals hardly eschewed rules and boundaries. On the contrary, they were exquisitely well ordered, and many of the rules they observed could be traced back to the most advanced and liberal thinking of an advanced and liberal era. "Exceptional" justice, Bourelly argued, was what was meted out in times of crisis, often arbitrarily, by *ad hoc* tribunals tasked with eliminating some specific and highly urgent problem (e.g., the military commissions instituted in 1795–1796 to deal with counterrevolutionary Chouans, or those decreed in 1812 to punish unauthorized capitulations). Such proceedings were rightly feared. The army's justice, however, was something else entirely. It was indeed "a consequence of its organization, of its needs, and of its mission." Yet its character was "not that of an exceptional justice but of a *special* justice, which is quite different. . . . Far from contradicting civil justice, it is the auxiliary of it."[4]

But if Bourelly correctly scored some reformers' depiction of French military justice as an artifact of the age of unreason, his own representation of the historical record omitted a great deal. The system's foundations were indeed the work of committed constitutionalists, legalists, and republicans of the revolutionary era. In the end, it was they who contrived to seal military justice from external, unmilitary, political imperatives. Yet on another level, there were few institutions in France more profoundly political than her military tribunals—few on which the complex political experience of the revolution had been more deeply etched, few as tangibly shaped by political circumstances that had emerged then but persisted into the present. The men of the 1790s had, in fact, produced at least three distinguishable systems of military justice in the space of about six years, roughly corresponding to the moderate, radical, and conservative phases through which the revolution lurched in that tumultuous decade. Nothing so clearly suggests the deep imprint of "politics" on French military justice as its mutability during this, its formative period. In fact, the "unpolitical," or unaccountable, character of the final version was itself simply an artifact of the particular political conditions that surrounded it.

The architects of French military justice were nothing if not flexible: testing measures conjured from theory against the shifting configurations of power in both France and Europe, experimenting, reforming, submitting all proposals to the acid test of efficacy. "Liberty, equality, and fraternity" had encapsulated no less shining a moral vision for them than the "military spirit" did for Bourelly. But, at least as regards military justice, they had been much more willing than he to adapt shining moral visions to an imperfect world. They were pragmatists, he a purist. Oddly, it was their pragmatism, their responsiveness to political circumstance, that laid the groundwork for the system that he, in his purism, dreamed of setting beyond the reach of political currents.

From the revolution's inception in the summer of 1789 to the following August, the French army had undergone what one historian has described as "a year of disintegration."[5] Finally, in August 1790, disorders within the military came to a head with a multiregimental mutiny in the garrison at Nancy, inspired by claims that officers were absconding with enlisted men's wages. Repressing the mutiny would require twenty-three death sentences and the disbanding of two whole regiments. It was hardly surprising to members of the National Assembly sitting in Paris that the army's old methods of self-regulation were not working. The old patchwork of overlapping jurisdictions was clearly irrational, the old punishments clearly barbaric, the old estate privileges enjoyed by officers clearly indefensible. Delegates recognized that they could counter incipient anarchy within the ranks only by bringing the rule of law, properly understood, to what had been a functionally lawless world. They would have to create a rational and enlightened system of military justice, where the brute force monopolized by officers would be replaced by equitable rules equally binding on all and invested with moral legitimacy through authorship by the nation's representatives. But determining the content of that law and effectively administering it were not easy tasks.

The army was not like the rest of France, and the National Assembly's delegates knew it. What French society as a whole needed was the full flowering of liberty, equality, and fraternity. What its army required, on the other hand, were discipline and good order, no less under the new constitutional regime than under any other—perhaps even more so. Delegates could see that discipline and good order were likelier to issue from the prompt and severe punishment of transgression. The problem was how to secure that sort of regimen without betraying the revolution's own basic goal of transforming Frenchmen from passive subjects of the king into rights-bearing citizens of the nation. Would the commitment to equality before the law not be hopelessly compromised by the creation of a legal subsystem for the army explicitly designed to prioritize order and discipline over rights and liberties? In short, how to reconcile the lofty goals of the revolution with the institutional needs of the military?

The National Assembly's response was a pragmatic admixture. It announced that the soldier, while indeed a citizen, must accept a "sort of privation of his rights" and the necessity of "passive" obedience while in service.[6] Yet those admissions were offset by new practices and institutions introduced by legislation of September and October 1790, through which the new, progressive brand of justice the National Assembly hoped to bring to the nation as a whole would be only minimally qualified for the army. For most offenses, the vicious punishments of old were eliminated, replaced mainly by some form of prison time. The arbitrary power of officers was tempered by a provision permitting soldiers to bring suit against them for wrongful punishment—a major innovation. Most striking of all were the new *cours martiales* (courts-martial), which were to replace the summary judgments of regimental *conseils de guerre* with proper jury trials. In fact, the courts-martial represented the first attempt to introduce jury trials, explicitly based on the English model, to France. Civilians wouldn't share the procedural rights that the National Assembly devolved on soldiers until the following year.[7]

To ensure thoroughness in deliberations, the designers of the court-martial were willing to accept a rather clunky two-jury system. Complaints were initially brought to a panel of three commissioners, who would then instruct the commanding officer of the unit involved whether to convene a nine-member jury of accusation. If convened, that body would determine whether legitimate grounds to prosecute existed. If so, another nine-member jury of judgment would be empanelled to assess the facts and determine guilt after hearing not only the evidence against the accused but his defense as well. Both those juries were to contain two jurors bearing the same rank as the accused, alongside seven higher grades. The jury of judgment could consider motive as well as fact, effectively entertaining the notion of extenuating circumstances. Whatever finding on guilt the jury reached, final sentencing was reserved for the same panel of commissioners who had initiated the process. Those three could prescribe death only in restricted cases and only through unanimous accord.[8]

Officers were disproportionately represented on the courts-martial, and the requirement that they announce their judgments aloud, starting with the lower ranks, severely diminished the likelihood of truly independent judgment. Defendants had as yet no right of appeal, in order that the system's judgments, once concluded, could be expeditiously, and publicly, enforced. In these ways the legislators of 1790 deferred to the imperatives of hierarchy and celerity as practical means of maintaining discipline. Yet they also recognized the importance of avoiding arbitrariness and respecting the elemental requirements of justice. Perhaps most significantly, the National Assembly took special pains to minimize the scale of the military jurisdiction itself. The courts-martial had no standing in peacetime. In wartime their reach was confined to a set of specified military offenses (e.g., desertion, cowardice under fire, trafficking with the enemy, insubordination), which were explicitly distinguished from civil ones. In fact, the 1790 statute took pains to stipulate publicly that the latter "fall within the scope of ordinary justice, even when they will have been committed by an officer or by a soldier."[9] The legal principle at work was thus *rationae materiae:* the parameters of the jurisdiction were to be determined by the types of offense to be adjudicated, not the type of person involved (the latter sort of system falls under the heading *rationae personae*). In 1790 delegates could still hope that the "privation of rights" military personnel had to undergo might not be too severe, or required beyond the narrow confines of the barracks in wartime.

Those hopes, however, had to be tempered over the next two years. Military disorders seemed to actually widen, as more officers deserted and their replacements struggled to establish authority. A surprised but adaptable National Assembly would modify the 1790 law twice, first in September–October 1791 and again in May 1792. By the latter date war had broken out, and after considerable soul-searching the (Legislative) Assembly prosecuting it decided that the maintenance of discipline would require a substantially more coercive, more streamlined system of military justice than that inaugurated in the hopeful days of 1790.[10] No less than fifteen of twenty-three articles denoting punishments for specific offenses were rewritten to provide the possibility (although not the requirement) of death sentences. At the same time, officers' on-site authority was reinforced in several ways. They were provided with *tribunaux correctionnels* (correctional tribunals), where infractions of discipline less severe than those addressed by courts-martial could be handled summarily by three-man panels.[11] Soldiers' opportunities to hold officers accountable for unfounded accusations were significantly narrowed. Such complaints would be heard only after the penalty had been administered, and only by separate hearing boards composed of officers—who could, if they chose, also *augment* punishment.[12] Yet even while strengthening officers' control over enlisted men, the Assembly was unwilling to return to the days of a privileged officer caste. It reminded them that they were servants, not masters, of the revolutionary state by penalizing them more heavily than their subordinates for some of the same offenses.[13]

By 1793 circumstances had changed yet again, this time far more dramatically. The king was dead, the First Republic had been declared, and elements more radical than those holding power in 1790 were in ascendance. The nation was engaged in armed struggle with both domestic insurgents and foreign powers. This fight was clearly to the death, and the new governing body, the Convention, would undertake it with the most thorough mobilization of eligible manpower and resources the nation had yet seen—the *levée en masse.* The Convention needed both iron discipline and unquestioning loyalty within the army and aimed to secure both by reconfiguring military justice yet again. Legislation of May 12, 1793, ominously declared that it was "the honor as well as the duty of true republicans who defended the fatherland to expel from their ranks all who have tried to corrupt through infidelity, cowardice or treason the purity of the principles that made them act," and that this honor and duty could be fulfilled only by "giving the armies of the Republic some prompt, just, and severe means of delivering the guilty to the blade of the law."[14] The system this language announced was unlike anything that came before or after.

The Convention began by legislating even harsher punishments for military offenses. Of the twenty-nine different varieties of insubordination the 1793 statute specified, eleven were punishable by death.[15] Its most striking innovations, however, concerned the organization and competence of military courts. It began by suppressing the courts-martial in favor of new bodies, the *tribunaux criminels militaires* (military criminal tribunals), and attached two to each army.[16] What was new about those military criminal tribunals was their incorporation of a civilian element, three *juges de paix militaires* (loosely, "military justices of the peace") chosen by the Executive Council of the Convention and confirmed by its Committee of Public Safety. Those civilians, vetted by legislators in Paris, were to be deeply involved in the administration of military justice in the field, their responsibilities overlapping those assigned in the old *cours martiales* to the all-military jury of accusation and to the all-military three-commissioner panels. They were the first auditors of accusations, entitled to determine whether further investigation was warranted. If so, they would add two military men to their own number, one superior and one equal in rank to the accused, and then proceed to a decision on whether military law had been violated and actual prosecution before a tribunal was warranted. If it was, the case would be brought before a nine-man jury of judgment—which, after legislation of *3 pluviôse an II* (Jan. 22, 1794) was a very different one than had been established in 1790. According to that newer legislation, four members of the jury of judgment would also be civilian. All would be selected by the civilian justices, who would also determine the sentence in the event of conviction.

The Convention's work in the area of military justice was complex. On the one hand, it rendered military courts even more distinctively "military" by the draconian character of punishments it prescribed for military offenses. It also granted those courts a broader jurisdictional range. For the duration of the war, the Convention ruled on January 22, 1794, military personnel would face military criminal tribunals for offenses against civil as well as military law, if they were committed within military administrative districts. Civil tribunals retained jurisdiction over both types of offenses when committed by military personnel outside those districts; and the jurisdictional change pertained only to wartime. Nonetheless, it was the Convention that initiated military justice's movement away from the *rationae materiae* principle, toward *rationae personae*—a potentially momentous change heralding precisely the sort of extensive military jurisdiction the men of 1790 had carefully tried to avoid.[17]

Yet the sterner and broader military justice configured by the Convention was also tied more closely to the civilian world than previous versions, indirectly monitored by elected officials. Newly created military justices of the peace served as a tangible conduit back to the Convention itself, and especially to the Committee of Public Safety. In fact, the military criminal tribunals the Convention established for the army functioned not unlike the *tribunaux révolutionnaires* (revolutionary tribunals) the Committee of Public Safety established in the civilian order—and for similar reasons: to submit real, perceived, or even potential enemies of the revolution to the full wrath of the "people's justice"; to purge not only active foes but lukewarm friends; and to forge the nation, both armed and unarmed, into the united, determined, merciless phalanx that alone could triumph over its myriad enemies.[18]

The Convention's system of military justice was thus a highly political product, reflecting both the general ideological orientations of its leaders and the desperate real-world circumstances they faced. Ideologically the new tribunals were said to represent a "democratization" of military justice—a debatable claim although, to the degree that "democratization" entails a measure of social leveling, not an entirely implausible one. The Convention certainly did prioritize the accountability of officers, requiring even generals to answer charges brought by any military personnel or by any civilian attached to the new military criminal tribunals. The stated motive behind this was "to avoid the effects of intrigue and of the influence that these officers could have on the tribunals attached to each army,"[19] that is, to prevent military justice from becoming a self-contained system, with generals and other officers selecting and staffing its courts while remaining unaccountable themselves to representatives of the people.

In practical terms, the Convention undertook its reconfiguration of military justice fully mindful that the instrumentality with which it hoped to defeat both the combined weight of monarchical Europe and a substantial insurgency within France was a "people's army" in ways no other French force had been. Legislators' introduction of ongoing political oversight—even political accountability—of military courts might be interpreted as a pragmatic adaptation to unprecedented pressures and entirely new circumstances. French soldiers were fighting for the first time as citizens, often enough as electors. Indeed, their military effectiveness was by all accounts greatly enhanced by their realization that they were defending rights of their own, not prerogatives of their betters. For reasons both moral and military, military courts could not be allowed to vitiate the meaning of citizenship. The authority of officers in those courts, which had already been strengthened, must not go unmonitored and unchecked lest it regress to *l'arbitraire*. How could that be assured without bringing military tribunals under the gaze of the people's representatives?[20] Defenders of the Convention's reforms could note that under its regimen the morale and fighting effectiveness of the army were sufficient to prevail against what had seemed like hopeless odds.

Critics, of course, would see in those reforms an intolerable politicization of military justice, the intrusion of politicians bearing political agendas into what should be a field of exclusively military judgments. By their reckoning, from its inception French military justice had been built to serve the army's need for discipline and order, not legislators' schemes to advance social egalitarianism or popular empowerment or anything else. To the degree that the system was opened to incursions from the political world, it would be bent to serve political ends and its original purpose necessarily corrupted.

Those critics would find the system's next configuration far more congenial. It was the work of a new government, led by a five-man executive authority called the Directory, which was formally installed with the passage of a new constitution on 5 fructidor de l'an III (August 22, 1795). The nation remained at war, but military circumstances were far more favorable: invaders had been driven from the fatherland, while French forces took the fight to Austria, their remaining Continental adversary. The army was proud and robust—and potentially a highly valuable tool in achieving what the Directory defined as the essential political tasks of the moment within France herself. These included ending the radical phase of the revolution; dismantling the "Terror" the Convention had inaugurated (by replacing it, in some measure, with a conservative or "white" Terror of its own); restoring order and hierarchy to society; and ending the chronic instabilities of revolutionary governance.

In fact, the army was about to become something like the arbiter of the political destinies of the nation, with the Directory's reliance on it increasing. The spring of 1795 witnessed the first deployments of army units against Parisian insurgents. In October the army was mobilized to put down a substantial royalist uprising. Repeatedly used to quash outbreaks, its value to the new government grew precisely as the Directory's own basis of political support in the nation narrowed, with political disaffection deepening on both right and left. In the fall of 1797, with victory over Austria in sight thanks to the successes of General Bonaparte, the army was used to expel royalist deputies elected to provincial assemblies. The elections of 1798 would again return forces hostile to the Directory, and those results were again annulled with the help of the army. By 1799 two Directors were prepared to conspire with Bonaparte to end the charade of democratic government and install the army's most illustrious general in power (this despite the failure of the latter's project to strike at an intransigent Britain through Egypt). Bonaparte's use of troops to expel deputies still loyal to the constitution in the *coup d'état* of November 9, 1799, simply confirmed what had been clear for years. A new era had indisputably dawned in civil-military relations in France. It was the beginning of a long period of active military involvement in the internal life—specifically, the political and social struggles—of the nation.

Unsurprisingly, a new system of military justice had grown up alongside that new civil-military relationship. If under the Convention the pendulum had swung toward a "democratization" of military justice, under the Directory it had swung far in the other direction, toward a system organized to enforce discipline and maintain "the military spirit," with minimal interference from outside and minimal rights granted military personnel on the inside. Given the Directory's growing isolation and reliance on the army to prop itself up, its willingness to gift that vital institution with broadened jurisdiction and effective autonomy for its courts was not without a certain logic.

Once again, the prior regime's tribunals were disbanded and new ones created. Attached to divisions, they were first denoted *conseils militaires* (military councils) and later, in a striking regression to the prerevolutionary nomenclature, *conseils de guerre*. These tribunals were much grander than those created during the revolution's earlier stages, with dramatically enlarged competence. Article 290 of the constitution of 5 fructidor de l'an III (August 22, 1795) stated that "the army of land and sea is submitted to particular laws, for discipline, the form of judgments, and the nature of penalties," while specifically declining to add—as had statutes of 1790, 1791, and 1792—"regarding military offenses." By the omission of that phrase the Directory signaled its intention to elevate fully and unequivocally the *rationae personae* principle over that of *rationae materiae* in the military jurisdiction.[21] That intention would be formally realized through Article 85 of the constitution of 22 frimaire de l'an VIII (September 13, 1799), which stipulated that all military personnel were now justiciable before military councils for any and all offenses, civil or military.

So concerned was the Directory to endow the *conseil de guerre* with a competence befitting its function that for a time even civilians alleged to be complicit in the felonies of military personnel were hauled into military courts. A statute of 1796 ended that particular practice; but the Directory was not so chastened that it would ever restore prior laws holding that, in cases where the same felony was the work of both civilian and military personnel, the civil jurisdiction would obtain. There would be no backtracking. On the contrary, with the legislation of 13 brumaire de l'an V (November 3, 1796)—probably the single most sweeping reform of military justice until 1857—the Directory took the enormous step of extending the jurisdiction of its new tribunals *jusqu'à la paix* (as far as peacetime). That was the first admission of a permanent, peacetime jurisdiction for military courts in French history.[22]

That 1796 legislation also dramatically altered the composition and procedures of military courts, effectively ending jury trials as those bodies had conducted them since 1790.[23] The civilian element introduced into the system by the Convention was abruptly ended, but the Directory didn't stop there. The jury of accusation itself was disbanded, its auditory and investigative functions devolved onto military *rapporteurs* (investigators) who were attached to the permanent court and appointed by the divisional commander. That commander also appointed the officer serving as *commissaire du pouvoir exécutif* (commissioner of executive power), who prosecuted cases brought to the jury of judgment. The divisional commander was now, in fact, the real oracle of military justice. It was he who decided which cases would proceed to a jury of judgment and which representatives of the various ranks prescribed by law would sit on that jury.

The jury itself was trimmed from nine to seven members, and the specification of ranks eligible to serve was permanently fixed to exclude all but the defendant's superiors. The juridical principle that the assessment of facts be separate from the determination of culpability and appropriate sentence, and entrusted to different personnel, was abandoned. Henceforth, the same panel that determined the truth of the case also determined punishment in the event of conviction. Yet despite the importance of their work, military juries were provided with surprisingly few binding procedural guidelines. The trial's direction was essentially left to the officer serving as president of the jury.

Gross violations of form could draw the attention of a newly created appeals court, the *conseil de révision*. But only such procedural violations could serve as grounds for appeal, never the jury's assessment of the evidence, its determination of guilt, or sentence—never, in short, the justice of its conclusions. If, for instance, the *conseil de guerre* had been incorrectly constituted, or some other grave procedural error occurred in a *conseil de guerre* proceeding, the appeals court could immediately remand the case to a second *conseil de guerre* also attached to the division. But, since it was deemed vitally important that the entire matter be concluded as expeditiously as possible, appeals courts were not inclined to intervene.[24] Nor was appeal beyond military courts to a civilian appellate tribunal a viable option. The Directory did endow the civilian judicial system with a high court of appeals, the *Tribunal de cassation* (literally, the "annulment tribunal"). It could quash lower-court judgments and require a retrial when law or procedural form had been egregiously violated. But Article 77 of the enabling legislation denied military personnel the right to appeal judgments of military tribunals in civilian appellate court. In the end, wrote one student of the system, "in the absence of precise rules as to their functioning and procedure, revision was still an illusory formality, abandoned to the caprices of chance."[25]

With the reforms of the Directory, celerity, hierarchy, and discipline had been definitively elevated over deliberative caution, defendants' rights, and equitability in French military justice. Moreover, juridical autonomy had triumphed resoundingly over political accountability. First under the consulship that Napoleon dominated and then under the empire he ruled, those priorities were deepened and extended to the numerous special tribunals now attached to units below the divisional level for summary judgments of cases outside the purview of the *conseils de guerre* themselves. These included cases involving prisoners of war, varieties of espionage, and military relations with civilian populations, all of which expanded enormously amid the nearly constant warfare of the Napoleonic period.[26]

French military justice had begun with a grudging admission that an army in combat will inevitably experience a few carefully defined situations where relief from ordinary civilian legal norms must be temporarily and narrowly granted. By the advent of the First Empire in 1804, it had evolved into an extensive legal subsystem that unashamedly departed from the basic principles of jurisprudence prevailing in the civilian sphere. It had become a separate juridical universe indulged by the state, where discipline was permanently prioritized over rights and liberties. Yet it was not clear at the time that the new configuration of the military jurisdiction would be permanent.

Oddly enough, the ever enigmatic Napoleon expressed a paradoxical interest in scaling it back by reviving the *rationae materiae* principle—at least provisionally, or when practical. "Justice is one in France," he observed; "one is a French citizen before being a soldier." The emperor's view was that "if, in the interior, one soldier assassinates another, he has doubtless committed a military crime, but he has also committed a civil crime. All offenses must be submitted first to the common jurisdiction whenever it is present."[27] As it happened, this sentiment was abandoned in the Criminal Code that Napoleon actually promulgated in 1808, Article 5 of which specifically excluded military crimes from its procedures. But the emperor's awareness that some of the principles French military justice had come to incorporate were at least debatable was shared by important figures in subsequent regimes, and the system was repeatedly reconsidered following his fall.

In fact, the 1814 Charter promulgated by the Bourbon monarchy that allied armies restored to France annulled most of the special, sub-*conseil de guerre* tribunals of the Napoleonic period. The new regime went on to assemble a special commission to consider French military justice as a whole. By then, there was much to consider.

The nation had experienced a far broader range of military actions than could have been foreseen by the men who had inaugurated a separate legal jurisdiction for the military in 1790. These included civil war at home and ongoing conflicts abroad, with both volunteer and conscripted armies, including the military administration of conquered territories. The men of 1790 had tried to confine that jurisdiction to specifically military crimes, which, in turn, they had tried to delimit to those carrying serious implications for discipline and order among uniformed personnel. But experience had tested the practical meaning of those boundaries.

Was ordinary theft, for instance, really so ordinary when committed in a military setting? What if the stolen item held military value? If military justice was intended to repress acts that subverted military order, were soldiers who robbed and assaulted their own comrades not undermining the cohesion and morale of their units? Did that not render these "ordinary" offenses military crimes? In that case, was the proper jurisdiction not the military one? Should it not remain so whenever unit morale was affected, even if the malefactor was a civilian? Desertion in the face of the enemy was obviously a military crime. Was not desertion from sentry duty another, albeit lesser, one? If desertion, why not drunkenness? If outright drunkenness, why not mild inebriation? How about dealings with civilian populations, especially conquered ones? If a sacked village, in its rage, were to support insurgents, was the pillage that produced this effect not a crime with specifically military consequences? If so, should the pillagers not be brought before military courts? If pillagers, why not pilferers?

Theoretically, any and all of these questions could be resolved either in favor, or at the expense, of the military jurisdiction. The penalties selected for them could, by their harshness, serve the "exemplary" quality of military justice; or they could be calibrated to reflect the specific circumstances and context of each case. The procedures by which they were adjudicated could, in the interests of celerity and exemplarity, be streamlined; or they could be structured to allow time for careful deliberation. The courts administering those procedures could be closed to the civilians who actually legislated the measures those courts applied; or they could be held either indirectly or directly accountable to the political branches. Theoretically the system could go either way.

By 1814, however, the internal logic of the army's "exceptional jurisdiction" generally tended toward extending the jurisdiction's reach, rather than contracting it; toward the mechanical administration; toward the mechanical administration of uniformly harsh penalties, rather than the accommodation of mitigating circumstances or the special circumstances of individual cases; and toward maintaining a *cordon sanitaire* between military justice and the civilian variety, rather than submitting the former to any sort of political oversight. The question was: would that logic and that system be retained? With the end of the First Empire and the reduction in scale of France's military forces, political circumstances were changing. Should military justice not change as well?

This question was posed repeatedly in the years that followed, as military justice was studied by one commission after another, under no fewer than three separate regimes. The restored Bourbons assembled panels to study and report on the military jurisdiction in 1819, 1822, and 1827. No proposals produced agreement, and no reforms were undertaken. In 1830 that regime was overthrown and replaced by the "July Monarchy" of Louis-Philippe (Orleans), which initiated yet another study in 1831. But the "July Monarchy" likewise took no action. That regime, in turn, was overthrown by revolution in 1848 and replaced by the Second Republic. The subject of military justice was on the new regime's agenda as well. However, it was unable to proceed very far because in 1851 Napoleon's nephew, Louis-Napoleon Bonaparte, who had been elected president of the republic in 1848 secured dictatorial powers through a military *coup d'état*.[28]

France's new ruler, the self-styled Napoleon III, would formally inaugurate the Second Empire in 1852, which would last until it was toppled by the Germans in 1870. Five years after that regime's inception, French military justice finally secured the full, formal approbation that prior regimes had been unable or unwilling to supply, by means of legislation that would effectively undergird the system from 1857 until 1928, when it was refashioned yet again. But there was little that was actually new in that 1857 legislation; its principles were fundamentally those of the Directory.

Remarkably, the system that had been configured by that government and then entrenched by Napoleon survived all subsequent changes of regime more or less intact. Military justice had been shaped by external political dynamics throughout its formative period, the 1790s. In fact, it had been exquisitely responsive to political circumstances: each of its several configurations had been a function of the particular political situation in which its framers had found themselves. How, then, did the rise and fall of four separate political regimes after 1814 leave so little imprint on it?

The answer is that a Rubicon of sorts had been crossed in 1796 with the conferral of internal political responsibilities on the army by the state. The license granted then to intervene in the domestic political life of the nation had, in fact, been renewed by each regime that followed the Bourbons. In both 1830 and 1834, the Orleanist monarchy deployed the army to repress rioting silk workers in Lyons. In 1848, the Second Republic, which had replaced that monarchy, turned to General Cavaignac and the army to crush working-class insurgents in Paris who would have pushed the new regime toward a social radicalism its founders could not countenance. They, in turn, were undone by Napoleon III, who owed the power he had secured by 1852 almost entirely to the support of the army. In a politically unstable nation, the civilian state, whatever its ideological coloration, had learned the importance of the military as an internal political prop. It is hardly surprising that such reliance would be accompanied by an unwillingness to offend military sensibilities or intrude on military prerogatives. One of the most important of those was military justice, by which the army preserved its own internal order and character. Oddly, it was the restored Bourbon monarchy that was least dependent on its military, and it was this regime that devoted the most energy to reconsidering military justice (although ultimately to no avail). The others owed the army a great deal and knew when to defer to it.

The complex, varied experiences of the 1790s had produced several configurations of military justice, but it was the final one that endured. A function of the new civil-military compact (i.e., state-army relationship) forged as the great revolution wound down, its basic terms would be retained by successive governments throughout the first half of the nineteenth century. This system of military justice was fully instantiated by legislation enacted in 1857 and would, in fact, last well into the twentieth century—as did, of course, the basic terms of the civil-military compact within which it was nestled.

General Bourelly and other defenders of the system proudly described it as "unpolitical" to denote (and applaud) the system's imperviousness to external political agendas and pressures. It was indeed unpolitical in that immediate sense. But it was profoundly political in another, historical one. The basic contours of the system itself really represented the most conservative of several politically generated alternatives that had emerged from the Revolution. French military justice was thus nothing if not "political," in the sense that it was at all times a function of the broad set of power relations by which the army was bound to the state, and both related to French society in particular, politically contingent ways.

Having ascended to power on the army's shoulders, Napoleon III naturally wanted no one else hoisted there. Generally speaking, the emperor's interests were served by closing all avenues linking the army to the political universe except the ones that led directly to himself. The army of the Second Empire was to be an *armée de métier*—a force that relied on career soldiers serving long terms rather than one that culled enough manpower from broad demographic swathes of the nation to permit shorter terms. This sort of army needed fewer points of contact with the civilian world and could be more easily sealed off from it.

The new *Code de Justice Militaire* (*CJM*) finally adopted on June 9, 1857, comprised the sealant. Authored mainly by Jacques Langlais, deputy of the Sarthe in the Second Empire's *Corps Législatif* (Legislative Body), it detailed French military law, specified penalties for breaking it, described the structure of military tribunals, and prescribed the procedures to which they must adhere—all with a thoroughness and clarity not previously attained.[29] The system of military justice it limned would remain closed to unauthorized political incursions for generations. Indeed, until the last decade of the nineteenth century, the operations of French military justice were for the most part barely visible to the civilian world, let alone vulnerable to civilian interventions. For that matter, they were barely visible to soldiers.[30]

The juridical universe actually delineated by the 1857 *CJM* was one in which most formally juridical actions were not the work of courts or subject to "adjudication" in any public setting at all. Most applications of military law simply consisted of summary punishments for infractions of discipline, inflicted on the spot by officers according to terms carefully specified in the *CJM*. These infractions included acts bespeaking a lack of respect for military authority or superiors; the public expression of opinions prejudicial to the interests of the nation; acts compromising discipline; loss of professional dignity; drunkenness, brawling, hazing; inertia, laziness, or "bad will" (*mauvaise volonté*); neglect of duties; improper attire or misuse of military insignia; and the like. Officers were authorized to rule immediately on any act that, by their own lights, represented one of these stipulated offenses and to pronounce stronger or weaker penalties within a range provided by the *CJM* and varying by rank (generals could at will pronounce summary penalties of up to sixty days of imprisonment and alter the punishments set by subordinates). Enlisted men could thus come to know French military justice very well indeed without ever setting foot in a *conseil de guerre*. They would find themselves before a tribunal whenever an infraction was deemed sufficiently grave by commanding officers to rise to the level of *délit pénal* (penal offense), or accompanied in officers' view by "aggravating circumstances."[31]

Beyond these misdeeds, the *CJM* specified others that the military jurisdiction would consider under its purview. These were carefully ranked, from *délits* (offenses) to outright *crimes* (crimes), according to the degree of peril posed to military order and consequently to the security of the nation. These ranged from illegal requisitions, military theft, abandonment of post, insubordination, refusal of orders, and assault or "outrages" toward a superior to unauthorized capitulation to the enemy, desertion, mutiny, espionage, and treason. Various qualifying conditions and circumstances were painstakingly specified for each.

But the 1857 *CJM* went beyond the specification of military offenses, into the realm of the civil: it resoundingly confirmed the principle of *rationae personae* and, in fact, extended it. For generations, military courts had enjoyed jurisdiction over civil offenses committed by soldiers while in service. After 1857, those offenses fell within the military jurisdiction when imputed to military personnel whether they were acting in service or out of it. With this *CJM*, the army had won the right to administer nearly the entirety of the civil code in its own courts, many of that code's provisions having been amended to provide for a sterner set of penalties in the military jurisdiction. This was the single most innovative feature of the 1857 *CJM*, and the single most controversial one.

To Langlais the exigencies of discipline required that soldiers view their officers as the *only* source of authority, the *only* power in their lives during their term of service. Any jurisdictional encroachment by civilian courts on military space would submit soldiers to a parallel, civilian legal order; and any such exposure must inevitably dilute or even subvert the authority of the army's own *conseils de guerre*. It was crucial that soldiers know only one form of justice while in uniform—and that it be, always, swift and terrible. Langlais's view was that allowing certain offenses to come before civilian tribunals—with their deference to defendants' rights, their softer punishments, and their glacial procedural pace—would be "to take away from the penalty what strikes the soldier, what renders it exemplary and stinging, its rapidity."[32]

Critics, of course, argued that, to the degree that military courts administered civil codes, military law had absorbed or suborned the civilian variety. To them the system was no longer a regrettable, albeit delimited and more or less defensible, qualification of civilian rule. Granted the power to absorb civilian law, it had evolved into something genuinely dangerous to it. One critic, likening the army to society's "watchdog," proposed that Langlais had "conferred on the military watchdog society's whip: the laws. When a dog carries his master's whip in his mouth, he no longer has to worry about the corrections he merits."[33] The system of military justice configured by the 1857 *CJM* may or may not have been bestial. It certainly was largely untethered from civilian institutions.

If an offense went beyond routine disciplinary infractions, it would draw the attentions of investigatory and adjudicatory machinery the *CJM* outlined in considerable detail. Each division of the army was to have two permanent *conseils de guerre,* and two permanent *parquets* (prosecutors' offices). Each of these offices, in turn, was to be headed by a *commissaire du gouvernement* (public minister), most often a battalion commander in active service or retired. The office of the public minister represented the one point in the system where the hand of civilian political authority might be felt. He was appointed by the war minister; and in addition to conducting actual prosecutions in cases where offenses were thought to require a full *conseil de guerre* trial, he was delegated to represent the interests of state and society in general. But in its overall contours, the system minimized his role and maximized those of officers whose principal or even sole responsibility was the maintenance of discipline within their units.

For all the talk of "celerity" in military justice, its pretrial procedures as delineated by the 1857 *CJM* were actually rather cumbersome. When evidence suggested that a specific article of either the military or civilian criminal code had been violated by a member of the armed services, the officer commanding the relevant company, squad, or battery was required immediately to report the presumed offense to the officer (captain or above) commanding the detachment. That latter officer automatically assumed responsibility for the initial investigation, under the title of *officier de police judiciaire* (police judicial officer). This initial investigation was taken seriously. Delegation of responsibility for it by the detachment commander was discouraged in any case and confined to high-ranking officers when absolutely necessary.[34] It was to be based on the formal interrogation of anyone deemed knowledgeable by the police judicial officer. Interrogations were to be carefully transcribed by a *greffier* (recording secretary) and attached as *procès-verbaux* (depositions) to the final report, which was delivered directly to the general commanding the division. If the police judicial officer were to conclude that the case merited the attention of the *parquet,* he would include that recommendation with his report.

The rest of the process, in fact, was almost entirely in the general's hands. If he decided, on the basis of the initial investigation, that full *conseil de guerre* proceedings might eventually be warranted, he would instruct the public minister of the *parquet* holding jurisdiction to activate a fuller and more extensive inquiry (i.e., the general would announce to the minister his *mise d'informer*). That inquiry would be conducted by a special *rapporteur* attached to the *parquet*, who, like the police judicial officer, would be assisted by a secretary. This investigator's counterpart in the civilian system was the *juge d'instruction* (examining magistrate), but the military investigator was kept under far tighter procedural reins. Technically, a military investigator was appointed by and accountable to the public minister. But this minister could not authorize the investigator to have anyone arrested or held in custody, to conduct supplemental interrogations, to order tests (e.g., of the accused's mental state), or to contextualize or widen his inquiry significantly without securing the permission of the general beforehand. Nor could the investigator play any official role in *conseil de guerre* hearings should the case proceed to one. In actuality, the entire investigation was conducted under the "surveillance" of the general.[35]

When the investigation was concluded, it would be resubmitted to the public minister, who would pass it on to the general with his own recommendation that the general either order a full *conseil de guerre* trial (i.e., announce a *mise en jugement*) or drop the prosecution (i.e., announce a *non-lieu*). That decision, however, belonged to the general alone. He was not required to follow the advice of the minister. The latter, however, *was* required to conduct the prosecution, whether or not he had recommended one, if the general decided to order a *mise en jugement*.

Critics of the jurisdiction would argue that the designers of the 1857 legislation had an unwholesome reason for inserting the divisional general into the pretrial procedure twice (first to decide whether to order a full-scale investigation and then to decide whether to order a full trial), however cumbersome that might seem. The rationale, they suggested, was to enable the general to monitor the course of the investigation carefully enough so that he could avoid open *conseil de guerre* trials in cases where officers' actions might be implicated in some way deemed unhelpful to the maintenance of discipline. In such cases, the general could skirt the trial with a *non-lieu*, while still punishing the malefactor by exercising his own prerogative to order disciplinary actions within the limits set by law. Whatever the truth of that charge, there was no question that the *CJM* assigned an enormous juridical role to the divisional general. Significantly, that officer's own superior, the general in command of the corps, could not modify juridical decisions taken by his subordinate. In fact, the war minister himself could not intervene in the process unless the accused held the rank of colonel or above.[36] Withal, the role of the divisional general in French military justice was so extensive—and it so dramatically curtailed the independence of the public minister and investigator—that one commentator described it as "quite a remarkable derogation of the theory of the separation of powers."[37]

If the general did indeed order a *mise en jugement*, there was never the slightest pretense that the accused would face a "jury of his peers" in court: in no case would the seven-man *conseil de guerre* panel be composed of any but the defendant's superiors. The selection of specific officers to serve on the tribunal, as well as their substitutes, also fell to the general. That selection was significant, since in a military court those men would act as both judge and jury. Officers comprising it would simultaneously rule on the facts, determine the degree of culpability, and assign punishment. Notably, those officers "were not bound by the conclusions of the minister, whatever they might be" (i.e., they were not required to acquit even if the prosecuting minister were to decide to drop the case).[38]

The court's own procedures were consistent with the "inquisitorial" model common in continental Europe, which meant that the course the proceedings took would be set not by the clash of prosecutor and defense advocate but by the particular priorities of the tribunal. Rules of evidence were loose, basically *ad hoc* and determined primarily by the tribunal's presiding officer or president. The latter could require new testimony or debar witnesses put forth by the prosecution or defense based on his own determination, in consultation with his colleagues, of how truth might best be served. All members of the court were to familiarize themselves with the details of the investigator's report, plus the minister's recommendations or comments, before the trial opened. That was a significant disadvantage for the defense since, as one attorney observed, it would be "quite rare that the incidents of the trial come to modify the view of the affair that judges will have taken in the act of accusation."[39]

That was hardly the only liability defendants encountered. The 1857 *CJM* had made no provision for legal counsel at the time of the initial investigation, only following a *mise d'informer*. During the initial investigation, which often provided the basic case that the *rapporteur*'s subsequent inquiry simply elaborated, neither the questions to be posed in interrogations nor any other measures undertaken by military investigators had to be made known to defense counsel. The 1857 *CJM* offered defendants no possibility of bail, or any sort of provisional liberty (in fact, once an alleged offender had gone into custody, not even the general commanding the territory could terminate it). It denied the possibility of extenuating circumstances as a defense. It maintained military appellate courts (*cours de révision*, structured much like the *conseils de guerre* and staffed entirely by officers) but confined the right of appeal to the narrowest of procedural grounds: only a violation of written procedures "to the point of nullity" of the findings of fact, or the explicit failure to rule on a right claimed by the defense, could provide a basis for appeal. It further discouraged appeals by providing only a twenty-four-hour window of opportunity for submitting one and required that the sentence be administered within twenty-four hours of the conclusion of legal proceedings.

Here, in the trial and punishment phases of the process, is where "celerity" truly was prioritized in French military justice. It was achieved mainly by curtailing the ability of defense counsel to slow down the proceedings.[40] In the eyes of the system's architects, after all, the trial was clearly not the central part of the process. The prior investigations were; that was where guilt would usually be determined. The tribunal's primary function was to prevent gross lapses of form and to determine the sort of punishment that might have the most salutary effect on the unit (i.e., assign punishment with an eye toward its broad exemplary value).

At the conclusion of the process, the primacy of the divisional general in the entire jurisdiction was again confirmed. Responsibility for the execution of all judgments was conferred on the general, not, as in the civilian system, on the public minister of the *parquet*, or on a separate penitential administration. The general was even permitted to delay execution of the sentence if he so chose. In fact, he could conditionally delay even informing the minister of his actions regarding the administration of sentences. This was telling. Theoretically, the minister retained the power to pardon prisoners. But, in granting the general the right to delay implementing such an order, the *CJM* instantiated "a veritable dismemberment" of that ministerial prerogative.[41]

Broadly political circumstances, then, had devolved onto the army a legal subsystem quite carefully protected, in its day-to-day operations, from contamination by "politics" in the quotidian sense. Screened from prying civilian eyes, it entrusted all key procedural decisions to officers:

the police judicial officer; the *rapporteur*; the president of the tribunal; and the divisional general, who exercised broad oversight over the entire system. The only avenue through which any other considerations might conceivably intrude was the office of the public minister, since that led back to the war minister (and through him to the cabinet, and indirectly to the entire parliamentary world). But that avenue was highly constricted. Once appointed by the war minister, the *commissaire du gouvernement* held a very limited range of responsibilities within the system.

No one acting on behalf of a civilian constituency or bearing a nonmilitary agenda could substantively affect the decision on whether to initiate an investigation; or how it should be conducted; or whether to proceed to trial; or how the tribunal would be constituted, or conduct its hearings, or decide the case. On this operational level, the military jurisdiction was insulated from direct political interventions far more effectively than most French civilian courts, where the principle of judicial independence remained tenuous. In fact, the military jurisdiction actually minimized the input not only of political agents but of civilian personnel of any sort. Indeed, it accommodated civilian juridical norms only in highly qualified form: Henri Barboux, basically a defender of the system, noted that only France—unlike Germany, Austria, Italy, and even Russia—left the investigation of military crimes to officers untrained in interrogation or investigative procedures and entirely uncounseled by civilian experts.[42] Agents of military justice could attend to their primary function—the maintenance of discipline—pretty much as they saw fit. They were accountable to no one and nothing except the rules that had been set for them in 1857. Indeed, most jurists, prosecutors, and other agents of the law today can only dream of what these men enjoyed: the untrammeled power to administer a legal code that expressed moral values in which they believed, with no exogenous pressure to compromise.

In fact, the social locus of that power was about to expand greatly—not, oddly enough, as a consequence of martial success but rather in response to the French army's decisive defeat at the hands of German forces in 1870. For this defeat occasioned the collapse of the Second Empire and its replacement by the Third Republic, which, in turn, would replace Napoleon III's comparatively small army of long-serving professionals with a larger force of citizen-soldiers. At this point, the question would be: could a system of military justice designed for the army of an authoritarian regime effectively regulate that of the nation's new democracy?

The View from the Left

If there was anything France's Third Republic did not lack, it was enemies. For the first decade or so after the new regime's troubled inception in 1871, most Frenchmen would probably have named their recent conquerors as the most significant of those. Indeed, to much of France, invasion, defeat, and above all, the loss of the provinces of Alsace-Lorraine had raised the newly federated German Empire to the status of blood foe. The new army that legislators began fashioning in 1872 was entrusted with the task of confronting that foe. For a while, it could bask in the esteem and confidence the nation bestowed on it.[1]

Yet the regime faced internal enemies as well, forces antagonistic to either the theory or practice of republicanism as finally specified by the constitutional laws of 1875. On the right of the political spectrum stood monarchists of various stripes as well as ultramontane Catholics, an aggregation of traditionalists angrily opposed to the basic principles of popular, sometimes simply laic, government. On the left stood democrats and social egalitarians rooted in the working-class movement, profoundly embittered by the brutal repression of the Paris Commune in the wake of the war with Germany. The Third Republic, leftist activists commonly thundered, had been born in working-class blood. It was an ersatz, "bourgeois" republic, the rule of capital constitutionalized.

The traditionalist right at first seemed the more dangerous element, electorally formidable (ironically enough, given traditionalists' philosophical opposition to democratic processes) and mobilized to thwart the Third Republic's elevation of parliamentary governance over executive power. But its own internal divisions would preclude success, and by 1879 it was essentially spent. The left would not begin to recover from the disaster of the Commune until the 1880s, as the republic began lifting the proscriptions it had initially decreed against workers' organizations. After 1884, with trade-union and strike activity finally fully legalized, leftists could rebuild their organizational sinews. But the left, too, was beset by internal divisions. Anarchists dreamed the death of the state, while various denominations of socialists sustained the hope of state-based social leveling envisioned by Saint-Simon and, before him, by Gracchus Babeuf and even Robespierre.[2]

The ideological center was represented mainly by parties denoted "Opportunist" (later the "Moderates") and "Radical," which were basically dedicated to the stabilization of the republic itself. Regarding social policy, important components of both groupings favored ending the church's monopoly over French education, while Radicals specifically represented themselves as champions of "the little man" (i.e., rural smallholders). The clearest victory for the political center came in the late 1880s with the defeat of the odd political movement that gathered itself around the charismatic general and war minister Georges Boulanger. Boulanger first came to public attention as a vigorous proponent of *revanchisme* (vengeance for the defeat of 1870) precisely when zeal for a settling of scores with Germany seemed to be fading. He would go on to attract a disparate group of supporters from both the right and left of the political spectrum, unified mainly by contempt for parliamentary government and, in particular, by dismay at the waning zeal of republican politicians for a military reckoning with Germany.[3] This "Caesarist" movement was effectively dispersed by 1889, but it did leave ripples.

They included a "new right" of secular nationalists, which would gradually displace the old one of monarchists and clericalists. Its program was essentially sociocultural: cultivation of an almost mystical veneration for the nation, conceived in quasi-spiritual terms ("the land and the dead," in the formulation of novelist-politico Maurice Barrès); hostility to cosmopolitan and pacifist forces held to compromise national solidarity and purpose;

contempt for the legalism, scientism, and individualism that seemed to characterize the republic's governing class; and a recovery of manly, martial virtues.[4] All this was to steel the nation for the inevitable struggle with Germany over Alsace-Lorraine, which must be recovered at all costs. Unlike the old right, this new element was not monolithically antirepublican (Barrès himself wasn't). But genuinely committed republicans, mindful of the army's role as incubator of the Boulangist movement, were disquieted by the attraction that the "integral" nationalism now swirling on the new right seemed to hold for military personnel. The Boulangist episode was over; but a degree of concern with the question of "praetorianism," or unwholesome involvements by the military in political affairs, had begun penetrating the political center, even as centrist parties turned their energies toward reducing the power of the church within state and society.

That discomfort with the army's perceived political orientation was matched by other sorts of unease with the military that had taken root within certain quarters of the rural and urban middle and lower-middle classes, whose values the centrist parties basically represented. The clearest and oldest was a pacifist sentiment, fairly well established in France since the end of the Napoleonic era and represented by organizations committed to international arbitration and ultimate disarmament, such as the *Ligue Internationale et Permanente de la Paix* (Permanent International League of Peace) and the *Association de la Paix par le Droit* (Association for Peace through Law). The 1880s, however, witnessed the stirrings of a more pointed critique of the army as an institution, one that moved beyond the question of war to that of daily life in the barracks. During that decade, a set of novelists and journalists described that life as one of chronic degradation, cruelty, and moral turpitude (especially alcoholism and pederasty). The novels, including Abel Hermant's *Le Cavalier Miserey* (Trooper Miserey) and Lucien Descaves's *Sous-offs* (Noncoms), reflected in part the discomfort of educated young bourgeois forced into harsher material circumstances (and more egalitarian social ones) than any they had known. Indeed, the number of unwilling recruits had greatly expanded by the end of the decade, as the state began closing the legal loopholes that had enabled the comfortable classes to avoid or minimize their military service.

But another and much more deeply rooted variety of antimilitarism was developing on the left. Beginning in the 1880s and gathering steam in the next two decades, this was distinguishable from other strains by its explicit linkage of "the military Power" to the class struggle, and by its overt challenge to the basic terms of the civil-military compact that had privileged the army's role within the polity for generations.[5]

Leftists saw themselves as the primary victims of that compact and expected to remain so until it was fundamentally recast. The army, after all, had been deployed against working-class insurrectionists in Lyons twice and in Paris in 1830, 1848, and 1871—the last with particular lethality. Now, the "bourgeois" Third Republic was evidently prepared to go even further than its authoritarian predecessors, targeting not only insurrectionists but demonstrators and strikers as well. On May 1, 1891, an infantry regiment killed nine people in the textile mill town of Fourmies. It was only the first in a long series of interventions by the French army on one side of the class struggle during the 1890s and early 1900s.[6] Leading leftist theoreticians began to devote special attention to "the Military Power" and the threat it posed to working-class emancipation. The more closely they examined military institutions and the state's use of them, the deeper and broader they recognized that threat to be.

The army, activists argued, was the single most formidable instrumentality of the class enemy, used to serve bourgeois interests and crush workers on every conceivable front. Abroad it served no purpose but the defense and extension of empire, all in the interests of capital accumulation. The end result of that capitalist aggrandizement could only be war—itself simply the organized slaughter of one country's workers by another country's workers. At home the army's crimes against working-class demonstrators were exacerbated by the fact that it used working-class conscripts to perpetrate them, crushing the dream of class solidarity as brutally as it crushed particular strikes and demonstrations. There were dissenters within the army, of course: workers who recognized that their real enemies were their own masters rather than the native forces who resisted empire or the workers at home and abroad on whom their guns were trained. But the army had long ago learned to channel the violent impulses that class-conscious soldiers harbored against their officers outward, against the (false) enemy. In fact, some argued that the army's tolerance or implicit encouragement of the pillage and rape of civilians in Algeria, to take one example, was consciously designed to provide a sort of catharsis for chronically enraged soldiers.[7]

But there was something else, something less visible, more insidious, maybe even more destructive than all this. There was military justice.

The left's analysis of the army's special jurisdiction was just as multitiered as that of General Bourelly and his fellow conservatives; leftists, too, embedded their juridical analysis in a broader moral and political sensibility.

Publications des « TEMPS NOUVEAUX » — No 17

LE MILITARISME

PAR

DOMELA NIEUWENHUIS

Prix : 10 centimes

Aux Bureaux des « TEMPS NOUVEAUX », 4, rue Broca, Paris

The nexus of capitalism, imperialism, and militarism, as seen on the radical left.

But that sensibility and that juridical analysis were the absolute antithesis of Bourelly's. For on the left, military justice was an abomination—simply bourgeois justice in microcosm. It was, at its core, a system for the domination of labor (soldiers) by administrators and managers (officers), themselves paid functionaries of an institution (the bourgeois state) owned, through various fronts (political parties), by the ruling class (the bourgeoisie).

The most impassioned articulations of this perspective came from the pen of Georges Lhermitte, an attorney/journalist of varied radical engagements.[8] To Lhermitte the operational efficiency of this hideous jurisdiction was cause for a kind of horrified admiration. For the genius of the system was that, from top to bottom (from *CJM* to tribunal, *parquet* to penal institutions), class dominance was so brazenly, so unashamedly enforced that anyone with eyes to see must recognize it. But few did, and those few could do little about it because the daily work of the system was so effectively screened from public view and immunized against public accountability. To Lhermitte those screens and that immunity were standing affronts to the democratic ethos. Yet the forces that would dismantle them were invariably routed—in fact, with insulting ease. Defenders of the system needed only assert the self-evident imperative of *discipline*, and the attacking forces simply melted away.

Military discipline, Lhermitte argued, was a grotesque joke to anyone who had seen the system's operations from the inside. Military discipline existed only for enlisted men. Officers knew none. Lhermitte stressed the codification, in the 1857 *CJM*, of entirely different ranges of punishment for officers and enlisted men convicted of the same offense: loss of rank, fine, or dismissal for officers; public degradation, imprisonment, or hard labor for enlisted men.[9] Furthermore, he found that such penalties as could legally be applied to officers rarely were. A particularly galling example to Lhermitte was the heavily publicized case of one Colonel de Saint-Rémy, who had refused even to answer a direct order from a republican prefect to march a squadron to a site in Brittany where local residents were violently resisting the closure of a religious order. Legally, Lhermitte argued, the citizens' action constituted "armed insurrection." This meant that, under Article 234 of the *CJM*, Saint-Rémy had refused to obey a direct order in the presence of an armed enemy, the penalty for which could actually have been death. Instead, he was practically cheered for his refusal "to carry out an order that offends my feelings and faith." In this instance, noted Lhermitte, the basic republican principle of civilian control of the military had been at issue—and the results had been, to say the least, disquieting.[10]

Lhermitte went on to document in great detail instances where entire groups of enlisted men had died for lack of medical care, died of food poisoning, died of physical beatings—all cases where the negligence, incompetence, or outright criminality of officers had been clear, or at the very least, plausibly alleged, yet where no disciplinary action against those officers had been undertaken (in fact, the officers were rarely even investigated).[11] He further attested to cases of financial irregularities in military budgets that would surely have provoked inquiries by the relevant cabinet minister had they occurred in any other department of government—but they provoked none, by any war minister, when attributable to officers.[12] Yet while officers literally got away with murder, soldiers brought before the *conseils de guerre* faced the full fury of the law—especially in Africa. The two divisional tribunals of Oran, for instance, had jointly pronounced 3,120 condemnations, amounting to 9,043 years of prison time, in 1897 alone; 23 men had been sentenced to death, and 5 had been executed. Only France, Lhermitte stressed, was so quick to mete out the death penalty in her military courts, especially for assaults against officers. Other countries' military courts might admit extenuating circumstances in at least some such cases: in Italy if there had been "prior calumny" by the officer; in Austria in cases of mental impairment. Even Russia, Lhermitte noted, treated that as a capital crime only in time of war.[13] In effect, "military justice" was simply code for institutionalized caste privilege, and class oppression.

What was particularly sinister to Lhermitte was the fact that this monstrous jurisdiction had been aggrandizing itself, extending its tendrils beyond the military sphere to encroach upon civilian juridical space. The ground had been prepared long ago, with the Directory's establishment of permanent peacetime tribunals—the first instantiation of standing judicial bodies beyond the reach of civilian authority. Those bodies had begun expanding their competence in 1857, when the architects of military justice had decided they could not be content with the unmonitored enforcement of an increasingly inequitable military code and secured the power to administer civil law to military personnel as well. That, Lhermitte argued, represented an ominous eclipse of the civilian juridical sphere, and one with disastrous consequences for enlisted men. For, in his view, officers routinely violated both the letter and the spirit of the civil codes that had been entrusted to them. Military disdain for the basic principles of civilian law, Lhermitte proposed, was indicated all too clearly by the case of a soldier named Sablayrolles—who ran afoul of French military justice for doing something that French law specifically guaranteed him the right to do.

In 1889 legislation had restored the right to vote and to register a public opinion to soldiers not on active duty. In August 1899, at the height of the Dreyfus Affair, Sablayrolles availed himself of this right by shouting "Vive Dreyfus!" while on convalescent leave and out of uniform in the town of Albi. Informed by the police chief of this affront to the honor of the army, his commanding officer had arranged with the chief to vitiate the protection the law ostensibly afforded the soldier. Sablayrolles was jailed for public drunkenness, whereupon divisional General Mibielle invoked a ministerial edict authorizing the summary cancellation of leave for any soldier incurring a civil penalty out of service. Since he was returned to active duty, Sablayrolles's commanders managed to discover blameworthy aspects of his conduct that had somehow escaped prior notice, and he was dispatched to a military prison.[14] Thus, proposed Lhermitte, did the military jurisdiction evince its regard for civil rights and for civilian-made law.

"Our army," liberal monarchist Odilon Barrot had observed in 1872, "distinguishes itself with eminent qualities, but I daresay that it lacks one essential one, that of respect for the civil power."[15] This, contended Lhermitte, was putting it mildly. By his own account, "the Military Power" was overtly contemptuous of civil authority, and nowhere was that contempt more manifest than in the actions of the military jurisdiction. In fact, the long arm of military justice had been reaching further and further into the civilian world, suborning civil authority by incrementally expanding both the categories of crimes justiciable in military courts and the range of people who might be hauled before them.

With the inception of universal military service in 1872, of course, all French males were theoretically subject to the military jurisdiction while in active military service. But with the refurbishing of that legislation in 1889, the shadow of the *conseil de guerre* fell over them even when their term of active service was completed and they were reclassified as reservists. Reservists would henceforward be covered by the terms of the *CJM*—not only when activated but even when inactive, for certain offenses (treason, espionage, rebellion, and most notably "provocation to desert") committed within six months of any period of activation.[16] Next, the military jurisdiction had stretched its talons to fully decommissioned soldiers, who were informed that they could and would be prosecuted by military courts if accused of offenses against military personnel on active duty (Lhermitte made much of cases like that of ex-soldier Amédée Huss, who made the mistake of thinking that his civilian status enabled him to insult his former sergeant without fear of prosecution by a military *parquet*).[17]

But the jurisdiction hadn't stopped with inactive reservists, or even with ex-soldiers. Since 1857, for example, civilians complaining of mistreatment at the hands of military personnel had to bring suit in military tribunals rather than in civilian ones. The argument had been that if civilians were allowed to bring complaints against military personnel before civilian juries, officers in particular would face a never-ending stream of nuisance suits brought by disgruntled former soldiers and civilians seeking to feather their nests at the government's expense. To preclude that, those cases had been remanded to military courts—where, by Lhermitte's statistical reckoning, civilians' chances of securing judgments against officers in military courts were next to zero. Indeed, he claimed, a notorious 1897 acquittal of officers accused of beating a newspaper editor was all too typical of the kind of justice civilians could expect in military courts.[18]

With "provocation to desertion" definable as a military offense, the potential utility to the bourgeois state of this jurisdictional aggrandizement became clear. For, by that device, the "Military Power" had licensed itself to drag some of the army's growing number of critics from their sheltered niches in the civilian world into the hostile setting of a military court. The journalists and novelists now alerting the public to the true nature of military life often published their critiques after they had completed their own active service, that is, while themselves still technically on reserve duty and subject to reactivation. Theoretically, noted Lhermitte, they could be reactivated whenever the army so chose—and it might very well so choose whenever it wanted to haul an offending author before a military tribunal rather than a civilian jury for "provocation to desert." This was what Francis de Pressensé, the prominent Dreyfusard and luminary of the League for the Defense of the Rights of Man, had in mind when he decried "the menace of the incessant extension of this exception" to ordinary law, railing against "the pretensions of the praetorians" to submit as many Frenchmen as possible, in one way or another, to the rigors of its special tribunals.[19]

But, leftist activists claimed, it wasn't just military courts that were extending the shadow of the "exceptional jurisdiction" over the civilian world. That shadow was lengthened by the actions of military prisons and penal procedures—they, too, had extended their orbit well beyond the military sphere. In fact, it was in its penal operations that the military jurisdiction's effectiveness as an instrument of class oppression was most chilling.

Any sentence to a military jail or prison was transmitted to the public prosecutor's office in the offender's area of residence, where it was entered into the offender's job registry. The stigma this record carried in the eyes of employers could never be expunged.[20] But what military prisons could do to a worker's reputation was not nearly as bad as what they could do to his body, given the ease with which he could be snatched from the civilian world and dispatched to one of the notorious *Bataillons d'Infanterie Légère d'Afrique* (African Light-Infantry Battalions), or *Bats d'Af.*

The first couple of these units had been commissioned in the 1830s, well before the days of universal conscription. From the beginning they had served as military halfway houses: combat units mainly composed of men who enlisted after having incurred felony convictions in civilian life, as well as soldiers who had incurred repeated disciplinary infractions after enlistment.[21] These men were thought to represent a potential danger, moral or physical, to the body of the army. The idea was to quarantine them and shape them into reasonably reliable soldiers through a particularly rigorous disciplinary regime. With the expansion of France's North African empire, deployment of the *Bats d'Af* to build roads, fortifications, and other public works seemed logical enough, assuming sufficient numbers of suitable men could be found. With the arrival of universal military service, they could. By 1910 there were five of these units, where civilian felons were joined by soldiers who, convicted of military offenses, had served their sentences but not completed their term of military service.

Leftists argued that conscription simply provided a kind of cover, behind which the army was able legally to raid the ranks of working-class youth to fill what were essentially military *corvées* (forced labor assignments). The legal mechanism was simple. Over time the range of civilian offenses that triggered an automatic *Bat d'Af* experience was steadily increased, while the scale of penalties that qualified a conscript for one was steadily lowered. The joint effect was a considerable widening of the pool of potential *Bat d'Af* conscripts. According to the terms of 1905 legislation, young men facing conscription after convictions for theft, swindles, abuse of confidence, public outrages to decency, assaults on morals, or vagabondage, with sentences totaling no more than six months, could be sent to a join "*les joyeux*" (the merry ones) of the *Bats d'Af.*[22] Strikers and working-class activists were often prosecuted on one or another of those charges—indeed, in some cases (e.g., with "aggravating circumstances") as little as three months of jail time could trigger assignment to a *Bat d'Af* upon the felon's conscription. That was why such measures were seen on the left as mere adumbrations of the infamous *lois scélérates* (villainous laws) designed to repress working-class militance amid the wave of anarchist violence through which France and Europe had passed in the 1890s.[23] Radicals were absolutely incensed to see their brothers-in-arms removed from the struggle for social justice in France and impressed into the service of empire in Africa, along with the common criminals the system funneled into these units. To these activists, the *Bats d'Af* represented at best a further blurring of the line between civilian and military justice, at worst an explicit militarization of a civilian criminal-justice system already heavily weighted against the poor.

Within the military, the *Bats d'Af* were viewed as *corps d'épreuve* (trial units) for men who had demonstrated moral weakness in the civilian world (there were so many pimps in their ranks that special care had to be taken with the departure of *Bat d'Af* conscripts from Paris because of the number of young women who came to say goodbye).[24] In these special units, such men would be afforded the opportunity to rehabilitate themselves. Reintegration into a regular army corps was theoretically possible for those who could boast flawless records for eight months or who distinguished themselves during combat (the combat record of the *Bats d'Af* was indeed impressive).[25] The units' notoriously grueling marches and labor regimen were thought to help build character. So were the recurrent lectures by which conscripts were apprised of the evils of alcoholism and the meaning of country, as well as the sporting facilities and libraries with which they were provided.

But officers of the *Bats d'Af* appeared to find severe and chronic punishment a far more powerful spur to acceptable behavior than any sort of educational resources. Behavioral problems were countered with deprivation of food, drink, and leave; with solitary detention; and with particularly onerous or dangerous work details. Theoretically, officers were legally bound to stay within general guidelines set by the *CJM* (occasionally supplemented by a decree from the war minister) in administering disciplinary measures. But enforcement of those guidelines in the remote locations where most military prisons were situated was very difficult.[26] At any rate, men deemed incorrigible troublemakers faced something much worse than what was ordinarily on offer even in most *Bat d'Af* units. For them there was "Biribi."[27]

The name was derived from the Italian *Biribosso*, a simple game of chance played on a board consisting of seventy squares. Players bet on which of those squares would serve as receptacles for the sixty balls rolled onto it.[28] The term came to denote what was in effect a military gulag situated in the most remote sections of French North Africa and elsewhere in the empire. It encompassed *compagnies de discipline* (disciplinary companies) attached to particular *Bat d'Af* units, as well as special *sections d'exclus* (sections of the excluded) for men against whom civilian legal actions had pended at the point of conscription, and special *sections des mutilés* (sections of the mutilated) for self-mutilators and chronic malingerers. These penal institutions were held to be every bit as arbitrary as any game of chance—and considerably more lethal. Biribi was, in truth, the real nadir of France's entire system of military justice.

Its most informed critic was Gaston Dubois-Desaulle, who would author a series of chilling reports on conditions in Biribi after concluding his own sentence in a *compagnie de discipline*. There were several types of disciplinary companies, but the most important were set up in remote sectors of France's Algerian and Moroccan holdings. Men who had incurred significant infractions within a *Bat d'Af* could be summarily dispatched to one, as could soldiers in regular units found guilty of what were considered particularly serious violations of discipline. Some of these violations were clearly defined, such as insubordination during combat. Others were vaguer, falling under such shadowy rubrics as "depraved conduct" and "setting a bad example." In fact, what most appalled Dubois-Desaulle was the secretive, arbitrary process by which so many men found themselves transported to Biribi. And the process was all the more hideous for the fact that an ostensible republic countenanced it.

The identification of these "troublemakers" and the determination of their sentence was not necessarily the work of the divisional *conseils de guerre*, which at least followed well-defined procedures and held open hearings. As Dubois-Desaulle revealed, each regiment was also endowed with its own *conseil de discipline* (disciplinary council), composed of five officers interpreting the terms of the *CJM* by their own lights and determining the disposition of cases that, in their judgment, required action even though they didn't entail crimes specifically falling within the competence of the *conseil de guerre*. The procedures of these sub–*conseil de guerre* bodies had scarcely evolved since 1819; they could be convoked by officers ranking from captain to colonel. Defendants saw no charge in writing; had no defender, no right to confront their accusers, and no right of appeal even to a military court. They were not even told the council's decision until it had dispersed, whereupon guilt was usually written into their military *livret* (record book) and they were dispatched to whichever penal unit the council saw fit to send them. The council did not have to justify its decision or explain its reasoning. Of course, the divisional general signed off on its decisions.[29]

Dubois-Desaulle was particularly galled to recall how far French military justice had degenerated since its origins during the Revolutionary era. France's earliest military courts, he noted, had been places where soldiers could actually bring charges against their officers. That measure of equity was utterly alien to the *conseils de guerre* of the Third Republic. Now, military courts were administrative bodies masquerading as judicial ones, designed not for judgment in any real sense but for punishment pure and simple—and often overtly sadistic. To Dubois-Desaulle the *conseils de guerre* of the Third Republic were simple streetwalkers, whose corruption was public knowledge; and the *conseils de discipline* were their pimps—more shadowed, more unscrupulous, more dangerous.[30]

Indeed, Dubois-Desaulle protested that the whole idea of law was grossly violated by Biribi, which he claimed had never been authorized by specific legislation but simply allowed to devolve from executive actions licensing the army to maintain its own penal institutions and practices. The first had been a royal edict of 1818, the second a ministerial decree of 1890. The Third Republic, then—the bourgeois republic, the *faux* republic that had been established to tend to the needs of bourgeois society—had "filled in what the Bourbons in 1818 left blank." Worse yet, a decree issued by the war minister on November 24, 1894, had announced that the minister himself reserved the right to personally consign to disciplinary companies soldiers who had engaged in "collective acts of indiscipline" or had committed "one or several offenses the gravity of which, by virtue of their particular character or the circumstances that accompany them, renders repression by simple disciplinary penalties insufficient."[31] Leftists insisted that the "troublemakers" identified by war ministers were usually men who held the wrong political opinions—revolutionary socialist or anarchist beliefs, or even simply reformist ones. Dubois-Desaulle claimed that, in fact, he himself had been dispatched to Biribi for political reasons.[32]

According to Dubois-Desaulle, what happened within the *compagnies de discipline*, within Biribi, was almost beyond imagining. By the time he was writing, all of them were located in Algeria or Tunisia—deep in the *bled*, where firm walls didn't even have to be built to prevent escape. Contained most often only by a simple palisade, prisoners were armed and trained like other troops, but only lightly and briefly. Their time was consumed mainly by meaningless tasks intended either to exhaust them (cleaning, cooking, repairing equipment) or to enrich nearby settlements and, on occasion, their officers (roadwork, brick making, ditch digging, muleteering, construction).

These occupations were punctuated by repeated forced marches. Prisoners were given meatless soup in the morning and bread at night, which they ate with their hands. They could receive neither visitors nor gifts of any sort, and their mail was opened. Whether housed in tents or huts, there was no possibility of privacy. Those who resisted this life in any way incurred various sorts of penalties, beginning with confinement on reduced rations, sometimes within individual cells. The worst of the latter was the *silo*, a sweltering hole in the ground with not even a bucket to dispose of human waste. Beyond confinements and reductions in food and drink, there was the *peloton de punition*, a punishment detail, which might include the manual of arms conducted at *pas gymnastique* (rapid-time) under the desert sun for hours.

But the worst tortures of the *compagnies de discipline*, according to Dubois-Desaulle, were psychological and social. The sentence was not subtracted from a prisoner's terms of military service, and each lived in constant terror that his could be extended by further *conseil de guerre* actions. Some prisoners spent years or even decades in Biribi, with sentence heaped upon sentence. The *gradés* (noncommissioned officers and higher ranks) who maintained the camps tormented prisoners with that possibility and with other humiliations, including constant shavings. These, Dubois-Desaulle insisted, were not only physically painful (razors were often simply chipped stone, and the potash in the soap worsened the effects of razor cuts) but psychologically debasing. Facial hair was a masculine signifier in *belle époque* France; its loss was intended to stigmatize. Some among the "veal heads" of the disciplinary companies, according to Dubois-Desaulle, were quite deliberately feminized and suffered enormously as a result.

For Biribi, in Dubois-Desaulle's account, was also the site of incalculable sexual degradation. He claimed that the rank promiscuity of the camps was not only tolerated but encouraged by camp authorities, who carefully distinguished "active" from "passive" homosexuals (i.e., rapists from victims) in their care and were not above intervening in prisoners' sexual arrangements—abetting or impeding opportunities, providing or withholding protection—as a means of exercising control. To Dubois-Desaulle, the likelihood that men who had undergone even a few years of this exploitative and unnatural life would return to the civilian world and experience anything resembling sexual normalcy was very remote. One emerged from Biribi "no longer a man, not even an animal," but rather "a machine."[33]

Throughout the 1890s and early 1900s this depiction of Biribi as an organized torture chamber was amplified and disseminated through French popular culture by the music of Aristide Bruant and the graphics of Théophile Steinlein. The latter described the typical denizen of Biribi as "a unique type of pathetic outcast, suffering a thousand deaths under the blows the *chaouches* [slang; loosely, "underlings"] set upon him."[34] But no one ever presented a more bitter or detailed portrait of it than the anarchist writer Georges Darien in his seminal work *Biribi* (1890)—part novel, part memoir, and totally horrifying. Impassioned and personal where Dubois-Desaulle's was analytical and objective, Darien's account provides the single finest representation of what military justice meant, viscerally, to the most committed antimilitarists of the left. To them it was the refined essence of bourgeois society; and only Darien, himself converted to anarchism by his experience in Biribi, spoke the truth about what would be required to destroy it.

Darien had entered the service in 1881, when the term of duty was still five years. He would be one of the first soldiers to be sent by a *conseil de discipline* to the *compagnie de discipline* of Gafsa, in Tunisia. "This is a true book," his account began. "*Biribi* has been lived."[35] Speaking in the first person as the character Froissard, Darien describes himself as ill-suited to military life from the beginning, both unwilling and unable to adjust to a world in which "the intelligence of a man is so often judged according to the degree of gleam and polish that he can impart to an iron tip or a piece of leather." After a few weeks in his artillery regiment, Froissard finds himself slipping little by little into "a totally machine-like life. . . . I no longer thought. I was almost a thing. I had nearly become a soldier."[36] Small disciplinary infractions result in disproportionate penalties, until he finally dares to leave the barracks without permission and returns to Paris simply to confirm that he has not yet been broken and reduced to a passive automaton like his fellow conscripts. He is jailed for that offense, then reassigned to Tunisia. Ever defiant, Froissard draws eight days in jail there for an unnamed offense, smiling knowingly when the sergeant who escorts him to his cell conveys the captain's message that "it's not me who's punishing him, it's the rules."[37]

His real problems begin when he is summoned to the regimental *conseil de discipline*. Officers explain that he is being sent to a disciplinary company simply because "someone who has been punished as often as you deserves to be punished severely." Froissard protests the injustice—indeed, the madness—of the decision: he is to be punished simply for having already been punished (in truth, he insists, for having been repeatedly bullied by officers). He loses all composure when told that his fate will serve as a salutary example to others. But Froissard won't realize what real dehumanization means until he actually arrives at the camp.[38]

It begins with a strip search and full-body shave. He is then given ill-fitting prison garb and told to keep the vest, in particular, clean for inspections (the vest, Froissard knows, is what is customarily worn in regular units for the lowest work details, such as cleaning latrines). Above all, he is apprised of the disciplinary methods favored by officers in a disciplinary company when confronted with anything resembling insubordination. Beyond the various deprivations, confinements, and work details sanctioned by law and described by Dubois-Desaulle, the authorities of Biribi deploy a set of restraining devices that have been formally outlawed: *les poucettes* (a sort of handcuff with thumbscrews); *les menottes* (manacles with pressure bars to crush the wrists); and *le baillon* (a woolen gag with a wooden bit, fastened behind the head and capable of suffocating). Most notorious of all is the *crapaudine*. The latter is inflicted when the prisoner's hands and feet are gathered together and manacled behind his back, a posture that guards can make as excruciating as they choose and in which the prisoner can be left for as long as they choose. Utterly helpless, he can eat and drink only by lapping at sustenance like an animal. He can relieve himself only in his clothing. He can protect himself from neither the scalding force of the sun in daytime nor the gelid temperatures of a desert night.[39] If guards choose to apply *le tombeau*, he will be *crapaudined* under a tent with only his head and legs exposed, his mind exquisitely focused on the damage the elements are doing to those specific parts of his body.

Biribi, Froissard soon learns, is no less a social hell than a physical one, the ranks of prisoners filled with informers, degenerates, and psychotics. Officers are hardly models of integrity; many are assigned there as penalty for offenses of their own. Their corruption and sadism, however, are exceeded by the bestiality of the *chaouches*, mostly Corsican non-coms and native *tirailleurs* (auxiliaries) who actually inflict the punishments officers assign. Froissard does make one friend—Queslier, a worker and confirmed socialist who ran afoul of officers only after they learned of his political inclinations. ("I'll show you how I treat communards," his commanding officer had told him.) Queslier was sent to Biribi after being falsely identified as the author of some revolutionary graffiti on a barracks wall.[40]

By Bernard Naudin, from *L'Assiette au Beurre,* August 5, 1905.

Together Froissard and Queslier will experience the full hell of Biribi. They will witness what happens to prisoners who fall ill or fail to keep up the pace during forced desert marches (they are dragged by mules). They will experience deliberate starvation (one soldier, Lucas, falls to his death down a well while searching for pigeon nests). They will be confined in irons, they will be beaten. Above all, they will recognize with agonizing clarity how profoundly alone they are, without advocates, without shield of any sort against the assaults of *chaouches* and officers. They are hardly, in any real sense, French citizens, deprived as they are of any recourse to justice.

Indeed, Darien's assessment of the *conseils de guerre* was widely shared by radical antimilitarists: they are cruel mockeries of judicial bodies, institutions that exist for no purpose other than to confirm the utterly rights-less condition of soldiers, in general, and military prisoners, in particular. In the novel the prisoner Loupat realizes this when, having lost a couple of cartridges, he is accused by grinning *chaouches* of stealing and selling ammunition—a charge that must land him before a *conseil de guerre*. Loupat's accusers are simply arranging a few days' diversion in the city for themselves. But the prisoner knows that the tribunal will certainly extend his time in Biribi. He also understands that the stigma of so lengthy a prison term will condemn him to pariah status when he does return to civilian life. Loupat elects to hang himself.[41]

Another incident involving the *conseils de guerre* eerily prefigures the Aernoult-Rousset Affair. A prisoner, Barnoux, has been killed by *chaouches*, and the camp begins to hum with mutterings of revolt. Hoping for some semblance of justice from a duly constituted court, Queslier and Froissard undertake to deliver to the divisional general a letter bringing charges against Barnoux's assailants and complaining about the treatment of prisoners in general (the camp's commandant, Captain Mafeugnat, threatens them at gunpoint but backs down when he realizes the depth of the prisoners' resolve). The general promises to launch an investigation then sends the complaining prisoners back to their captain—where their workload is doubled. Prisoners take heart when they learn that the assassins will indeed be called before the *conseil de guerre*. But their hopes are dashed when the tribunal not only acquits the defendants but commends their action.

A bit later, Queslier will himself be called before a *conseil de guerre* when an officer accuses him of feigning illness while on a march (he was disciplined at the time with a stint in *le tombeau*). The hallway selected as the site of the trial puts Froissard in mind of an abattoir, an impression confirmed by the mechanical, perfunctory dispatch of the several cases preceding Queslier's. Disgusted to see that Queslier's judges are to be his commanding officers, Froissard watches the proceedings with mounting cynicism. Witnesses are permitted to answer only the three questions the president of the tribunal sees fit to ask. The *commissaire du gouvernement* can barely exert himself to read a list of Queslier's prior punishments, which he asserts confirm the prisoner's dangerousness. Finally, the trembling young sublieutenant assigned to defend the hapless Queslier drops all pretence of advocacy and agrees in short order that the maximum penalty of two years would indeed be appropriate.[42] By this time it is abundantly clear that the *conseil de guerre* represents not the possibility of justice but the final extinction of hope.

How could such conditions be endured? For, Froissard realizes, many prisoners will emerge from Biribi only marginally human. Indeed, the most shocking scene in Darien's book occurs when Froissard and others, driven mad with thirst on a march, kill an old Arab man and a young Arab boy for their water—an event that barely troubles Froissard as he recollects it years later.[43] But Froissard also finds that there are means by which at least some prisoners maintain some faint sense of worth and agency. One of them lies in the homosexual subculture. In Darien's original text of *Biribi*, edited from the 1890 edition, Froissard describes it in some detail and with considerably more sympathy than Dubois-Desaulle.

In the novel, at least a portion of that subculture is healthy: transgressive, but only against the insane norms of Biribi; adaptive; even therapeutic. Froissard notes the semiformal marriages and *ménages* through which those still capable of trust or concern for another find some measure of comfort:

> They don't seem ashamed. They don't blush. They hardly carry on their brow the stigma of their vices. . . . They have themselves tattooed, generally on the arms, their enlaced initials mounted in a heart pierced by an arrow; and when they really want, in intimacy, to lift a little corner of the curtain that hides the mysteries of the domicile, they confess artlessly that they are quite content with one another. . . . One envies their lot.

To be sure, there is a less savory side to that subculture: "The whole troop of low-downs, the streetwalkers by need, the Gitons by instinct," a world of sexual commerce that is anything but clandestine. But this world, Froissard decides, is mainly an artifact of officers' pathologies, not prisoners'. "No prudes, besides, these officers," Froissard says scornfully. "Not so dumb!

By Bernard Naudin, from *L'Assiette au Beurre,* August 5, 1905.

They prefer to laugh with the clowns whose habits they know and whom they call familiarly by their names."[44]

Froissard's own survival strategy is quite different. He has learned to hate, learned the life-sustaining force of hate, recognized its odd but indisputable symbiosis with hope. He has learned, further, to forge his hatred into a general social stance, a kind of politics. On his release from Biribi, Froissard is informed by a relative that the entire family is deeply ashamed to learn that he has spent much of his term of service in prison. He responds defiantly that he looks forward to the day when he can move from *indiscipliné* to insurgent. He is, now, proud to pronounce himself an enemy of bourgeois society. In fact, he has come to understand that individual officers and *chaouches* are not the real authors or essence of Biribi; nor would their assassination, which he unashamedly fantasizes, end it. Biribi is a function of bourgeois rule. It is simply the logical terminus of militarism, and militarism the most effective strategy for maintaining the bourgeois order.

And in articulating what Froissard has learned, Georges Darien summed up as well as anyone ever would the militant left's retort to General Bourelly, and his idea of discipline as moral anchor.

> I understand a lot of things today I didn't understand yesterday. I know that the Disciplinary Companies, the Public Works camps, are the immediate and necessary consequence of permanent armies. . . . I know why bourgeois society, to safeguard its interests, makes a soldier out of a citizen, and makes a convict out of a soldier the day he tries to shake off the yoke of the crushing discipline that humiliates and brutalizes him. It's because it needs, like all usurping societies, to support its domination on terror, because it needs to make itself feared. . . .
>
> What it wants, at all cost, is a passive and blind obedience, a complete brutalization, a limitless debasement, the obedience of the machine in the hand of the mechanic, the submission of the trained dog to the trickster's stick. Take a man, make him abdicate his free will, his liberty, his conscience, and you have a soldier. . . . And this is understood. The army, that's the keystone of the actual social edifice; it's the force sanctioning conquests by force; it's the barrier raised less against the attempts of foreigners to invade than against the claims of the nationals. The soldiers, those sons of the people armed against their fathers, are neither more nor less than *gendarmes* in disguise. Instead of blue breeches, they wear red pants. That's all. The goal of their leaders, the pimps of the State, is to get from them, word for word, "an absolute obedience and instantaneous submission, discipline being the principal force of armies."

By Bernard Naudin, from *L'Assiette au Beurre,* August 5 1905.

Now, discipline—it's been said—discipline, *that's fear.* The soldier must have more fear of what's behind him than what's before him, he has to have more fear of the execution squad than of the enemy that he's supposed to fight. *It's fear.*

And if he laughs, if he gets indignant, if he speaks, if he thinks, if he's not afraid, then so much the worse for him! He's undisciplined: discipline him! He's an insurgent: humble him! Provide an example for the others! To prison! To Biribi![45]

The Dreyfus Affair and the Debate over Military Justice

Antimilitarism was common currency across the entire French left, but there were significant differences in both tone and content. Those differences roughly corresponded to the key divide between the *première gauche* (first left) of Socialists oriented toward the conquest of state power, and the *deuxième gauche* (second left) of anarchists and syndicalists who disdained the political arena in favor of ground-level actions against capital. Enamored of the idea of insurgency, this second left was deeply mistrustful of the politicians within socialist ranks. Indeed, some of the *enragés* (militants) in those precincts approximated the ideas of General Bourelly in terms of the depth of their convictions regarding the corrupting influence of politics.

Socialists themselves were further splintered into Proudhonists, who defended artisanal labor from the onslaught of the factory system, and Marxists, who adopted a more forward-looking, "scientific" critique of industrial capitalism. Among the latter, divergent interpretations of Marxist theory occasioned countless doctrinal splits, especially over the exact purpose of political engagement. A commitment to Marxism, after all, meant a commitment to revolution, at least in theory. Forming a political party and competing in the electoral arena would have to be justified as a means to that end, a necessary evil. There were several variations on this theme. Some Marxists offered a sort of embarrassed defense of political action, arguing that a proletarian political party was regrettably necessary to protect workers from the blandishments of bourgeois politicians. Others actually suggested that the ultimate value of political action would lie precisely in its entirely foreseeable failure to alter the capitalist order substantially—whereupon it would "free the proletarians of their last reformist illusions."[1] Still others, including followers of such militant figures as Jules Guesde and Jean Allemane, offered a rather more robust defense of political engagement, theorizing that the expropriation of bourgeois political power was the unavoidable precondition of an effective expropriation of the ruling class's economic power.[2]

One strain of socialism, however, felt less need for the apologies and elaborate defenses of political action undertaken by those who approached both state and nation as inherently bourgeois constructions. Its spokesman was Jean Jaurès, a teacher first elected to the Chamber of Deputies from the *département* of Tarn in 1893. Jaurès saw France in a much more positive light than did many of his fellow socialists. To him, the nation was the birthplace and bearer of the most humane political currents Europe had yet known; and that France, the real France, was in his view only temporarily in eclipse. In Jaurès's judgment, socialism was perfectly compatible with French patriotism, if the latter was properly directed toward a Jacobin, egalitarian vision of *la patrie* and fully distinguished from the reactionary, authoritarian nationalism of contemporary rightists. Accordingly, he did not disdain the Third Republic. Rather, he believed that if it could be pried from the grip of the bourgeois parties and rendered more responsive to working-class interests, it might become an effective instrumentality of socialism, incrementally legislated. What Jaurès did disdain was the romanticization of class warfare that prevailed on the second left and even in some quarters of the first.[3] By 1905 he would finally succeed in attracting all but the most intractable socialists—even the followers of Guesde—into a unified Socialist Party, formally known as the *Section Française de l'Internationale Ouvrière* (French Section of the Workers' International), or SFIO.

Like most socialists, Jaurès was an internationalist and near-pacifist, firmly committed to negotiated settlements of national conflicts. Unlike many socialists, however, he distinguished wars waged to advance capitalist interests from legitimate wars of national defense, and he took quite seriously the potential threat that Wilhelmine Germany posed to France. Jaurès believed that French security could be assured without saber-rattling or provocative action, and he would labor for years to produce detailed proposals for the sort of military organization that could do so. Eventually he would present a serious, highly ambitious blueprint for the construction of an alternative army—a democratized, "people's" army in the tradition of the great *levée en masse* that, in his view, had advanced the cause of French and indeed human freedom during the revolutionary era. In fact, the Jaurèsian vision would constitute the fullest and most far-ranging articulation of the notion that *L'Armée, c'est la Nation,* calling for the almost complete replacement of the standing army with a permanent militia of citizen-soldiers. This scheme had many innovative features: military training was to begin at age thirteen; troops were to be stationed close to their own homes, a full commitment was to be made to a defensive strategy, a portion of the officer corps was to be recruited from labor organizations, and others.[4]

A military vision leavened with socialist principles, Jaurès's plans for thoroughgoing military reform naturally entailed a full reconfiguration of military justice. He had been interested in that subject from the beginning of his public life: one of his first legislative proposals, co-sponsored with Guesde in 1894, would have restored to soldiers the right to bring suit against officers in military courts.[5] Certainly, his notion of discipline differed substantially from that held by most defenders of the military jurisdiction. Under Jaurès's plan, discipline would be inculcated gradually and equitably from earliest youth rather than imposed violently and suddenly on men unaccustomed to the rigors of service. Discipline would also be redefined. Instead of forced submission to the dictates of officers, it would now entail voluntary assumption of sacrifice on behalf of the nation. Its dimensions and means of enforcement would be determined legislatively by the nation itself, through the democratic processes the republic had established, rather than by a narrow and publicly unaccountable caste of military hierarchs. In this scheme, in fact, there would be scant need of a separate military jurisdiction to preserve discipline. Citizen-soldiers would move easily between the military and civilian worlds, and for the most part the same laws and courts would apply in both.

But an entirely different variety of antimilitarism was also emerging on the left, especially in those trade unions, union federations, and labor exchanges where anarchists and syndicalists held sway. In those quarters the fundamental assumption of Jaurès's entire worldview, the compatibility of patriotism and socialism, was scornfully rejected. "The nation" was a reactionary fantasy, necessarily in conflict with the ideals of a workers' state and international brotherhood. Workers must indeed fight, but never in a national army for the "fatherland" that enslaved them. Their war was *la guerre sociale*—the social war, the revolutionary struggle against their capitalist masters. And if patriotism was a bourgeois deception, militarism was simply its repulsive terminus. Jaurès's notion that military organization could somehow be made compatible with revolutionary goals, especially as anarchists conceived them, was beyond naïve. "Discipline" could never be rendered emancipatory. Agglomerations of armed men primed for mass slaughter could never be rendered wholesomely democratic.

To radical theoretician Gustave Hervé, an uncompromising antimilitarism was the only conceivable cornerstone of an authentic radicalism, the one reliable marker of true opposition to the state and social order the military protected. A schoolteacher, Hervé established himself as a force to be reckoned with in radical circles—and, in fact, made quite an impression on the public in general—when he suggested in 1901 that the best way to commemorate Napoleonic military glory would be publicly to drag a flag through a dung heap.[6] Those sorts of remarks, along with his contributions to the antimilitarist journal *Le Pioupiou de l'Yonne,* cost Hervé his teaching position and led to several prosecutions (in one of which he was defended by Aristide Briand).

Formally enrolled in Jaurès's pre-SFIO grouping (the *Parti Socialiste Français*), Hervé's ceaseless demands that socialists foreground the problem of militarism and endorse the most aggressive tactics in opposing it (encouragement of desertion, sabotage in the event of war) created considerable friction with Jaurès. The latter could hardly agree with Hervé's analysis of patriotism as the core pathology from which war, armies, and militarism itself all sprang. In fact, even Jules Guesde, the main exponent of Marxist militance within the party and an old antagonist of Jaurès, bitterly opposed Hervé for the near obsessiveness of his antimilitarism. Hervé, Guesde argued, failed to realize that armies and war could only end with the construction of a socialist society, not prior to it. Worse yet, the sorts of antimilitarist activities and propaganda urged by Hervé did the socialist cause no little damage by providing an easy rationale for governmental repression of radicals.[7]

Yet Hervéism was a real force, especially on the second left. In the early 1900s organizations exclusively devoted to the antimilitarist cause (*La Ligue Internationale pour la Défense du Soldat, L'Association Internationale Antimilitariste*) emerged, drawing considerable attention from the government before eventually fracturing through a combination of repression and internal fissures.[8] Hervé himself, from jail, would eventually found a new journal, *La Guerre Sociale*, as a vehicle for the expression of his own perfervid loathing of the army and the social atavism that was patriotism. It reflected his own conviction that the depth of one's hostility to militarism bespoke the depth of one's hostility to bourgeois civilization itself. To Hervé it was perfectly obvious that Jaurès's and his fellow reformists' rancor toward both was nowhere near deep enough. Under the pen name *Sans-Patrie* (Without-a-Country), he would certainly be heard: the pages of *La Guerre Sociale* were filled with his attacks on the Socialist Party and calls for a closed, antipolitical organization of revolutionary insurrectionists to supplant it (Hervé would eventually be formally reprimanded by the Executive Commission for subverting party unity).[9]

If reformist, parliamentary Socialists were troubled by these attacks on their left, however, they were gratified by political opportunities that were opening up on their right. By the end of the century many political centrists were moving from a vague Boulangist-era unease with the army's general political orientation to genuine alarm. Forces within the Radical Party, in particular, evinced a willingness to entertain more ambitious measures to republicanize military institutions, including those of military justice, than had ever been considered. If Socialists could find a way to work with those forces, however bourgeois, the prospects for reform seemed better than ever.

The reason for all that was, of course, the Dreyfus Affair, which riveted the nation's attention on the operations of military justice. In fact, it was mainly the Dreyfus Affair that inspired a decade's worth of detailed measures for reform of the military jurisdiction. It forced even the jurisdiction's defenders, including General Bourelly, to consider whether there might be something seriously wrong with its organization, or even with the values of the men in control of it. In the wake of the Affair (that is, from 1898 to 1909), no fewer than twenty-one *projets de loi* (legislative proposals) for the reform of military justice would be debated in parliament—an explosion of reformist energies that is scarcely comprehensible without a full reckoning of what, exactly, the military jurisdiction revealed about itself between, especially, 1897 and 1899.[10]

It all began with the conviction of a Jewish army captain, Alfred Dreyfus, for espionage by a military court on December 22, 1894.[11] Convinced that the conviction had been both unjust and illegal, Dreyfus's family and a few supporters initiated efforts to secure a reconsideration of his case. They began by reaching out to sympathetic journalists and politicians. But they never anticipated the explosion of popular anti-Semitism their efforts would trigger, or the tenacity with which military personnel would resist any attempt to undo Dreyfus's conviction.

To key officers, the fate of one man was infinitely less significant than the insularity of military justice itself. By their reckoning, the matter was "a strictly military affair, affecting military security, coming within the sphere of military justice, involving the larger interests of the army . . . something in which the civil authorities had absolutely no business."[12] What was vital was that the *chose jugée* (rendered judgment) of a military court not be undone by exogenous pressures, and that the *cordon sanitaire* shielding the military jurisdiction from the political world be maintained.

But what really problematized that political immunity was the fact that it was initially and repeatedly violated by military men themselves and their most zealous supporters. Indeed, in an affair replete with ironies, the single most striking one is surely the juridical act that triggered it. For at Dreyfus's December 1894 trial in Paris, the tribunal experienced precisely the sort of politically motivated ministerial intrusion that military jurists denounced in principle and that the 1857 *CJM* had been designed to minimize in practice. Incredibly, not only would the tribunal itself willingly accommodate that intrusion, but important sectors of the officer corps, including nearly the entirety of the General Staff, would commit their strength and honor to maintaining the results.

In November news had been leaked to anti-Semitic publisher Édouard Drumont that a Jewish member of the General Staff had been under investigation for passing military secrets to the Germans since early October. In his journal *La Libre Parole* (loosely, *Free Speech*), Drumont kept up a drumbeat of criticism directed at the war minister, General Auguste Mercier, for opening the General Staff to a Jew and for permitting a general expansion of Jewish influence in the army. Drumont was soon joined by other polemicists opposed to both Mercier (a man of republican and generally liberal views) and the government he served.[13] General Mercier was not accustomed to public vilification or skilled in the deflection of political pressure. Faced with assertions that failure to convict Dreyfus would reflect a malign and growing Jewish influence in the army, Mercier decided to act. He informed the press that he was certain Dreyfus was guilty and would be convicted forthwith. But this insertion of his own opinion and the weight of his office in the tribunal's deliberations was actually the less egregious of the minister's interventions in the military jurisdiction's handling of the Dreyfus case.

Concerned that the evidence against Dreyfus might not be compelling enough, Mercier distributed to the seven military judges a "secret dossier" of allegedly incriminating items on the last day of the trial. The defense was not permitted to see or rebut it. Not surprisingly, the minister got the unanimous conviction he wanted. But his communication of secret evidence unseen by the defense violated Article 329 of the Code of Criminal Investigation, which Article 128 of the *CJM* had incorporated and applied to the procedures of military courts as well. Dreyfus and his attorney knew nothing of the secret dossier and therefore had no solid procedural grievance with which to appeal to the military *cour de révision*. But news of it would leak out subsequently, apparently from the tribunal's judges.[14] As it became known that Dreyfus had been condemned through an illegal procedure, disquiet about the verdict set in among a few journalists, politicians, and academics—even before anyone knew that important documents in the secret dossier had actually been forged.

The concern both deepened and widened with subsequent reports, made public by the Dreyfus family, that evidence was accumulating to implicate another officer, Commandant Count Ferdinand Walsin-Esterhazy, of the crime for which Dreyfus was rotting in solitude on Devil's Island. However, there was great resistance within the military to the idea of prosecuting Esterhazy, and some officers undertook to shield him. Most military men familiar with the matter genuinely believed Dreyfus guilty. In addition, some of the protectiveness toward Esterhazy reflected alarm, not entirely unjustified, at the actions of his nemesis, Colonel Georges Picquart, then commanding the army's counterintelligence service.

Picquart's superiors were concerned that he may have used questionable methods, including unauthorized surveillance, in collecting the evidence incriminating Esterhazy. Worse yet, they believed he was leaking that information to the press and/or to the Dreyfus family's attorney. Picquart would vigorously deny this charge. But to the degree that his fellow officers believed it, their fury was understandable—he had, in their view, breached the wall sealing military courts off from the political world. Yet the juridical assault on Picquart that was to follow reveals the odd state of thinking on the relationship between juridical and military imperatives among the oracles of military justice. Why had they not shown the same outrage at Mercier's earlier breach of that same wall?

The answer may lie in Mercier's and Picquart's respective institutional positions, each of which was distinctive. Mercier was the first officer to serve as war minister in years. Every inch a soldier, he seems to have been seen less as the army's political regulator than as its own representative in the alien milieu of politics. In considering his delivery of secret information about Dreyfus's guilt that would otherwise have been unavailable to them, the officers who decided Dreyfus's case (and later their defenders in the General Staff and throughout the officer corps) evidently saw this particular war minister not as a politician meddling in their jurisdiction but, rather, as a fellow officer bearing vital intelligence from field assignment in government. Trafficking military secrets to the Germans, after all, constituted the unforgivable crime of treason. The gravity of the charge could have mitigated, in officers' judgment, whatever offense the war minister had given in crossing from his cabinet position to the inner sanctum of a *conseil de guerre.* Picquart's situation was entirely different. Functioning deep within the institutional recesses of the army, he had breached the precious insularity of the jurisdiction from the inside. He was the quintessential enemy within, a sort of institutional *doppelgänger* of the Jew who had betrayed France while wearing a French captain's uniform. Many officers, in fact, could not help but conclude that Picquart was in the pay of the Dreyfus family or of French Jewry in general. How else to explain his willingness to forswear his own well-attested anti-Semitism and to act so vigorously in defense of a Jew?

In any event, Mercier was lionized, while Picquart was nearly destroyed. Charges that he had forged documents with which to implicate Esterhazy were supported with documents that were themselves forged. Yet the several military tribunals to which he was summoned found the evidence persuasive enough. Picquart would be expelled from the service and spend eleven months in prison. In fact, some of the most egregious examples of military malfeasance in the Dreyfus Affair—forgeries, perjury, and a conscious connivance at them by a number of highly placed officers—occurred as part of the effort to silence Picquart (and, correspondingly, to protect Esterhazy).

The army's critics would attribute these crimes to what they called "the spirit of caste." By this they meant thinking shaped by the organizational structure of the military rather than by the facts of the case; an instinctive closing of ranks around the most senior officers (Mercier, and the General Staff that abetted the assault on Picquart); and a willful sacrifice of men, juridical principles, and ultimately common decency in their defense. The targets of those critics' wrath did indeed earn it. Some were overtly anti-

Semitic, while others were woefully ignorant of the laws they were entrusted with administering (not one of the military judges who initially convicted Dreyfus was aware that consideration of a "secret dossier" unseen by the defense was a violation of law).[15] But there was more involved than the ethical or intellectual shortcomings of officers, despite Dreyfusard attempts to reduce the issue to that.

Some of those officers sincerely believed Picquart and his supporters to be abetting a wider politicization of the case, an act they correctly understood to be incompatible with the entire theory and structure of French military justice. In fact, Dreyfus's case was attracting the interest of more and more men who found it instrumental in advancing political agendas extending well beyond his own fate. These included Radical politician and journalist Georges Clemenceau, a former minister driven from public office by Drumont and others through accusations of financial chicanery during the "Panama scandals" of the early 1890s.[16] Clemenceau found Dreyfus's cause highly worthy of his involvement, and he was hardly the only public figure to so involve himself. Indeed, the military jurisdiction was on a collision course with the political world. But what the guardians of military justice could not understand was the way their own actions accelerated that collision. Or they may have been simply unable to stop, once the die had been cast. In the end, it would be the most impassioned defenders of military justice, both within and outside the army, who would do it the most damage.

Officers' efforts to squelch the controversy could not succeed largely because the popular press—especially the journal *L'Aurore* (*The Dawn*), where Clemenceau was an editor and contributor—kept questions about the Dreyfus matter before the public. By January 1898 Esterhazy himself finally demanded a *conseil de guerre* hearing to quash the persistent rumors and clear his name. The tribunal would, in fact, exonerate him despite the evidence Picquart had assembled, and French military justice finally seemed to have done with the Dreyfus case. But this was the point at which the novelist Émile Zola chose to force the entire business to the forefront of public attention by removing it from the shadowy deliberations of military courts into an open, civilian jurisdiction. Clemenceau was glad to offer *L'Aurore*'s pages as a forum, and Zola would use them to publicly accuse various officers of perjury, forgery, and other illegal acts relating to the Dreyfus matter.

The novelist hoped that the libel trial he was deliberately provoking would amplify public pressure for a reconsideration of the Jewish officer's case.

Despite his defeat in court, the sensational proceedings did generate all the public controversy Zola had anticipated—and more. For the next two years the Dreyfus Affair roiled the nation like no other issue in the history of the Third Republic. Naturally, the more intense public pressure for revision grew, the more determined officers were to resist it: by this point any revision of the original Dreyfus verdict could and would be interpreted as a concession to exactly the sort of political pressure the military jurisdiction had been specifically designed to resist. Governing cabinets, staffed mainly by representatives of the centrist parties, understood this as well and shared the army's interest in quelling the controversy. Indeed, as public agitation intensified it could plausibly be argued that more than the insularity of the military jurisdiction was at stake. As the Count de Mun put it: "If a verdict cannot be accepted by citizens except on condition that it may be revised in all its elements by public opinion at the pleasure of whoever would put it in doubt, there would be an end to all justice, civil or military."[17]

Yet it is difficult to imagine anything more subversive of the insularity of military justice than the action taken by one cabinet minister, who believed there was only one way to silence the persistent clamor of the Dreyfusards. In July 1898 a new war minister, Godefroy Cavaignac, decided to answer "revisionists" demanding a retrial for Dreyfus by openly mobilizing political support on the army's behalf. He took the entire Dreyfus matter to the Chamber of Deputies (and, indirectly, to the electorate), where he affirmed his and the government's absolute confidence in the validity of the original verdict and unshakeable commitment to maintaining it. In his dramatic address, Cavaignac made specific references to three of the secret documents that had helped convict Dreyfus in 1894.

The war minister was willing to complete what Zola had begun—the transfer of the Dreyfus case from the juridical to the political arena—because at that moment he knew the political current was running in his and the army's favor. But he hadn't anticipated the revelations of military malfeasance that occurred shortly afterward (specifically, the confession of Colonel Hubert Joseph Henry that he had forged one of the documents Cavaignac had brandished before the Chamber of Deputies and the colonel's subsequent suicide). Those revelations naturally eroded the war minister's support in the legislature. Now that the case had basically been submitted to the judgment of the political world, he could do little but stand and watch helplessly as the political current began to shift.

The prize, to be awarded to whichever side could muster the most political support, would be the jurisdiction that would definitively decide what were by then a host of legal matters related to the original case (including Picquart's dismissal from the service and incarceration). Anti-Dreyfusards agitated mightily to keep as many as possible within the purview of the military jurisdiction, where they could still hope that the principle of the *chose jugée* would be respected (the jurisdiction's *cours de révision* could quash a *conseil de guerre* judgment only if the lower court's procedural errors were so severe as to render its verdict a "nullity," and even then a retrial would be held in another military court). Dreyfus's supporters, no longer the small band of 1895, agitated just as hard to get his case, in particular, out of the military jurisdiction and before the civilian system's *Cour de Cassation* (High Court of Appeals). This did not at first seem like a promising avenue.

At the time, only the most extraordinary circumstances could require the High Court to take up a case originating in the military jurisdiction—for instance, a determination by the justice minister himself that "the interests of law" demanded it.[18] In weighing those cases, any minister would have to be guided by the basic grounds for retrial in the civilian jurisdiction, grounds that had been defined very narrowly in 1808 (e.g., the conviction of someone else on a charge for which a defendant had previously been convicted; the conviction of a prosecution witness for perjury in the case). The Dreyfusards' trump card was legislation of 1895 that had somewhat enlarged the legal grounds for appeal by adding new or previously unknown documentation tending to prove innocence to the list of errors that rendered a lower court's verdict a "nullity." Lucie Dreyfus's invocations of this legislation in her earlier petitions to the Ministry of Justice had been rejected, mainly on the grounds that evidence improperly gathered or leaked (i.e., by Picquart) was not admissible, and that the 1895 legislation was not clearly retroactive to Alfred Dreyfus's 1894 trial. But the Henry revelation gave her claims new life.[19]

It was the shifting politics of the moment that led to the drama's next act. Public opinion seemed to be turning, and Premier Henri Brisson sensed that the time had come to align his government with the revisionist cause. He wanted his justice minister to endorse Lucie Dreyfus's petition to the High Court. But antirevisionists were hardly ready to concede defeat, and their perspective was widely shared inside Brisson's cabinet. War ministers Cavaignac, Zurlinden, and Chanoine resigned in succession, and Justice Minister Jean Sarrien opposed Brisson's initiative as well. In the end, Sarrien was essentially compelled to endorse Lucie Dreyfus's appeal to the High

Court when Brisson forced his entire cabinet to vote on the subject (an exercise of executive authority that one scholar has described as "a serious interference in the normal legal process").[20] In late October 1898, the High Court finally agreed to hear it.

Enormous political pressure would be exerted on those magistrates as they went about their deliberations. Street demonstrations, often violent, were ongoing. Press vituperation by both sides was constant, fed by illegal leaks of confidential materials. On February 23, 1899, the archnationalist Paul Déroulède tried unsuccessfully to instigate a military *putsch* during funeral ceremonies for Félix Faure, President of the Republic. A crescendo of sorts was reached in March, when feverish agitation by antirevisionists led to special legislation requiring that the case, actually in the bailiwick of the High Court's Criminal Chamber, be considered by all three of its chambers meeting in joint session—the Civil and Penal Chambers presumed to be better stocked with antirevisionist judges. By that point the threat to basic rule of law seemed strong enough that in June a new premier, the Moderate René Waldeck-Rousseau, would have to form a new, center-left cabinet of "republican defense." It even included a Socialist, Alexandre Millerand, to the disgust of militants, who never forgave Millerand—or, for that matter, Jaurès—for approving his action.

Most scholars have treated the High Court's deliberations under these exceptionally trying circumstances—and especially its June 3, 1899, decision, which quashed Dreyfus's 1894 conviction—as shining moments in the history of French jurisprudence. Civilian justice had upheld the rule of law against political passions that had reached unimagined intensity and might well have compromised it permanently.[21] In remanding Dreyfus's case to a military court for retrial, the High Court gave military justice, in its turn, an opportunity to derive some honor from the entire affair. Georges Clemenceau, in particular, delighted in the possibility that "the error of soldiers might be repaired by soldiers."[22] But the men on that military tribunal would find this difficult to do, and their incapacity said much about the priorities and, indeed, the essential nature of military justice itself.

The second Dreyfus trial convened on August 9, 1899, in Rennes and held the attention of not only France but the entire world until its conclusion a month later. General Mercier was the dominant figure there, repeating in great detail the case against Dreyfus. Much of the evidence he cited had by then been publicly tainted. Some of it was entirely unsubstantiated, in particular his allusion to documents confirming intimate knowledge of

Dreyfus's activities at the highest levels of the German government and his repetition of an old myth that Dreyfus had confessed prior to his first trial. An honest reckoning with the evidence presented, removed from all extraneous considerations, would clearly have led to Dreyfus's acquittal. But, even if they had been willing to openly defy Mercier, how could the officers on the tribunal have exonerated Dreyfus without seeming to yield to the political pressure of Dreyfusards? How could justice be served without conceding victory to the civilian tormentors of the military jurisdiction? If Dreyfus were really innocent, then the political insularity of the jurisdiction had thwarted justice for five years. The value of that insularity, that unaccountability, could never be defended quite as confidently again.

The remarkable thing is that two of the seven military judges, including the tribunal's president, were willing to vote for acquittal (in fact, with votes rendered orally and from junior to senior officers, it is conceivable that the more junior officers may have rendered the judgment of guilt they thought their seniors expected of them, while the senior officers actually voted their conscience). At any rate, the guilty verdict was scarcely redeemed in the eyes of Dreyfusards by the tribunal's invocation of "extenuating circumstances," which were never explained; or by its announcement that Dreyfus's sentence would be lightened to ten years, five of which had already been served.

Anti-Dreyfusards took the Rennes verdict as a victory of sorts, but it was a short-lived one. At the urging of Waldeck-Rousseau, President Loubet granted a pardon to Dreyfus ten days after the end of the trial. Over the next few months the government took further steps toward "liquidating" the public tumult, chief among them the granting of a blanket amnesty to all defendants in litigation occasioned by the Affair. This benefited Picquart and Zola but not Déroulède (who was tried, convicted, and sentenced to ten years' exile by the Senate sitting as a High Court), or other accused plotters against the government. Those actions, plus general exhaustion, began the process of ending the public melee.

The hazard to the current system of military justice, however, was just beginning. Its political insularity had been dramatically compromised—from without but, initially and in fact repeatedly, from within as well. Its investigative, adjudicative, and even penal procedures had been exposed and publicly contested. Several court judgments had been functionally (if never formally) reversed. Mistrust of the jurisdiction, long-standing on the political left, was now considerably more widespread, and it seemed clear that substantial reform was in store.

But what kind of reform? That would depend on interpretations of the Affair, and its lessons. Had it demonstrated that the basic principles of military justice needed to be revisited? Or had the system simply witnessed an unfortunate confluence of human failings? If so, how should they be understood? Should the measures by which legislators had tried to insulate the jurisdiction from political accountability be abandoned—or, rather, reinforced? Did this autonomous legal realm preserve something precious to France? Or something potentially toxic to her?

As early as October 25, 1898, Socialist deputy Édouard Vaillant and colleagues brought before the Chamber of Deputies a proposal that would have simply eliminated the entirety of the 1857 *CJM*, including the *conseils de guerre*, and remanded soldiers to the civil jurisdiction for any and all offenses.[23] Vaillant and other Socialists certainly knew that so radical a measure had no chance of passing (in 1893 some of them had actually presented a proposal for the complete suppression of the army itself, and its conversion into a set of sedentary national militias).[24] But they also knew that public skepticism about the quality of military justice was deepening (Colonel Henry had committed suicide in August following the revelation of his forgeries, and Esterhazy's flight to Belgium in September had suggested guilt despite his acquittal by the tribunal). In particular, they knew that the lengths to which the army and its supporters were willing to go in defense of this lacuna within the republican legal order were beginning to frighten even moderates (on that very day, in fact, an anti-Semitic demonstration in Paris's *place de la Concorde* resulted in 150 arrests). On November 4 Socialist Alexandre Zévaës and other deputies followed Vaillant's proposal with another one, milder only in that it would have countenanced military tribunals in times of war while advancing a reorganization of them along the lines established by the Convention.[25] It was self-evident, argued these bills' supporters, that the proper venue for the adjudication of ordinary, civil offenses committed by military personnel was the ordinary, civil courts. But even specifically military crimes (desertion, cowardice under fire, etc.) could and should be remanded there because there were items of the civil code that covered defiance of a duly authorized representative of the state, under which those military offenses could easily be subsumed. There was simply no other way. The republic could not continue to maintain a jurisdiction that, in its unashamed elevation of discipline over all other juridical principles, undermined the very idea of law.

Termination of the jurisdiction, of course, was an extreme position. Socialists were still a marginal parliamentary force, and these proposals were defeated easily enough. But there was an aspect of their critique that resonated in the political center as well, especially after the Rennes verdict: the claim that officers, by virtue of their training and their functions within a hierarchy, were simply incapable of competently exercising judicial functions. This argument was effectively advanced by the celebrated microbiologist and Dreyfusard Émile Duclaux.

Appalled by what happened at Rennes, Duclaux scrutinized the "military spirit" so extolled by Bourelly and pronounced it a juridical abomination. The willingness to subordinate individual needs and interests to the well-being of the corps, acknowledged the scientist, was a necessary and, indeed, noble quality on the battlefield. But it was absolutely disastrous in court. It was what led offers to subordinate the merits of an individual case to questions of its broader exemplary value, its potential implications for the maintenance of unit discipline and morale. In particular, Duclaux contended that the principle of judicial independence, an obvious prerequisite of justice, was impossible to even approximate when officers composed the tribunal. Officers lived their entire professional lives deferring to superior ranks in the military hierarchy; indeed, respect for hierarchy was perhaps the single most powerful component of their professional ethic. They could hardly be expected to elevate their own independent judgments above those of higher-ranking judges during temporary service on a *conseil de guerre*. All this, claimed Duclaux, constituted "the spirit of caste" to which even the best officers were inclined in court. The Dreyfus Affair had demonstrated the sheer power of this "caste" spirit, which had led officers to conflate the reputations of particular members of their fraternity with the honor of the army in general; to insist, against all reason, that its institutional honor would be irredeemably stained by any admission of error; and even to arrogantly hold the entire nation's public life hostage to their intransigence. "You should not be judges," he sternly admonished them, and to many Dreyfusards it was as simple as that.[26] If military justice was not to be fully suppressed, then judicially untrained officers must yield to professional jurists in administrating it. This would mean either ceding jurisdiction over at least some civil offenses to civilian courts (i.e., qualifying the *rationae personae* principle in favor of *rationae materiae*), or somehow involving civil jurists and incorporating the principles of civilian jurisprudence into the operations of the military jurisdiction, or some combination of the two.

The minimalist position within the reform camp was that the provisions of the *CJM* must be aligned more closely with those of civil codes, and the procedures of the *conseils de guerre* with those of civilian courts. This was the view of liberal humanitarians who applauded recent ameliorations of those civil arrangements and urged their extension to the military. *Le Temps* expressed it succinctly in a November 22, 1899, editorial on the state of the military jurisdiction. "Since the code of military justice was promulgated about a half-century ago, a profound change has been operating in the spirit of our public morals," the editorialist began, adding a bit smugly that "military justice cannot stay foreign to this movement." Recent legislation had, in fact, granted judges more latitude in tailoring sentences to individual circumstances. Perhaps more significantly, the fairness of pretrial investigations had been enhanced by conferring on defendants access to the services of an attorney from the moment an investigation was formally opened (access previously granted only during the actual trial period). There had indeed been a parallel procedural modification within the military jurisdiction, although there even this modest reform had been diluted: opponents, arguing that absolute secrecy was vital to uncovering the truth in those preliminary investigations, had seen to it that defense attorneys would be granted only eventual, not immediate, access to information the police judicial officer and *rapporteur* gathered from interrogations, and that any information the public minister regarded as particularly sensitive would be seen only in chambers.[27] *Le Temps*'s editorialist didn't dwell on this, perhaps in recognition that, however qualified, this was a reform that would certainly have benefited Alfred Dreyfus, who, after all, had been entirely unrepresented during his initial investigation, when handwriting samples that would help convict him were elicited under false pretenses.

In fact, several more specific reform proposals were already under discussion in a commission specially assembled the previous December by the head of the General Staff, acting at the behest of Charles de Freycinet, the new war minister.[28] They included replacing the army's own appellate courts, the *cours de révision*, with the civilian High Court of Appeals; the admissibility of attenuating circumstances as a defense in at least selected cases; and measures to elevate the level of legal expertise on military courts, including the possible attachment of some number of civil magistrates to them. There was, then, a broad range of ideas for the reform of military justice under discussion by the closing phases of the Dreyfus Affair, ranging from the extreme (total suppression) to the moderate (reduction of the jurisdiction's competence, closer alignment with civil law and procedures) to the mild (softening certain penalties, granting more rights to the defense).

Could the French political process find the right path among these? Could both critics and defenders of military justice learn the right lessons from the Dreyfus Affair? The first major test came on July 9, 1899, when left-leaning Radical Louis Massé and sixty-eight co-sponsors brought forth the first major proposal for comprehensive reform of French military justice. The High Court had quashed Dreyfus's 1894 conviction only a week earlier, and Massé and his supporters were buoyed by that expression of the supremacy of civil power. In fact, they were prepared to acknowledge a degree of sympathy for the intent of the Vaillant and Zévaës proposals. The proposal began with an open indictment of military justice as, in effect, a violation of citizens' equality before the law. The bill's authors also conceded, however, that "the nation has not yet sufficiently broken with the entire conception of military law, of its necessities and of the rigors that the needs of discipline impose on it."[29] The proposal was intended to specify those aspects of the 1857 *CJM* that required immediate attention, while awaiting the nation's further maturation on the subject.

The first was the lack of judicial professionalism in military courts. Article 8 of the Massé bill directly invoked the travesty of Dreyfus's 1894 trial by penalizing any communication of information by the president of a military tribunal to its judges outside the official dossier of the case. Moreover, in an effort to graft civilian juridical standards onto the military jurisdiction, the proposal further enjoined military judges to conduct all votes in secret and to accompany their decisions with written explanations of their reasoning and their understanding of the legal provisions they were applying. Failure to do so would automatically nullify their decisions. The Dreyfus Affair had also revealed the willed obduracy and narrowness of the army's appellate system, and Article 7 of the Massé bill took direct aim at it. It proposed the complete termination of the *conseils de révision* and their replacement by the civilian High Court of Appeals in peacetime ("the utility of which, a recent affair has demonstrated").[30]

Finally, a serious deficiency in the *CJM* had been reflected by the attempt by military judges at Rennes to soften their judgment with a legally unwarranted reference to attenuating circumstances. Actually, as Massé and other students of the system knew, it was not uncommon for military judges to seek out various means of qualifying the sentences they delivered—too often, judicially maladroit means. Judges understood as well as anyone that they were enforcing a code written in a pre-democratic age, for a pre-democratic French army. In fact, when judges found its penalties too harsh in light of the defendant's past record, value to his unit, or absence of premeditation, they quite often preferred to simply acquit, regardless of the evidence of guilt. The time seemed right to formally address this matter, and Massé's bill proposed the formal admission of extenuating circumstances in the adjudication of military offenses (the *CJM* already permitted them in civil offenses).

There was an overall design and intent to the Massé proposal, from which its specific provisions issued: it aimed to modestly trim (by ending its appellate component) and professionalize the jurisdiction rather than to end it. In fact, it was a very mild package, particularly in its omission of any provision for the remanding of civil offenses to civil courts. Sophisticated defenders of military justice appreciated this. Some were willing to engage in good faith with at least those provisions of the bill where they found the promise of benefit to the jurisdiction. Their observations deepened the discussion and widened the range of reform options.

General Bourelly was one of them, publishing an extended, two-part consideration of the past, present, and future of military justice in *Le Correspondant de Paris.*[31] He was particularly interested in the question of the admissibility of attenuating circumstances in the adjudication of military offenses, and his discussion of the question was both thoughtful and thorough. The basic argument against this proposition, Bourelly explained, was that defendants' prerogatives were already protected by the *minorité en faveur* provision of the *CJM*, by which conviction required the vote of five out of seven *conseil de guerre* judges. Soldiers were read provisions of the code at regular intervals, and Bourelly, like most defenders of the jurisdiction, believed firmly that they must never come to see it as flexible, or military judges as sources of mercy. But this, unfortunately, was precisely what happened when judges simply refused to apply penalties they considered too harsh. Bourelly was therefore willing to endorse the admissibility of extenuating circumstances in one particular military offense: physical assault against an officer. He noted that three out of the four types of assault the code described (against various ranks, with particular intents) carried the death sentence. This, he submitted, was entirely too harsh. Extenuating circumstances, including the possibility of provocation by the officer, could and should be entertained in the three categories where intent to kill was lacking, a reform that would still leave French military law considerably less tolerant of this offense than, say, the German code. There might be other offenses where such circumstances should be factored into judges' reasoning, Bourelly suggested; but it was important that individual judges not be licensed to determine when and how. Rather, the code's descriptions of categorical offenses ("outrage" toward a superior by word or deed, for instance, and refusal to obey an officer) should allow for subcategories, where particular extenuating circumstances were specifically delineated and appropriately diminished penalties specified. Thus could justice be served, even while the traditional imperviousness of military judges to *ad hoc* pleas for mercy was maintained.[32]

Bourelly also tried to advance the discussion of judicial expertise on military courts. He was absolutely convinced that officers must dominate the *conseils de guerre,* insisting that a thorough understanding of the military setting and of the duties and character of the men within it was far more important than formal legal training.[33] At the same time, he supported the notion that officers should comport themselves more "judicially" on courts. He endorsed the notion that final votes should be secret in order to render moot all considerations of rank within the tribunal and the idea that judges should be formally sworn in. He even grudgingly countenanced the presence of a couple of civilian legal "counselors" on the *conseils de guerre*, so long as their function remained strictly advisory. But Bourelly could not endorse the substitution of the civilian High Court of Appeals for the army's own appellate courts, on the grounds that celerity, vital to the exemplary quality of military justice, would be compromised. Instead, he offered to replace the *cour de révision* not with a civilian tribunal but with a single, reconfigured military appeals court, a *Cour de Cassation Militaire* (High Court of Military Appeals) permanently staffed by credentialed jurists granted special military rank. These, Bourelly submitted, could effectively monitor the judgments of *conseils de guerre* for legal form without privileging civilian norms or compromising the fundamental character of the jurisdiction.[34]

Valuable commentary on the Massé bill also came from jurist Henri Barboux, another champion of military justice. Barboux's commitment to the jurisdiction was just as profound as Bourelly's and founded on the same moral sensibility. "Now France doesn't need a very strong army only to defend its independence," he argued, since "the more the ideas, the tastes, the more of democracy invade us, submerge us, the more necessary it is that the generations to come find in the army the school and the example of discipline, of obedience, of respect, of sacrifice."[35] Barboux casually deflected the claim that the military jurisdiction violated the principle of legal equality with the lawyerly observation that, since all Frenchmen were now equally liable for military service, all were equally justiciable before military courts for its duration. Military justice, he asserted, was the final guarantor of those "male virtues," and anything that might dilute or impede its work was "a public danger," pure and simple.[36]

Yet Barboux also recognized that the jurisdiction had been weakened by the debacle of the Dreyfus Affair and went further than Bourelly in holding its own operatives responsible. Officers themselves "have put into the hands of the army's enemies the most redoubtable weapon with which it can be assaulted," he submitted, "because they have authorized them to say that the habit of discipline renders independence impossible and that *esprit de corps* can stifle the voice of conscience and take the place of impartiality."[37] Barboux was rather more anxious than Bourelly to address deficiencies in the legal training of military magistrates and, in particular, to enhance the sophistication of the jurisdiction's investigators. The latter problem had been amply attested by the inadequacies of the officers who conducted the initial investigation of Dreyfus.

Barboux, like many other commentators, openly acknowledged that "the military ha[d] gotten into the habit of considering the dispensation of justice as an accessory service, abandoned to those to whom military inadequacies or age prevent great ambitions."[38] "Professionalizing" these components of the jurisdiction would certainly strengthen it—in fact, he argued that Massé and his fellow reformers had been entirely too timid in this area. Their proposal simply required the investigators and public prosecutors attached to *conseils de guerre* to be credentialed with law degrees (*licencié en droit*). Barboux, for his part, noted that the German, Austrian, Italian, and even the Russian systems went much further to ensure investigatory competence, in particular, creating special investigatory offices within each military court and surrounding the military staff within them with several legally trained functionaries. The professional standards of military judges needed enhancement as well, and Barboux lauded the proposal's stipulation that they be required to defend their decisions in writing. This would require open deliberations, which rendered secret voting superfluous.

Barboux also departed from Bourelly in his willingness to jettison the army's appellate courts, a component of the military jurisdiction that he felt had proven indefensible in the Dreyfus Affair. He explained that the authors of the 1857 *CJM* had actually fashioned the *cours de révision* in a spirit of respect for the juridical maxim that judgment of facts and application of law should be separate functions in a tribunal. They had seen the *conseil de guerre* as a sort of jury, concerned with the former, and had established the *conseils de révision* to see to the latter by monitoring the lower courts' rigor in applying the code. However, the 1857 legislation had entrusted that vital juridical task to untrained and uncredentialed men. It then compounded this error by creating entirely too many *conseils de révision* (eight, until their recent reduction to two), with inconsistencies in appellate jurisprudence the predictable outcome. The results had hardly been helpful to judges on *conseils de guerre,* whose task was actually weightier than that of civilian judges since the *rationae personae* principle devolved jurisdiction over both civil and military questions onto them.

The Dreyfus Affair, argued Barboux, had left military personnel with an exaggerated fear of the civilian High Court of Appeals. It was, after all, already the nation's final court of appeal, even though the military route to it had barely been traversable since 1857. In fact, he suggested that military men should recognize that there is "quite an advantage to sharing the accidental charge of applying the law and judging men with those who are by profession the supreme arbiters of all contestations."[39] Barboux concluded that the Massé proposal was entirely right to shear the military jurisdiction of its own appellate dimension. He allowed that remanding appeals to the civilian sector might indeed compromise the celerity upon which military justice relied. But he nevertheless argued—with surprising sharpness, for a defender of the overall structure and purpose of the system—that "regarding justice, it's not a question of doing it quickly but of doing it well; we have to reject a punitive justice that would put its honor in its rapidity, and one can well ask those who want this expedited justice whether they would prefer being shot in six weeks over being acquitted in three months."[40]

Barboux's and Bourelly's careful, detailed considerations of the Massé proposal and suggestions for alternative or supplemental measures demonstrated that even to the most impassioned defenders of military justice, reform was theoretically conceivable—even, in some ways, desirable. Yet it didn't happen. The Massé proposal was not constructively amended; it simply went down to defeat, unable to dent the parliamentary opposition that gradually solidified against it. In fact, Barboux and Bourelly both understood perfectly well what motivated that opposition. It was a concern they firmly shared, even if they had shown a certain suppleness in their own applications of it.

It was the principle of *rationae personae*. The crucial, overriding question for most defenders of military justice, especially in the legislature, was that of the jurisdiction's competence. Military personnel must fall under the jurisdiction of military courts—and military courts alone. Those courts' authority simply could not be shared with civilian courts, nor could they tolerate incursions by civilian personnel. Indeed, Barboux had begun his own consideration of the Massé proposal by announcing forthrightly his intention to "repulse all restriction of the competence of the *conseils de guerre*."[41] He and Bourelly had been willing to countenance particular reforms that either didn't challenge *rationae personae* or potentially even strengthened it by neutralizing the arguments of its critics. They recognized that the Massé bill was actually nonthreatening and were prepared to engage with it for that very reason. But the problem other champions of military justice saw in it was less its specific provisions than its philosophical provenance.

Massé, after all, had made his intentions clear: this was to be the beginning, not the end, of a process whereby military justice would be incrementally "civilianized." Today, only the *cours de révision* would be eliminated. But what additional surrenders of jurisdictional competence might be proposed tomorrow? Massé and his sort were no friends of the "exceptional jurisdiction," and no proposals issuing from them could be trusted—they were intended to be steps toward the ultimate extinction of military justice.[42] In that assessment of reformists' intentions, defenders of French military justice were quite right.

Yet they were nonetheless quite wrong to reject the proposal. In doing so, they replicated the fundamental error of those officers who first convicted Dreyfus in 1894: they confused the identity of a political agent with the actual threat his "politics" represented. In 1894, the oracles of military justice had failed to recognize that General Mercier's involvement in their deliberations was actually enormously threatening. They simply couldn't see that threat because he was, after all, *General* Mercier. In 1899, defenders of military justice thought they must oppose the Massé bill because of what Massé and his sort were: center-left politicians ill-disposed in principle to the military jurisdiction. Yet, as Bourelly and Barboux indicated, there was much in Massé's bill that, by disarming some of the most active critics of military justice, would actually have strengthened the jurisdiction and left it less vulnerable to further invasion by political forces.

There was something else those defenders of military justice didn't realize in 1899: they could do far worse than the Massé bill. For, thanks to the political skill of Jean Jaurès, Socialists were about to greatly expand both their numbers and their influence in parliament. Their own approach to military justice was considerably less modest than Massé's—and with their elevation, the possibility of full or partial suppression of military justice would become very real indeed. In fact, given Jaurès's sensitivity to the force of Hervéism on socialism's left flank, they could hardly settle for much less.

“Can the Judge of Liberty Be the Judge of Obedience?”

Jaurès lost his seat in the Chamber of Deputies in the election of 1898, but he was in some ways more politically effective out of office than he had been in it. Initially indifferent to the Dreyfus matter (shortly after Dreyfus’s 1894 conviction, he famously remarked that ordinary soldiers were routinely shot for less heinous offenses than Dreyfus’s), he would eventually enlist in the Dreyfusard cause. Once committed, he emerged as one of the most tireless of Dreyfusards, all the more fearless now that he was no longer accountable to voters.

In fact, for Jaurès (and, through him, for French socialism), the Dreyfus Affair represented a watershed moment. Until rather late in the Affair, most socialists felt that the fate of a quintessential bourgeois like Alfred Dreyfus—and a militarist to boot—had scant relevance to the class struggle. But Jaurès had decided that socialists would become Socialists and grasp the movement’s real meaning only when they had affirmed that suffering humanity was their ultimate constituency and general moral uplift their ultimate goal—that injustice and arbitrary power were their primeval foes, to be battled wherever and whenever they appeared. The fate of this well-to-do Jewish captain, Jaurès argued, was as integral to the socialist project for a humane civilization as that of a striking worker. By 1902, when he was returned to the Chamber, he had fully distinguished his own strain of socialism from that of other, more doctrinaire or class-bound ones, a vision he would etch into the program of the Socialist Party (SFIO) that finally coalesced around his leadership in 1905.

The legislative election of 1902 suggested the promise of that new vision, by which alliances with other progressive, albeit nonproletarian, forces could be undertaken in pursuit of particular goals. It brought to parliamentary primacy a loose alliance of centrist and leftist parties, the *bloc des gauches* (left-wing bloc), formed to check the power of the "new right" to which Maurice Barrès gave voice and various nationalistic and anti-Semitic leagues now gave institutional form. The right's ideological appeal to some unmeasured but significant portion of the army, as well as to conservative Catholics, had been clearly demonstrated during the Dreyfus Affair, as had the scale of some rightists' political ambitions. The Moderate Waldeck-Rousseau's government of "republican defense" had neutralized the immediate threats to public order, but a root-and-branch attack on sources of rightist strength awaited the mandate devolved on the loosely conjoined Moderates, Radicals, Radical-Socialists, and Socialists. The Jaurèsian brand of Socialists were strong enough to withstand the inevitable charges of apostasy when they authorized members to follow where Millerand had led and to fill cabinet positions.

The political situation, then, was very different than it had been even a year earlier, when the Waldeck-Rousseau government had assembled an extraparliamentary commission under the leadership of Senator Guérin to prepare another proposal for the reform of the military jurisdiction. The highly complex, lengthy bill the commission produced (374 articles) mainly targeted the harshness of specific military penalties and the organization of the *parquets*. It was promptly killed.[1] In 1902, however, the parliamentary center of gravity shifted leftward. Reformers had more clout and considerably higher ambitions—especially for remaking French military justice.

In fact, reforms that had seemed reasonable or even daring in 1899 and 1901 now seemed vapid and toothless. For example, the whole idea of "professionalizing" military tribunals by elevating the legal training of military judges, which had been an important plank in the reformist platform just a few years earlier, now seemed hopelessly naïve. Indeed, the idea had always struck Georges Lhermitte as ridiculous. "Certified or licensed in law, even doctors," he had written in 1900, "they would commit tomorrow the same iniquities with this single difference, that they would bring to their trials that much more ability, that, knowing the law better, they would be more apt to turn it, to conjure it away or to violate it. Their justice would not be more equitable, it would be more dangerous."[2] In fact, the entire program that Barboux had endorsed in 1899 had been denounced on the left as no more than a return to the status quo of 1793, hardly a "reform" in any meaningful sense.[3] With the expansion of the Socialist (and Radical-Socialist) presence in parliament, this view and the impatience underlying it could no longer be dismissed as the fulminations of a few hotheads. And if a program like Barboux's was now passé, one that had once seemed dangerously drastic—full replacement of *rationae personae* with *rationae materiae*, and a shearing of the jurisdiction's competence to specifically military crimes—now seemed a sort of moderate middle ground compared to the Socialists' goal of full suppression of the jurisdiction, at least in peacetime.

Socialists understood they might not achieve their maximum aims, but they could hardly settle for the minimum either. They were contending with militants to their own left, already excoriating them for participating in the charade of bourgeois government. Hervéists, in particular, found that charade especially cynical with respect to military justice. From their point of view, parliamentarians' focus on the procedures of the *conseils de guerre* and the provisions of the *CJM* were a cruel hoax. Military justice as it was actually experienced did not devolve from those sources. Specifically, military courts did not actively administer military justice. Officers did, authorized as they were to mete out draconian punishments for trivial offenses on the spot. The *Bats d'Af* did, as a part of the netherworld of prisons and work camps to which the republic's legal order systematically consigned the human detritus of French capitalism. The semi-clandestine *conseils de discipline* did, in their determinations of who would and would not experience the full fury of Biribi. Those were the active agents of military justice. Its norms and standards were manifest not in the public decisions of its tribunals but in the hidden *règlements* (rulings) issued by generals and war ministers, far from public view—edicts with the force of law for military personnel, rulings that in fact trumped regular law with impunity. Such edicts, noted Lhermitte, were what had enabled Sablayrolles's tormentors to mock the law that ostensibly protected his verbal support of Dreyfus. "Is it law that must cede to these rules or rules that must cede to law?" Lhermitte demanded.[4] Reformists, militants charged, were focusing on the visible institutions of military justice precisely so that its secretive inner workings would remain untouched.

But Socialists had every reason to expect that they would be able to show their constituents the tangible benefits of their parliamentary strategy in the form of some serious reform of the jurisdiction. After all, their new Radical partners' concern with "praetorianism" was surely real. Throughout the course of the Dreyfus Affair, in fact, no one had denounced military justice more vigorously than the Radical leader Georges Clemenceau, who had repeatedly shone the harshest light on the judicial chicanery of officers. "Judge and soldier, two contradictory terms," he had sneered back then, boldly asserting the moral and intellectual primacy of the former (who "knows no other servitude than that of the law" and "must be free to pronounce in the sovereignty of his conscience") over the latter (for whom "duty consists in obeying, in ignorance of reasons, under the yoke of an iron discipline that suppresses the two essential factors of human individuality: initiative, responsibility").[5]

With partners like that, Socialists certainly could hope for more than a mild refurbishing of an intact military jurisdiction. In fact, the first demonstration of the new climate and the evolving "mainstream" view was Massé's own submission in 1902 of a considerably amended bill, which no longer contented itself with the professionalization of military tribunals and *parquets* or the attenuation of military penalties but, rather, went further, proposing a direct reduction of the competence of the jurisdiction. Specifically, Massé's 1902 bill included a provision for the transfer of civil offenses committed "out of service" to civil jurisdictions.[6]

Significantly, the government itself endorsed this approach over the course of the next year. Waldeck-Rousseau's new war minister, General Louis André, assembled some of the measures Massé and others had already advanced into a three-pronged measure that would bear his and the government's own imprimatur. Like Massé, André proposed that the military jurisdiction's *cours de révision* be replaced with the civilian High Court of Appeals. André further proposed that military judges be drawn from the ranks of officers holding legal degrees. Most significantly, he echoed Massé's proposal that jurisdiction over civil offenses committed outside service (excepting assaults, outrages, and threats by military personnel to one another) be remanded to civil tribunals.[7]

As the century turned, then, it seemed clear that the military jurisdiction, which had stood unchanged in its fundamentals since 1857 (or even, arguably, since the days of the Directory) was about to undergo major surgery. The only question seemed to be how radical that surgery was going to be. At the very least, it seemed that the *rationae personae* principle was about to be tempered by some bow in the direction of *rationae materiae*, with jurisdiction over at least certain kinds of civil offenses shared with civil courts. Under the circumstances, defenders of military justice might have considered the advisability of a legislative bargain: a qualification of *rationae personae*, in return for continued jurisdiction over specifically military offenses (however those might be defined); and maintenance of tribunal procedures that elevated "celerity" and "exemplarity" over defendants' rights; and retention of a penal code that was both considerably harsher and less egalitarian than its civilian counterpart.

But the jurisdiction's supporters instead stiffened their resistance to change, refusing to cede any measure of *rationae personae* despite the new and markedly less favorable political circumstances they faced. Their resistance to any encroachments on the basic competence of the jurisdiction was largely based on fears within the military that reformists saw this as the beginning, not the end, of the process they had in mind. Those fears were hardly irrational. In fact, they were intensified by the overall campaign General André had undertaken from his position in the war ministry.

The Waldeck-Rousseau government had entrusted to André the larger undertaking of "republicanizing" the army, of which the reform of military justice was just one component. The key to overall victory, he felt, was breaking the power of the General Staff, which in his own and prior war ministers' views had gradually usurped policy prerogatives that properly resided with the war ministry. In 1890, War Minister Charles Freycinet had tried to emulate Germany's command structure by reconfiguring France's General Staff—no longer the "General Staff of the War Minister," it was to be the "General Staff of the Army." Freycinet had wanted a General Staff as insulated from civilian interference as Germany's. He urged his countrymen to imagine their General Staff as "a specific, autonomous service, essentially technical, which must remain sheltered from ministerial instability."[8] From this attempt to screen the army from cabinet and parliamentary influences, André felt, emerged everything that was un- or antirepublican in the French army, for the General Staff was the true center of resistance to the new political order. If that center could be neutralized, André believed, the entire program of *L'Armée, c'est la Nation* would fall into place.

Tactically he decided that the best site for this battle would be the promotion process, which was dominated by "classification commissions" affiliated with the General Staff. These commissions prepared annual promotion tables, which for decades the war minister had simply rubber-stamped. André's predecessor, the republican General Gaston de Gallifet, had described the process as an "absolute abdication" of the prerogatives of the war minister, indeed an implicit denial of the civilian government's supremacy over the military, and had begun reducing the commissions' role in it.[9] In 1901 André had simply abolished the commissions entirely. He explained that in returning promotion decisions to the office of the war minister he had essentially placed it all "in the hands of parliament," where it belonged.[10]

The effect of that sort of language on officers committed to the continued political insulation of military justice can be imagined. Did this, too, belong in the hands of parliament? The substance of André's proposed alteration of the military jurisdiction was only a reduction of its competence, a partial instantiation of the *rationae materiae* principle. Yet in light of his specific action on promotions, and the general philosophy known to be driving the broadly gauged military reform to which the government he served had committed itself, defenders of the system could hardly ignore the possibility that any victory by André and the Radicals must represent the beginning of full and unapologetic civilianization of the jurisdiction (i.e., the full "politicization" of it). *Rationae personae* must therefore be defended at all costs.

An enraged General Bourelly went so far as to argue that "the remand to common law of nonmilitary crimes and offenses, the attribution to the High Court of Appeals by military personnel, would be fatal."[11] Bourelly's argument, repeatedly echoed by like-minded defenders of military justice, was that allowing civilian courts any share of jurisdiction over military personnel must ruinously dilute the authority that military courts required to enforce discipline. "The day when the examining magistrate would come into the barracks to order proceedings, and when the red-trouser [soldier] would make an appearance at the bench of the assizes and in the civilian correctional facility," Bourelly warned, "we will have taken a decisive turn toward demilitarization."[12] That hardly seemed alarmist to Bourelly; after all, the triumphant Dreyfusards had made their long-range goal clear. In 1903, Bourelly noted, Clemenceau (elected to a senatorial seat the previous year) was supporting another bill that would not only further delimit the competence of the military tribunals but "completely recast the penalties of the military code and go so far as to efface all distinctions, regarding those penalties, between the officer and the soldier."[13] Military organization itself could hardly survive such measures.

Bourelly and other defenders of the jurisdiction were still strong enough to stem the reformist tide in those first years of the century. Indeed, given André's administrative priorities and the depth of opposition he generated in some quarters of the army, it is scarcely surprising that military justice underwent very little real alteration under his tenure, despite his own and others' determination to reform it and the generally propitious political climate. The small measures of 1901 (including a ministerial edict of that year whereby time served in preventive custody prior to trial could be deducted from whatever sentence a *conseil de guerre* might eventually impose) were not followed by more substantive reforms. The year 1904 witnessed only one more modest achievement: the legalization of executive reprieves and stays of execution (again, a measure enacted earlier for the civilian system and now applied to the military).

That, in fact, would be André's last year in office. He was politically undone by the celebrated *affaire des fiches* (index-card affair), a scandal that engulfed the government when news broke that the war minister had built a secret intelligence network from friendly Masonic lodges, amassing information about officers' private religious affiliations and political views and apparently using it in his promotions decisions.[14] The outcry cost André his position and helped eject Émile Combes from the premiership (which he had taken from Waldeck-Rousseau in 1902) as well.

But the process of legislatively "republicanizing" the army actually accelerated under new sponsorship. In 1905 *L'Armée* was brought much closer to *la Nation* when the term of enlistment was reduced to two years and all exemptions essentially ended. That 1905 law elevated the importance of the citizen-soldier and reservist, the ordinary Frenchman, over that of the professionalized careerist to a degree that provoked misgivings in even General André. Legislators were unapologetic and frank enough about their intentions. "To tell the truth," intoned Senator Rolland in the Chamber of Deputies, "we are infinitely more preoccupied with the question of principle than with the practical consequences. . . . This law, gentlemen, evidently opens for the army an era which I will dare to call . . . the era of civilianism."[15] In fact, the 1905 law would be complemented by a flurry of "decrees, circulars, committee reports" that were clearly intended to "desacralize" the army by, for example, deliberately diminishing the personal prestige attached to the uniform, a prestige that had served to compensate officers for their notoriously low pay.[16] It was no surprise that such measures would issue from a government that owed many of its operating principles to the Dreyfus Affair. As early as 1899, after all, Émile Duclaux had declared that "the honor of the army" was qualitatively no finer than the honor of, say, the university and pointedly noted that the nation paid soldiers to defend it "just as it paid professors to discipline minds."[17]

It was perfectly obvious that the effort to "civilianize" military justice at least partially would be renewed; in fact, its adherents could be expected to push harder than ever, and for more extensive reform. For if military men saw reform going too far too fast, the opposite assessment prevailed on the left of the political spectrum. There, pressure was building to go well beyond the proposals that had been advanced thus far. For example, militant socialists argued that André's proposal to remand civil offenses to civil courts had been fatally compromised by its provision allowing military courts to retain jurisdiction over civil offenses committed *in* service. Those "in service" cases, critics claimed, were precisely the most common ones in military courts and the source of the greatest iniquities. That weakness would hardly be compensated by permitting soldiers to appeal convictions to the civilian High Court rather than to military *cours de révision*. The High Court, like the army's own appellate courts, could rule only on procedural questions, which meant it could reverse only the verdicts of soldiers tormented by military courts in flagrantly illegal ways. The vast majority of those courts' victims were, in fact, destroyed with perfect legality, and this would continue to be the case until the jurisdiction's competence had been reduced far more drastically than anyone had yet proposed.[18]

Aware of the strength of those arguments on the "second left," Socialists knew they had to deliver considerably more substantive reforms than those on offer thus far. But there was a problem: their partners in the *bloc des gauches* were proving much less cooperative than the Jaurèsians had hoped. In fact, Socialists were growing impatient with the commitment of their Radical allies to social amelioration in general. Radicals, for their part, made no secret of the fact that their priority was church-state relations. Socialists generally shared the Radicals' determination to extrude the church fully from the state (formalized, in a wrenching process, in 1905). But they could not content themselves with action on that front alone and sometimes feared that Radical absorption in it was an all too convenient rationale for inaction on other, equally urgent, questions. Recognizing that antimilitarism was deepening on the left, Socialists had to produce tangible benefits for conscripted proletarians—and promptly. After all, military justice had been much discussed but not yet much reformed.

In 1904 participants at the International Socialist Congress meeting in Amsterdam decided to stiffen parliamentarians' spines a bit. Mindful of militants' hostility to parliamentarianism, delegates hoped to narrow the ideological divide on the left by urging parliamentarians to at least foreswear further participation in bourgeois cabinets or support for bourgeois governments. Jaurès's SFIO duly withdrew from the *bloc des gauches* and assumed a posture of principled opposition to the Radical cabinet. The hope was that reforms Socialists had been unable to purchase through support for Radical governments might be forced from them through confrontation.

In fact, an April 17, 1906, finance bill occasioned an especially lively discussion, as reformists succeeded in including a provision (Article 44) that finally ended the *conseils de révision*. To Socialists this was an opening salvo signaling their determination to secure real change in the military jurisdiction. Noting that the *conseils de révision* had been "one of the key components of the judicial armature of 1857," one Socialist credited the measure with having "brutally—one could even say revolutionarily—dispossessed" military justice of something vital—with, hopefully, much more to follow.[19]

Indeed, 1906 was a promising year for those committed to meaningful reform of the jurisdiction, and a depressing one for its defenders. Three years earlier Alfred Dreyfus had petitioned the High Court of Appeals to quash the verdict of the Rennes tribunal. In July 1906 it did so and then went much further. The court expressly refused to remand the case to a military court, or to any other, for what would have been a third Dreyfus trial. In fact, it declared him innocent of all charges. The decision may have represented questionable jurisprudence, since the court was permitted to present independent judgments only in very rare circumstances, which some argued had not been fulfilled.[20] The stinging rebuke it delivered to French military justice, however, was crystal-clear to everyone.

The year's most significant event regarding the future of military justice was certainly the assumption of the premiership by Georges Clemenceau, who was already interior minister, on October 25, 1906. Critics of the jurisdiction could take heart at this ascent to power of one of its most implacable foes. Defenders, on the other hand, had every reason to wish they had embraced some of the modest reforms Massé had offered in 1898, before the change in political circumstances had rendered those *passé* and more drastic ones likely. In fact, with the premiership of Clemenceau a demolition of the 1857 *CJM* seemed inevitable. Time and circumstance had never before so clearly favored such an outcome—and never would again.

In his very first ministerial declaration Clemenceau openly promised something like the abolition of military courts and their replacement by civilian ones.[21] His resolve seemed unquestionable, especially when he tapped Georges Picquart, of all people, to serve as his war minister. Picquart, after all, had been drummed out of the service and incarcerated for nearly a year under French military justice. Who understood its deficiencies better? Who could possibly be more driven to correct them? By January 1907 Picquart, along with Justice Minister Guyot-Dessaigne and Marine Minister Thomson, had prepared provisional legislation with which they hoped to settle the question of military justice once and for all.

Indeed, by that time even some of the system's defenders, including some of its own operatives, were prepared to accept serious restructuring, if only in the interests of political expediency. The army currently operated "judicial institutions whose complete transformation can't be retarded much longer," wrote one sympathetic military journalist, "given the attacks of which they are the object without being defended by anyone."[22] "Fragmentary reforms, especially in this matter," argued a sympathetic legal scholar, "are insufficient: new principles can have their effect only with a complete recasting."[23] A military jurist, Lieutenant François Bassieux, claimed that the piecemeal reforms enacted to date had actually softened discipline without advancing justice, and he went on to argue that the adoption of a *rationae materiae* standard was imperative if the system were to function with anything approaching effectiveness.[24] Certainly, the report prepared on Picquart's proposal, submitted by the Commission on Judicial Reform in May, shared that sense of both the urgency and magnitude of the task: "Everyone today recognizes that the old legislation in this area has had its time. . . . [A] special justice organized thusly appears to us today as an outmoded institution that must be radically transformed."[25]

What Picquart and his associates produced was General Bourelly's worst nightmare. "The military tribunals of the land and naval forces and the maritime tribunals are suppressed," their proposal stated bluntly. "All crimes, offenses, and contraventions committed by soldiers or sailors are remanded to the competence of the jurisdictions of common law."[26] Military justice as currently constituted would simply cease to exist. What the proposal's authors offered in place of the old jurisdiction was a complex array of measures whereby the enforcement of military discipline would be incorporated into civilian legal codes and enforced in civilian courts—with both codes and courts somewhat modified to allow for the accommodation of specifically military concerns.[27]

Picquart and his associates were nothing if not ambitious. The first task they set themselves was redefining the category of "military offenses," that is, acts with substantially deleterious consequences for discipline. The proposal they brought forth attempted to balance the *rationae personae* and *rationae materiae* principles. It reconfigured "military offenses" to include both acts that were offenses precisely because—and only when—they were committed by military personnel (e.g., abandonment of post, insubordination) and those that, while offenses in the civilian sphere as well (theft, assault), could carry special consequences when committed by members of the services. Both types of offenses were to be incorporated into various provisions of the civil and criminal codes, either through new provisions specifying offenses against military order or through new articles of existing provisions, disbursing harsher penalties when violators were military personnel (whose status constituted a new variety of the "aggravating circumstances" already admitted in ordinary law).

Enforcement of these new laws was treated at great length. Most military offenders would now wind up, like civilian offenders, in civilian courts—either correctional tribunals (for bench judgments) or assize courts (for jury trials), depending on the offense. But the proposal also created special mixed tribunals to adjudicate the military offenses it enumerated. After the charge had been brought and a civilian investigator had assembled a case, it would be heard by a newly created section of whichever civilian tribunal held jurisdiction over it. In those special sections civilian judges would be joined by their military counterparts. The exact number of each, as well as other important questions regarding the composition of these mixed tribunals (e.g., whether their presidents would be civilian or military), were left open in the proposal, to be determined by the normal parliamentary amendment process after a period of debate. Picquart endorsed suspension of the civilian principle that the determination of facts should be separated from the selection of penalty in these new, mixed tribunals; he argued for military input into both. However, in a separate report he prepared on the legislation in his capacity as war minister, he also made clear that the proposal's authors did not intend to grant military personnel decisive power in the new bodies. The system must actually replace the *conseils de guerre*, not simply reconstitute them in another setting.[28]

Some on the left feared precisely this and remained highly skeptical that the problem could be skirted. Socialist Gustave Rouanet, for instance, argued (*pace* Lhermitte) that French military judges had, in fact, never been particularly iniquitous in the administration of civilian law; it was, rather, their furious repression of specifically military offenses that had earned the opprobrium of the nation, and this was precisely the role to which they would be readmitted under Picquart's reform.[29] Invoking, as always, "the spirit of caste" as automatic disqualifier, Rouanet and others on the left insisted that officers be debarred from any judicial function whatsoever.

Nevertheless, the Picquart proposal could hardly be categorized as cosmetic. Regarding the penal dimensions of military justice, it broke dramatically with the status quo. Besides attenuating numerous punishments, it outlawed the death penalty for any military crime committed in peacetime, excepting violent assault, in service, on a superior or a sentinel; the direction of armed rebellion; or the organization of collective desertion to the enemy. It outlawed forced labor (i.e., "public works") as a form of punishment for military personnel. It began narrowing the gap between punishments meted out to officers and ordinary soldiers by toughening those devolved on the former (mainly substituting outright dismissal from the service for the milder loss of rank that had accrued to most of those officers unfortunate enough to be convicted by a military tribunal). Above all, it terminated the operation of separate military prisons entirely. Biribi was to disappear.

But what was even more distressing to military conservatives was what the proposal would mean for the political insularity of the jurisdiction. Conservatives had always thought that any sharing of responsibility for the enforcement of discipline with civilian institutions would subvert that insularity. The Picquart proposal actually went further. In remanding civil offenses to civilian tribunals, it seriously undercut the procedural role of the general, once the unquestioned primate of the system, whose monopoly over key decisions posed a formidable barrier against civilian influence. Furthermore, investigation would be handed over almost entirely to civilian authorities. The general could request initiation of an investigation after a complaint had been brought to his attention; but all further decisions fell to the public prosecutor—a decidedly secondary figure in the current system, and an appointee of the justice minister. One commentator felt that Picquart's reform put the divisional general in the same juridical position as an ordinary cuckold in civil law: apprised of the violation, he could take his complaint to the civil authorities and hope for redress but was strictly precluded from undertaking any action of his own. In fact, argued the same commentator, the general had somewhat fewer options than an aggrieved civilian. If the public prosecutor chose to dismiss a civilian complainant's grievance, the latter could appeal to a special *chambre des mises en accusation* (accusations board) for a reversal of that decision. Picquart's proposal afforded generals no such recourse.[30]

The proposal was first presented in January. The war and justice ministers submitted their own reports in May, and debate began in June. There was little likelihood that the entirety of it would have passed (there were several competing proposals in various stages of development). But there was no question that the left was about to make substantial progress toward its goal: the days of an entirely separate military jurisdiction, dominated by officers insulated from all political accountability, seemed to be nearing their end, at least in peacetime. With Picquart and Clemenceau in power, how could it be otherwise?[31]

But it was not to be. The *conseils de guerre* would be saved when, at the last minute, Clemenceau and Picquart themselves decided to abort the reform. In perhaps the strangest development in the strange history of French military justice to date, those two celebrated Dreyfusards would find themselves converted to the conservative position on military justice, after pondering the implications of an act of mutiny within the army itself.

Clemenceau's own antipathy to the army had been abating for some time, as he came to appreciate its utility in repressing strikes and other workers' actions when they took a violent turn. The Midi had seemed on the verge of serious labor violence since 1903, when viticulturists had begun protesting the collapse of prices for their product. By the spring of 1907, economic hardship in the area was generating large-scale, sometimes tumultuous actions. Clemenceau decided to deploy a cavalry regiment from outside the region to secure the arrest of some of the protests' leaders, and violence broke out in two separate locations.[32] On July 20 four people were killed in the town of Narbonne. But it was the behavior of the locally recruited soldiers of the Seventeenth Infantry Regiment that most concerned the government. These men, stationed in Agde, made common cause with the protesters, looted an arsenal in Béziers, and threatened to march on Narbonne, where five protesters had already been killed.

In the end, cooler heads prevailed. The soldiers were persuaded to return to the barracks at Béziers, and from there back to Agde. In fact, the commandant of the regiment would later evince some sympathy with the mutineers and confirm that officers had never been threatened. But neither Clemenceau nor Picquart was inclined toward leniency. The regiment was collectively punished with a harsh Tunisian posting, where several of its members would die.

The consequences of the event were felt well beyond the ranks of the Seventeenth Regiment. The incident gave Clemenceau and Picquart cause to reconsider the desirability of casting aside France's current *CJM* and entrusting military discipline to the good offices of her civilian courts and *parquets*. Arguably, this was hardly the time to experiment with a further "civilianization" of military justice; discipline needed to be fortified, not relaxed. Clemenceau's words might almost have issued from the mouth of General Bourelly himself as he addressed an astonished parliament: "There is a civil society founded on liberty and a military society, through which all citizens pass at a given moment, founded on obedience. It can't be helped; it's a fact. Can the judge of liberty be the judge of obedience?"[33] Ruefully, he concluded that the answer had to be no. To the horror of Socialists, the government withdrew the Picquart proposal from its legislative agenda. Clemenceau proceeded to confirm his shift rightward on military matters by appointing the Jesuit-trained Ferdinand Foch as the new commandant of the *École de Guerre*.

To be sure, Picquart would bring a similar measure back to parliament in 1909. In fact, there was a fairly vigorous parliamentary debate on the best means to guarantee the independence and professionalism of judges on the mixed tribunals Picquart once again proposed (must civilian judges themselves be veterans? should military judges be permitted to rule on motions for their own recusal?).[34] But the debate was basically meaningless, as Clemenceau in particular must have known: with Radical-Socialist estrangement now complete, the moment for substantive reform had passed, and the bill died a slow parliamentary death. Conservative forces in the Chamber of Deputies began the process by amending the measure to stiffen penalties and, in particular, to assure a preponderance of military elements in the proposed mixed tribunals (on certain offenses, nearly the entirety of the tribunal would be officers, with only its presidency left to a civilian jurist). Jaurès and the Socialists must have anticipated the opprobrium that Hervéists and anarchists would shower on them if they dared endorse such a watered-down measure—this, after all, was a bill that the Radical Deputy Lasies supported precisely because "it suppresses the *conseils de guerre* in the first article, but it reestablishes them in

Article 3 and the following ones."[35] In the end, Socialists' votes didn't matter anyway. Even the diluted reform passed by the Chamber of Deputies was too much for conservatives in the Senate, who opposed the role still left to civilian investigators and other aspects of the bill. Competing measures were eventually put forward by Senator Langlais and Senator Gouzy, all requiring further study.[36] In the end, nothing was done. The reform process had been effectively derailed.[37]

In the process, the standing civil-military compact had been affirmed. In fact, the defeat of the reform initiative reflected the deepening commitment to it on both sides: civil society's willingness—even enthusiasm—to countenance the repressiveness of military justice and the army's willingness to deploy those repressive mechanisms against elements that civil authorities feared. The conservative forces that had beaten back reform, despite an apparently irresistible alignment of political forces in favor of it, had been immeasurably aided by a darkening public mood regarding what seemed to be an expansion of crime and disorder within the nation—and the need to strengthen repressive machinery of all sorts in dealing with them.

This was the alleged "crisis of repression" that exercised not only criminologists, jurists, journalists, and legislators but a sizable sector of the public in the early 1900s.[38] Their concern was that under the general influence of that humane, "enlightened" sensibility that had devolved from eighteenth-century *philosophes* to contemporary republicans, French judges, police, and even prison administrators had been evincing an unwarranted solicitude for the well-being of defendants, suspects, even convicts—and that crime rates were expanding as a result. That softness, the argument went, must be reversed.

It certainly should not be further replicated in military courts. In fact, commentators on military justice could and did argue that the transposition to the military jurisdiction of initiatives originating in the civil sphere (e.g., more frequent reprieves, the subtraction of preventive detention from sentences, earlier access to attorneys by suspects, the admission of attenuating circumstances) had already weakened the administration of military justice. Indeed, there was no question that insubordination, desertion, and other offenses were dramatically up. On April 2, 1908, the war minister had taken the tribune of the Chamber of Deputies and announced that between 1904 and 1908 desertions had risen from 2,004 to 3,437, while unauthorized absences had risen from 4,600 to 10,630. A year earlier the army commission in the Chamber of Deputies had reported a rise in disciplinary infractions from 1,278 in 1898 to 2,052 in 1906, while citing a rise in common-law offenses from 4,238 to 6,323.[39]

To General Bourelly and to many others these trends were even more alarming within the army than outside it. After all, there was a qualitative difference between civilian and military criminality. The former might correlate to general economic conditions, but the latter reflected the general strength of a society's moral commitments.[40] For that reason, military discipline was special—and especially vital, as men like General Bourelly had argued for so many years. No nation, and particularly not a democratic one, could survive without "an ensemble of ideas, of sentiments or habits existing among individuals, able to produce in the collectivity a common orientation and a harmonious action." Discipline was simply the means by which individual interests and urges were subordinated to those collective ends—and military discipline was the model for all other kinds: "The discipline of the army is the common orientation, as general and absolute as possible, of all its individualities, supported by moral forces having the same goals, namely, public well-being and success in war."[41]

General Bourelly was hardly alone in arguing that staying even further the hand of military justice, carrying more deeply into the military jurisdiction currents that had already proven wrongheaded in the civilian sphere, would be disastrous. In this era of universal conscription (when socialists, anarchists, and career criminals were all brought under arms and commingled with healthier elements), the worst thing that could happen would be a further accommodation of the woolly headed humanitarianism that had unleashed a plague of *apaches* (hooligans) on civil society. "The contagion has reached the army itself," Bourelly wrote—and it had to be arrested.[42]

This concern and these conditions provided the backdrop to Clemenceau and Picquart's consideration of the mutiny of the Seventeenth Infantry Regiment, and their decision to defer, if not abandon, further "civilianization" of military justice. They must have shared, to some degree, the belief of Bourelly and others that the criminal disorderly elements in the army were functionally unredeemable and that only the sternest of repressive measures were appropriate for them. In granting military justice maximum latitude to do this, they not only renewed the civil-military compact but added a proviso to it.

And in doing this, they set the stage for the Aernoult-Rousset Affair. For every aspect of it—especially the unredeemability of France's *apaches*—would be contested by its key protagonists. What couldn't be modified effectively in parliament would now be challenged in the streets.

Djennan-ed-Dar, 1909

If Biribi was antimilitarists' vision of hell, the *compagnie de discipline* at Djennan-ed-Dar was its ninth circle.

The settlement was situated within the Figuig oasis, very near the Moroccan border, about four hundred kilometers south of Oran—a dangerous place in general. Life in the desert outside the oasis was precarious at best, and not much more secure within it. The territory was periodically contested by the sultan of Morocco, and rebellious Zenaga tribesmen had attacked no less a personage than the governor-general of Algeria in 1903.[1] Escape from Djennan-ed-Dar, then, was not a very plausible option.

The camp itself was located about six kilometers' distance from the *Bat d'Af* garrison at Beni-Ounif, within the military district of Ain-Sefra. In 1907, leftist journalist Jacques Dhur had described the camp as one of the worst in Algeria. In particular, he stressed the ravages of a certain Sergeant Iribarne, who delighted in clubbing prisoners whose heads were not tilted at the proper angle when saluting; and the attempted suicide of a cook named Steiner, sickened beyond endurance by his own forced participation in beatings ordered by Iribarne.[2] Dhur's account was not the only testament to conditions inside the camp. A former prisoner named Alfred Braucke, sent to Djennan-ed-Dar from Beni-Ounif in 1905, recalled vicious rifle-butt attacks on exhausted prisoners chained together following punishment exercises, conducted by native auxiliaries under the supervision of French noncoms.[3] Such stories might well explain a camp officer's observation that Djennan-ed-Dar's *gradés*, who were quartered in or near prisoners' barracks, were invariably insomniacs. They rightly feared, he said, nocturnal attacks.[4]

If Djennan-ed-Dar conformed to antimilitarists' general vision of military prisons, the short life of Albert Aernoult was a letter-perfect illustration of their depiction of the army as Moloch devouring proletarian youth—and of the special relish with which it consumed rebels and militants among them.[5] Aernoult was born in 1886 in the Parisian suburb of Romainville, where his father was a day laborer. Albert, too, was a manual laborer, a ditch digger who joined the *syndicat des terrassiers* (unskilled laborers' union, affiliated with the famously militant construction trades) and eventually came to work as a *couvreur* (slater/tiler). By 1905 he was one of many local workers employed in the construction of the Paris *métro*, until a strike temporarily halted work on the project. The crucial event in Aernoult's life was his participation at the end of that year in a labor action that turned violent. Specifically, Aernoult was involved in an attack on scab laborers. Such actions were hardly criminal in the eyes of working-class militants, who labeled them, somewhat blithely, "fox hunts" (a speaker at a rally in Bordeaux would later defend Aernoult's participation in the *chasse de renard* at Romainville by arguing that "well, you can't hesitate, when need arises, to fix a 'yellow' [scab] with a hobnailed boot").[6] The authorities, however, took a different view. Recognized and denounced to the police, Aernoult fled to the mining community of Courrières and was sentenced in absentia to two years in prison. A disaster at the mine forced his return to Romainville, where, still a minor and with no prior record, he appealed his sentence. It was reduced to ten months, to be served at *la Petite Roquette* (the Little Rocket) prison in Paris.

Aernoult understood that, with a reputation as a labor militant and a criminal conviction formally inscribed in the *livret* (passbook) he was required to show potential employers, his future was not bright. This might explain his alleged receptivity to the counsel of the military recruiter who, according to later accounts of his life in the antimilitarist press, visited the prisoner as his term at *la Petite Roquette* neared its end.[7] Aernoult would have been conscripted upon completion of his sentence in any event; but in these versions, he was persuaded to enlist voluntarily—apparently, in the hope that voluntary enlistment, followed by a good record in the *Bat d'Af* to which he would be posted, might make a favorable impression on prospective employers when he reentered the civilian world. Enlist (he was allegedly told), serve honorably, and your social standing will be refurbished. On March 26, 1907, he did just that.

But Albert Aernoult was not able to compile the sterling military record that might have elevated him from a *Bat d'Af* to a regular unit or brought smiles to the faces of prospective employers at home. Instead, he incurred the sorts of disciplinary infractions that led, inevitably, to Biribi. On July 1, 1909, he was transported by train from Mecheria to Beni-Ounif and from there to Djennan-ed-Dar, where he was to spend three days completing a sentence he had begun serving earlier. Aernoult may have been one of the prisoners who actually requested posting to a *compagnie de discipline* to finish such sentences (a brief spell at one of them could sometimes be substituted for longer terms in less forbidding institutions).[8] In any event, it appears that he was not entirely unknown to the staff at Djennan-ed-Dar. He had reportedly met one of its *sous-offs*, Sergeant Jean-Marie Beignier, in a prior posting at Colomb-Béchar, and the encounter had not been a happy one.[9]

The thirty-two-year-old Beignier was, like the camp's other noncommissioned officers, himself a *Bat d'Af* conscript who had earned his rank in service. He reported directly to Lieutenant Antonin Gabriel Sabatier, who was one year older, of the Fifty-Second Infantry. Djennan-ed-Dar's commanding officer, Captain Charles Léopold Finot, assessed Sabatier as an officer "very jealous of his own initiative," one who "liked to command by himself." But whatever misgivings Finot had about Sabatier's dislike of direct supervision were outweighed by the fact that the latter was "more energetic" and "more feared by the men" than the officer he replaced in conducting special punishment details, a certain Lieutenant Jeannin.[10]

Punishment details were designed to be more painful than the normal work assigned prisoners. At Djennan-ed-Dar they consisted of filling wheelbarrows, large oil cans, and other heavy containers with sand that had blown up around the camp's low-lying walls; carrying the loads (ordinarily at rapid-time) wherever a supervising *sous-off* commanded; emptying them; and repeating the exercise until officers decided it was concluded. Those terms were enforced by a contingent of native auxiliaries. Under the pitiless African sun, this could be an excruciating ordeal. Officers had jocularly nicknamed the courtyard at Djennan-ed-Dar where these details were conducted "the Court of Miracles," presumably alluding to the similarly

Albert Aernoult. *Archives Nationales*, F/7/12909.

named setting in Victor Hugo's *Hunchback of Notre Dame,* where seemingly disabled beggars performed physical acts that defied belief.

But by 1909 Djennan-ed-Dar's prisoners had discovered a means of "flanking" (*tourneur*) the officers conducting punishment details, and securing at least temporary respite from the Court of Miracles. They could deliberately provoke a *conseil de guerre* hearing by refusing to obey a direct order. This almost certainly meant additional prison time when the tribunal got around to hearing the case; but in the short run it also meant immediate placement in preventive custody, a confinement far preferable to the punishment detail. In addition, since passage of the 1901 law admitting extenuating circumstances as a form of defense, a *conseil de guerre* hearing might provide a forum for prisoners to level accusations of mistreatment against officers, accusations that were otherwise difficult to lodge. Officers believed that prisoners were gaming the system, using the tribunals' procedures as a form of leverage against officers properly administering perfectly legal punishments.[11]

They had been instructed to discourage the practice. Captain Finot would later recall having been apprised that prisoners deploying this tactic could often be induced to drop it if duly informed of the risk of a much longer sentence and provided plenty of time to think it over. Finot, however, would deny ever having been advised, or having authorized any serving officer at Djennan-ed-Dar, to skirt regulations precluding the use of physical force on recalcitrant prisoners.[12] The question at the camp on July 2, 1909, was whether Lieutenant Sabatier, as well as the other noncoms and auxiliaries who conducted the punishment detail on that day, observed those regulations.

Albert Aernoult's fate was essentially left to their discretion. Having arrived at camp after mess time on July 1, he was immediately put into a cell rather than fed. In fact, Aernoult had spent the previous six days in a cell, on reduced rations, and would be facing the punishment detail he was slated to undergo in a weakened condition. He was nonetheless awakened at around 2 a.m. and taken to the commissary to get his prison clothing. Around 7 a.m. he and another prisoner named Debon were brought to the Court of Miracles to begin the detail under the supervision of Sergeant David Casanova, who would observe the prisoners at a distance while a native auxiliary stood close by. For two hours Aernoult and Debon transported the heavy loads, at rapid-time, without incident. The courtyard faced a row of cellules, from which prisoners serving sentences could observe at least some of what was happening.

Other prisoners were engaged in various details in different parts of the camp. One of them was Émile Rousset, whose entire life would be altered beyond recognition by the events of the next few hours and his response to them.

Rousset's life up to that point had been quite different from Aernoult's. He was not a bona fide proletarian, although his background was humble enough. Rather, he was the classic *apache*, a career criminal. Born in Lyons, Rousset was part of a remarkably felonious family. He was twelve when his father died, leaving his illiterate mother, Antoinette Long, with "five or six" children to care for. She would incur nine prison terms for theft over the course of her life (she was serving her seventh in July 1909, while the events at Djennan-ed-Dar unfolded). Louis Rousset, a day laborer, was convicted twice for theft, while brothers Louis Théophile and Jean were both sentenced to forced labor (eight and five years, respectively) for homicides. Brother Aimé was the most virtuous; he had been convicted only once, for pilfering.[13] Émile, for his part, had been convicted of theft four times prior to his induction into the army. Physically slight, he was nonetheless a very formidable man: shrewd, tough, capable of sudden violence, and skilled with a knife.

Rousset had begun his military service on January 8, 1908, at the age of twenty-five (he would later describe gendarmes taking him, in handcuffs, directly from the prison, where he had just spent five years, to the induction center).[14] Within a month, while in transit from Marseilles to Blida, he incurred his first military penalty: fifteen days for fighting with a fellow inductee over a consignment of bedding straw. He would incur ten more penalties while winding his way from the garrison at Médéa to the penal institution at Boussauda, then the one at Djelfa, throughout 1908 and 1909. Rousset's offenses ranged from inexcused absences, to "insolent" responses to orders, to an unauthorized appearance "in a room other than his own" (where he "made the greatest difficulties" in leaving). He was nothing if not audacious, and he had a wicked sense of humor: on July 10, 1908, he enraged jailers and fellow prisoners alike by singing the "*Internationale*" at the top of his lungs throughout the night, denying everyone a moment's rest. On August 1 he escaped from that confinement and threw a bottle at one of the noncoms who rearrested him. Finally, in April 1909, a knife fight with a fellow prisoner at Djelfa landed him at Djennan-ed-Dar.[15]

If Rousset and his admirers are to be believed, three months later he stood on the verge of a dramatic personal transformation. By their accounts, his chronic, inchoate rebelliousness was about to find a suitable focus—or, rather, two of them: French military justice and his own moral shortcomings. In fact, by these accounts Émile Rousset was about to discover qualities within himself he had never known he had: solidarity with his fellow victims, a capacity for leadership, self-control—even a certain eloquence of expression. The *apache*, it would be held, had never been the real Rousset; merely a shell containing him. Within that shell lay a proletarian avenger—battler of class oppression, in general, implacable foe of the army and the torture chamber it called "military justice," in particular. This avenger was about to be awakened by the screams of Albert Aernoult.

The details of what actually happened in and near the Court of Miracles on July 2 would be hotly contested; but its general outline can be reconstructed clearly enough (see Appendix B). The tragedy began around 9 a.m., when Albert Aernoult decided that he could endure no more of the punishment detail and refused Casanova's direct order to continue. Casanova apprised Lieutenant Sabatier of the situation and Sabatier, as apparently was his wont, took it in hand personally. He simply refused to heed Aernoult's protestations of incapacity and repeatedly demanded that the prisoner resume his labors. An exasperated Aernoult finally responded by verbally abusing the lieutenant—thus compounding his refusal to obey with what was actually the graver offense of "outrage" toward a superior. What he couldn't have realized was that, no matter what offense he gave, Sabatier had no intention of allowing the prisoner to "flank" him and escape the detail.

Rousset and other observers would later insist that the lieutenant responded to Aernoult's verbal attack by beating the prisoner with his cane. This Sabatier and Casanova vehemently denied. They also denied having Aernoult placed in the *crapaudine*, as some observers claimed. But they did not deny returning the prisoner to his cell and tying him up there. That action was the first of several debatable measures the officers took in dealing with Aernoult. According to regulations, restraining devices were never authorized as a way to compel obedience; they were to be used only when a prisoner had become a physical threat to himself or to others, and then only for the duration of that threat. Sabataier and Casanova would insist that the unarmed and exhausted Aernoult, by then surrounded by several native auxiliaries as well as themselves, was indeed a menacing figure. Alone in his cell, Aernoult struggled futilely against his restraints for some twenty minutes, whereupon he agreed to return to the courtyard to complete his detail. He would perform his labors there for another fifteen or twenty minutes.

Émile Rousset, from *Comité de la Défense Sociale* (*CDS*) pamphlet, *L'Affaire Rousset*. *Archives Nationales* F/7/12909.

By regulation, all work, including special details, was to be suspended from mid-morning until 2 or 3 p.m. This was *sieste*, and Aernoult was duly returned to his cell, given some soup, and allowed to rest until about 12:30 or 1 p.m. At that time Sergeant Beignier returned to Djennan-ed-Dar from Beni-Ounif, where he had gone to fetch two prisoners (Caron and Létresor) newly arrived from Colomb-Béchar. He incarcerated the new prisoners in cells adjacent to Aernoult's and gave them food and water. Aernoult asked for water as well, a request to which Beignier may have responded violently:

some prisoners and auxiliaries would allege that the sergeant and a couple of auxiliaries entered Aernoult's cell, retied him, beat him, and filled his mouth with sand. Beignier and most of the auxiliaries vehemently denied this.

At any rate, Aernoult was returned to his punishment around 2:30 p.m., this time outside the camp's walls on the road to Beni-Ounif. Laboring alongside Debon, he transported heavy loads of sand for about another hour under Casanova and Sabatier's supervision. At that point he complained about his shoes, which were replaced. The afternoon was an extremely hot one (probably about fifty degrees Centigrade), but Aernoult's labors were continued until about 4:45 p.m. He obeyed orders but his performance was increasingly careless and desultory, and Casanova suspected that the prisoner was feigning illness even when he actually dropped to the ground. The sergeant summoned an auxiliary to help him force Aernoult back to his feet, but the auxiliary refused. Casanova then summoned both Beignier and Sabatier. Witnesses would later insist that the officers tied and badly beat Aernoult on the spot. They denied this, but whatever exertions they did undertake to restore Aernoult to his labors proved unsuccessful. He was finally carried back inside the camp by a set of auxiliaries under Beignier's direction.

Sabatier then made a curious decision. He elected not to return Aernoult to his own cell, later explaining that he feared adverse reactions among prisoners to the sight of Aernoult's limp body. Instead, he had him brought to another cell facing a smaller courtyard near the kitchen—cellule number 4, out of sight of the row of cells that faced the Court of Miracles. Sabatier's own orderly, a Zouave named Save, wandered into that courtyard seeking soup. He was brusquely told by Beignier to leave. Other prisoners would claim to hear cries of distress, although no one could see anything.

What really happened that evening in cellule number 4 would be fully known only to Casanova, Beignier, Sabatier, and the auxiliaries who accompanied them. They would testify that around 6:30 p.m. Casanova and an auxiliary brought Aernoult some soup, which he refused. At 7 p.m. Beignier and Sabatier visited his cell, where they found him seated on the floor and unresponsive to their inquiries about his health. Beignier returned for evening roll call at 8 p.m., later claiming that when he knocked on the door Aernoult responded "What is it?" in a perfectly "natural" voice. A half hour later, Beignier returned to recheck the prisoner's health. This time Aernoult was lying fully extended on the floor, unconscious. Beignier sent for Sabatier, and the two tried unsuccessfully to revive Aernoult. Informed of the situation,

Comité de la Défense Sociale (*CDS*) poster, Aernoult's ordeal.
(*Archives Nationales* F/7/12909)

Captain Finot tried to telephone Doctor Dorange at Beni-Ounif. But the phone was not working well, so Beignier was dispatched to bring the doctor back personally. Dorange arrived between 10:30 and 11 p.m., made a cursory examination of both Aernoult and his cell and pronounced the prisoner dead.

The head and body contained numerous ecchymoses. But Captain Finot, having heard accounts of the day's events from Sabatier, Casanova, and Beignier, attributed them to the restraining devices and to Aernoult's struggles against them rather than to violence deliberately inflicted by his officers. He informed Commandant Bonnelet, the public minister at Beni-Ounif, that he considered the death a natural one, probably related to the heat. Dorange was not instructed to conduct an immediate autopsy, and the body was left under guard in Djennan-ed-Dar that night.

But Djennan-ed-Dar's prisoners did not react to Aernoult's death quite as calmly as Captain Finot. An auxiliary told the prisoner Le Gleut about it around 5 a.m. on July 3, and by 9:30 a.m. Sabatier himself had confirmed the news. He could not have been pleased when prisoners, led by one named Allaire and another named Lavallée, asked to see the body.[16] In fact, for a brief period the camp hovered on the brink of open revolt.

The military jurisdiction afforded prisoners only the narrowest legal channels for the expression of grievances. Unable to bring charges of their own against officers, they could complain to the public minister in the hope that he would act, but they would be liable to prosecution themselves if the minister deemed their charges groundless. Allaire's demand for passage to Beni-Ounif to request a formal inquest was thus a rather daring act. Under the circumstances, Finot elected to permit him to go, accompanied by a sergeant and two auxiliaries. But when Allaire arrived, he would be placed in a cell—where, he later alleged, he was submitted to the *crapaudine* and other reprisals. Several regular-army soldiers temporarily stationed in Djennan-ed-Dar as cooks and orderlies would follow Allaire to Beni-Ounif, equally intent on complaining to Bonnelet. They, too, faced incarceration upon arrival. But the men's actions may not have been entirely fruitless. An autopsy was ordered, to be conducted by Dorange in the garrison infirmary at Beni-Ounif. A contingent of prisoners was assembled to transport Aernoult's remains there, and Dorange examined them late in the evening on July 3 (the heat precluded waiting until daybreak). Meanwhile, at Djennan-ed-Dar, auxiliaries leveled guns and bayonets at prisoners, whose public murmurings were effectively silenced. Privately, however, those men were far from resigned to accepting what many had concluded was an overtly homicidal camp regime.

Dorange's report was thorough, and a small masterpiece of ambiguity.[17] He was able definitively to attribute Aernoult's death to "cerebral congestion [stroke] seemingly due to exterior heat." But he also conceded that this condition "could have been hastened by some violent contusions" the prisoner had suffered on his head and torso, which the physician described in detail and attempted to explain. Some of the ecchymoses, he suggested, might have been caused by the restraints that had been imposed on Aernoult; others by his own struggles against those restraints; and still others by the slaps, tongue-pullings, and other measures Sabatier and Beignier had employed in attempting to revive him. Lastly, Dorange proposed that Aernoult might have administered some of those wounds to himself while in a state of "surexcitation" brought on by his stroke. Specifically, Dorange proposed that Aernoult might have banged his head against the wall of his cell during the onset of the stroke, although he had found no blood there. With those hypotheses on the origins of Aernoult's wounds, Dorange seemed to absolve the officers who had conducted his punishment detail. Yet by implicating those wounds in the prisoner's death, and by the tentative language he used throughout, he also opened the door to further investigation and alternative explanations.

Captain Finot seemed unmindful of those alternatives when he wrote to the mayor of Romainville on July 4, bluntly informing him of Aernoult's death and directing that his parents be apprised. They were stunned. Finot had supplied no details, and their son had written just a few days earlier, seemingly in good health and reasonably good spirits. Neighbors of the family wrote Finot to request an explanation, and on July 10 he finally provided one to Aernoult's parents. "Your unfortunate child," began Finot, "whose conduct left a lot to be desired, underwent a violent fit on the day of July 2 and, in the state of cerebral surexcitation in which he found himself, was struck down by the stroke that carried him off." The captain described Aernoult's worsening condition on the night of July 2, informing his parents that "despite the care that was lavished on him" their son had died of natural causes established by a physician's careful inquest. With Aernoult's remains now interred at Beni-Ounif, the incident, as far as Finot was concerned, was closed.[18]

But Finot's dispatches were not the only communications Aernoult's parents received from Djennan-ed-Dar. By his own account, Émile Rousset had actually snuck out of camp on the evening of July 4 and trekked to Beni-Ounif to deposit a letter to his brother Aimé in the garrison's outgoing mail, a letter that certainly would have been intercepted if posted at Djennan-ed-Dar.[19] Officers "have just assassinated one of our comrade [*sic*] and maybe tomorrow it will be my turn," Rousset wrote, adding that "we really wanted to have a revolt. But we aren't enough for that."[20] He included in the mailing some additional letters that Aimée, in turn, was to send to Aernoult's parents and to the Parisian journal *Le Matin*.

Those letters did have an effect. On July 13 *Le Matin* reported the allegation of homicide at Djennan-ed-Dar, without revealing its source. *Paris-Est* would shortly do the same. For their part, Aernoult's parents had contacted representatives of the unskilled laborers' union upon receiving Rousset's note and asked for their assistance. That body was part of a regional federation of unions, the *Union des Syndicats de la Seine* (Union of Seine Unions), which was in turn affiliated with a national federation, the *Confédération Générale du Travail* (General Confederation of Labor) or *CGT*, where syndicalists, anarchists, and other advocates of direct labor action exercised considerable influence. Through that channel, news of the Aernoult matter would reach and eventually activate elements of the radical left. At the same time, parliamentary Socialists and other reformists would be apprised of what had happened in Djennan-ed-Dar through Romainville's representative in the Chamber of Deputies, the Socialist Adrien Veber, who decided to take up the cause. The party's organ, the estimable *L'Humanité*, would maintain modest but persistent coverage throughout July and August of the allegations surrounding Aernoult's death. The possibility that yet another working-class conscript had been martyred in Biribi was thus brought to the attention of a not insignificant sector of the French public.

What would that public make of it? Would it react with sustained outrage and demands for further investigation? Or had the death of an obscure soldier in a remote Algerian prison camp, under unclear circumstances contested by a handful of felons, already elicited as much attention as could reasonably be expected?

The answer to that question would be determined by what transpired next at Djennan-ed-Dar. The atmosphere there remained edgy. Officers were furious at the leak and suspected Rousset as its source. When, by the prisoner's account, Sergeant Beignier threatened to make him "walk down the same road as Aernoult," Rousset became genuinely frightened, and fear may have loosened his tongue. On July 17 Captain Finot was informed that Rousset had publicly vituperated Djennan-ed-Dar's *gradés* as "a bunch of cows, a pile of bandits."[21] According to Rousset, he had done no more than verbally protest the treatment Casanova was meting out to fellow prisoner Marcel Moreau during the latter's punishment detail: "Sergeant, what you're doing is shameful, you've just assassinated one of our comrades and now you already need one more victim!"[22] But Finot immediately ordered Rousset put into a cellule for eight days, then he wrote General Alix, the divisional commander, to request that the general exercise his own authority and extend the prisoner's cell time to its maximum of sixty days.[23] Rousset was led to his cell by Sergeant Ravot and Sergeant-Major Finestre who, upon reaching the cell door, informed him of Finot's initiative. At that point, according to both *sous-offs*, Rousset exploded in a rage, threatening Ravot as the door was closed.[24]

Rousset would strenuously deny this, but he was glad to acknowledge another utterance that activated the machinery of military justice. On both July 18 and 19 he responded to direct orders that he report for work with flat refusals. Both Lieutenant Sabatier and Captain Finot came to his cell and urged him to reconsider, warning him that he could extend his sentence by as much as two years. But the prisoner was adamant and openly confided his intentions to Lieutenant Jannin, an officer he respected. Like Aernoult before him, Rousset aimed to provoke a *conseil de guerre* hearing—there to submit both Beignier's threat and the dispatch of Aernoult as extenuating circumstances for his offense. Captain Finot, in fact, would submit testimony from prisoners Pierre Daguerre and Baptistine Paul Marou on July 20, both of whom claimed to have heard Rousset specifically state: "Two years in prison, that's not too much."[25]

With this act, Rousset really initiated the Aernoult-Rousset Affair. Forcing the matter to the attention of a tribunal guaranteed that what had happened to Aernoult—and, of course, what was happening to himself—would not be buried with Aernoult's battered body in Beni-Ounif. Indeed, by activating the jurisdiction's investigative and adjudicative machinery, he gave dedicated critics of military justice in metropolitan France what they most needed and at the time least expected: an ongoing judicial drama with which they could resuscitate a campaign that had clearly either stalled or expired. Indeed, Rousset's timing could hardly have been better.

In the summer of 1909 all opponents of the military jurisdiction—from left-leaning Radicals to parliamentary Socialists to *enragé* anarcho-syndicalists—were seething in frustration at the failure of the reform initiative in parliament. What could be more welcome than another courtroom saga confirming—fully, dramatically, and above all, publicly—the sheer awfulness of French military justice? Judicial theater, after all, was the *sine qua non* of grand public "Affairs" in France. The innocent victim, the hideous deed, the gritty, truth-telling hero—these, woven into a compelling narrative, ensured extensive press coverage, which in turn catalyzed public demonstrations. And public demonstrations, if sufficiently large and numerous, would hold the attention of a government all too inclined to look away when street-level agitation had faded. From where antimilitarists stood, the Aernoult-Rousset matter held real promise. It might help them revive the movement to reform or even terminate military justice that the Dreyfus case had begun—this time without the distractions of the Jewish question, and with *dramatis personae* of impeccably proletarian background.

Rousset himself, however, was probably not thinking much past his own survival in that summer of 1909. He was a desperate man, and his own commitment to seeing through what he had started would waver more than once. The judicial machinery he himself had set in motion was grinding away, and the end result could not be foreseen. On July 19 a furious Captain Finot, acting in his capacity as police judicial officer, had written out his preliminary report on Rousset's refusal to obey, fulminating against the "deplorable" conduct of this prisoner, who was now "making a mockery of *conseils de guerre*" and did not "deserve the least indulgence."[26] On July 21 Finot formally submitted his report to General Alix, along with his official request that the latter order a full *mise d'informer* prior to a tribunal hearing.[27] On July 24 the general duly ordered Public Minister Bonnelet to initiate the investigation, which Bonnelet entrusted to his *rapporteur*, Captain Alix (no known relation to the general). Alix first interviewed Rousset on August 6.[28] He seems to have been unimpressed by the prisoner and his claims from the beginning.

Rousset clearly realized that his bid for a tribunal hearing was a high-stakes game. After all, that tactic hadn't worked very well for the unfortunate Aernoult, who according to Rousset "had said all the outrages possible" to Lieutenant Sabatier—eliciting only the chillingly prophetic reply "'You want to get to a *conseil*, you won't get there, but I'll make you go down another road.'" "[T]hat was 9 in the morning," Rousset observed bluntly; "by 5 at night [*sic*] he was dead."[29] Rousset told Captain Alix that he had personally witnessed Sabatier beating Aernoult with his cane (although he could not claim to have seen more); that he knew Debon and other prisoners had also been beaten on Sabatier's orders; and that he therefore had every reason to take Beignier's threat to "make him walk down the same road as Aernoult" very seriously indeed. He denied ever calling camp officers "a bunch of cows" and denied directing angry words at Ravot and Finestre upon being locked up. Yet when asked if he had anything to add, he muttered simply: "No. I regret having refused [to obey]."

Two more years in a military prison, even if removed from the particular nightmare of Djennan-ed-Dar, was a very long time—and would not be subtracted from Rousset's term of military service. By August 19 he was writing the public minister to explain that "today, having reflected on my wrong in a very careful way, I assure you that I actually have a sincere regret . . . for having committed this offense."[30] A week earlier his brother Louis had written to General Alix to argue that Émile was mentally incompetent. An uncle had been afflicted with mental illness, Louis explained, and in addition their mother was highly doubtful that Émile "has all his mental faculties" because of "very dangerous blows that he received on the head" as a child.[31]

The die, however, was cast, and the judicial proceedings were widening. On September 21 Captain Alix formally apprised Finot that Rousset had accused Sabatier, Beignier, and Casanova of killing Aernoult and asked him to share whatever information he had pertaining to those officers' actions on July 2. Finot responded that an inquiry had already been ordered by the divisional general into the circumstances surrounding Aernoult's death, and that its direct cause had already been clearly fixed as "cerebral congestion." Rousset, Finot submitted, could not possibly furnish any reliable information on the events of July 2, and his charges should not figure into the inquiry: "His declarations are just as false as the information presented in certain journals."[32]

But the alleged assassins would nevertheless be interviewed—possibly because in August both *L'Humanité* and Gustave Hervé's uncompromising *La Guerre Sociale* had publicly alleged a pattern of mysterious deaths in the army's Algerian prison camps (immediately after the publication of those reports, Deputy Allemane had made Biribi the subject of a pointed interpellation of the war minister). There were few surprises in any of the testimony the officers provided. They all insisted that no one had ever struck Aernoult, that Rousset had seen nothing, and that the matter had been milled into "propaganda" by professional antimilitarists.[33] Beignier denied ever having threatened Rousset, who was described by Sabatier as the ringleader of "the little revolt" the camp had experienced, "for which Aernoult's death served as a pretext."[34]

Yet the fact that this testimony was taken at all is significant. It meant that political developments in Paris had begun intruding on the operations of military justice in Algeria. Finot, Alix, Bonnelet, and others certainly resented antimilitarists' conversion of Aernoult's death into political capital, with which they hoped to influence procedures in Rousset's favor.[35] But their critics were no less convinced that sheer brute force was evading whatever modest restraints the terms of the CJM had ever imposed on the operations of military justice. Specifically, those critics would claim that the decision Alix and Bonnelet were about to make on the precise charges to be brought against Rousset was being influenced by their determination to simply destroy him.

Alix (and Finot, whom Alix delegated to act on his behalf) had diligently been adding testimony on Rousset's alleged blowup at Sergeants Ravot and Finestre upon being incarcerated on July 17 to the testimony they had collected on his refusal to obey, as well as on Aernoult's death. According to those officers, the prisoner had shouted (among other things), "You could have left the door open. I'd have committed a crime on your cunt of a mug, you pile of shit!"[36] That constituted an "outrage by word" to a superior, arguably even a direct threat, and this category of offense carried a maximum penalty of five years forced labor—much more, in fact, than the two-years maximum for which Rousset would be liable for his refusals to obey if the *conseil de guerre* rejected his claim that extenuating circumstances mitigated his guilt on those counts. On October 5, when Rousset had already been in custody for nearly three months, Alix formally asked Bonnelet to recommend that the general add an "outrage" charge to the "refusal to obey" charge Rousset already faced.[37] Bonnelet did, and in November the general would comply.[38]

Antimilitarists' claim that this offense was conjured up by officers long after its alleged occurrence was not exactly true—Finot had actually included the "outrage" allegation in his report of July 19, based on testimony Ravot and Finestre submitted at the time. Yet critics did have a point: the long delay in filing the formal charge was strange, to say the least. Alix and Bonnelet would account for it by explaining that the outrage charge had been the subject of considerable debate within the *parquet*, with some questioning the fairness of bringing it. According to Alix's final report on Rousset's case (dated December 27, 1909), the key question had been whether the door to Rousset's cell had actually been closed when he shouted at Ravot and Finestre. If the officers and prisoner had been physically separated by that door, then Rousset's words carried no substantive threat to the two *sous-offs*. According to Captain Alix, it had taken until October to conclude that "Underwriting this impunity because the men were on opposite sides of a door, and heard one another without seeing one another while knowing full well each was there, would be . . . a sort of juridical byzantinism."[39]

To Rousset, of course, the "juridical byzantinism" lay in bringing forth the "outrage" charge so late. Rousset would always insist that it had never happened, avowing that no mention had been made of it when Finot and Sabatier attempted to dissuade him from his refusal to obey on July 18 and 19. His fellow prisoners Marcel and Maurice Moreau, who occupied nearby cells at the time, would deny having heard him say anything of the sort described by Ravot.[40] He and his supporters would claim that the charge was simply a maneuver by Alix, a cudgel with which to force Rousset to drop all mention of Aernoult's death at his upcoming hearing (one of the most repeated claims of the pro-Rousset forces throughout the entire affair would be that Alix had the effrontery to openly tell Rousset: "Well, if you don't want to do a little favor for the army, Rousset, then the army won't do any for you").[41] In addition, Rousset's supporters in Paris would submit that Alix and his confederates used the new charge to prolong their investigation and delay the trial in the hope that the agitation over Aernoult's death would die down if denied the sustenance of trial headlines.[42]

If Alix and the *parquet* really did aim to defuse the situation politically, they did not succeed. On October 18 no less a personage than Francis de Pressensé, deputy of the Rhône and president of the formidable League for the Defense of the Rights of Man (then the world's largest civil liberties organization, founded at the height of the Dreyfus Affair) wrote War Minister Brun to express the league's concerns and to request a formal inquiry into the entire matter.[43] Brun replied that all would be clarified in the Chamber of Deputies on November 12, when he would formally respond to Deputy Allemane's direct interpellation on the subject. On that occasion Brun would assure the chamber that the matter had been carefully investigated and summarize the results of the inquiry he had ordered. The cause of Aernoult's death, Brun explained, had been medically confirmed as a stroke, and the inquiry had revealed Rousset's allegations to be groundless. But on November 15, Deputy Adrien Veber, whose district included Romainville, read a letter signed by fifteen of Rousset's fellow prisoners reasserting the charges. The matter could not be dismissed quite so easily.

A movement was indeed beginning to coalesce around the Aernoult-Rousset case. Yet for some time Émile Rousset himself would remain reluctant to accept the heroic role its spokesmen were anxious to assign him. Alix interviewed him twice on the "outrage" charge, on October 21 and October 29 (the second time in the presence of the prisoner's newly secured attorney, a young Oranese named Gandolphe). On both occasions Rousset took pains to shed the image of organizer or activist. He strenuously denied the least insolence toward Ravot or Finestre and identified prisoners who had occupied neighboring cells, prisoners who he promised would confirm his quiescence.[44] He further denied that he had been the ringleader of any incipient revolt at Djennan-ed-Dar. On the contrary, he had counseled prisoners to abandon plans for a work stoppage they had considered. He had indeed suggested that a representative go to Beni-Ounif to speak to the public minister. But the idea of writing letters to journals, Rousset insisted, was not his. And, he noted pointedly on October 21, those letters had not come only from him. There had been some seven in all, he claimed, signed by nearly every prisoner in the camp.[45]

But Rousset made a different impression on both his prosecutors in Algeria and his defenders in Paris. Both, for different reasons and with different inflections, deemed him a leader and a model. To the former he was a cunning criminal who had figured out how to politically orchestrate vengeance against authorities he had long feared and hated, indisputably "the creator of the legend of the tragic death of Aernoult and one of the authors of the agitation that followed that death."[46] The latter saw something rather more complex. One especially staunch champion, reflecting later, would paint a portrait of Rousset in these days as a sort of noble savage seeking, by the brave and disinterested act he had undertaken, entry to civilization—a moral child painfully entering adulthood, with its burdens and responsibilities. "There is no mystical illumination in him," wrote activist René de Marmande. "He's not an apostle. And on the road to Damascus, he has not been struck by the divine light that touched Saul." Instead, Marmande felt, "Rousset remained a *Man*"—or, rather, became one. His ordeal was nurturing not bitterness but "an altruistic sentiment" alongside "the thrill of avenging" injustice. "We discover in this strange boy," Marmande concluded, "the notions of human solidarity, of moral revolt against oppression."[47]

Rousset certainly had plenty of time to ponder such notions. He was incarcerated in Oran from late July 1909 until his trial—which would not occur until January 19, 1910. That long period of detention may have been, as Marmande claimed, "among the most fecund in Rousset's life, the fullest from the psychological point of view."[48] But in the end the court would not see fit to reward his internal evolution with an acquittal.

The actual proceedings were brief. The president of the *conseil de guerre*, Colonel Micheler, began by assuring Rousset that he was entitled to tell the court anything relevant to his defense. But when the defendant tried to explain his refusal to obey by describing Beignier's threat to "make him

Comité de la Défense Sociale (*CDS*) poster, Rousset's fate.
Archives Nationales F/7/12909.

walk the same road as Aernoult," he was curtly reprimanded: the Aernoult matter ("those infamies to which the Chamber of Deputies is doing justice") was not a matter under consideration by this court, asserted Micheler, and no reference to it would be entertained.[49] Rousset was not given the opportunity to confront Beignier, nor Casanova or Sabatier; none of them had been called to testify by the public minister (by then, an officer named Lussagnet). The court then turned to the "outrage" charge. The defendant denied it and was supported by the testimony of his fellow prisoner Maurice Moreau. But in the judges' eyes these disavowals did not outweigh the testimony of Sergeants Ravot and Finestre. In the end, Rousset was found guilty of both charges, sentenced to five years of forced labor, and dispatched to the prison camp of Douerá, some fifteen kilometers south of Algiers. He was lucky. Three of the seven judges concluded that he had not committed his "outrage" while in service, thus precluding conviction on that count by virtue of the *minorité en faveur* principle. Had one more judge thought otherwise, his sentence could have been ten years.[50]

News of the verdict was immediately telegraphed to the Socialist Party Congress at Nîmes. At the urgings of Pierre Renaudel, the congress passed a motion protesting it, demanding a new inquiry, promising an "energetic campaign" on Rousset's behalf, and renewing its commitment to ending Biribi.[51]

What had been a matter for military investigators and military courts was about to be seized by leftist politicians and journalists, labor activists, and public opinion. Another question of military justice was about to be dragged into the political arena. The Aernoult-Rousset Affair had begun.

The Aernoult-Rousset Affair

Terms of Engagement

Prior to their consideration of the Rousset case, delegates to the Socialist Congress at Nîmes had witnessed a heated debate on a legislative measure, sponsored by Jaurès, establishing retirement pensions for workers. The real subject of that debate, of course, was (once again) reformism itself. Jaurès, Renaudel, and Vaillant had defended the tactics of gradualism and state-sponsored ameliorations of working-class conditions, while Paul Lafargue spoke for orthodox Marxists in denouncing them as counterrevolutionary sops.[1]

But the most adamant critic of Jaurès's reformism was not an orthodox Marxist but the flamboyant antimilitarist Gustave Hervé. In fact, the latter's commitment to the party was nearing its breaking point (he would essentially strike out on his own after Nîmes). This development could not have entirely surprised or displeased Jaurès. He and other pragmatists had long felt that Hervé's single-minded concentration on the question of militarism was politically costly for Socialists. Jaurès had never accepted the *Sans-Patrie*'s claim that antimilitarism was actually the only way to draw France's rural smallholders away from the Radical Party, which would allegedly collapse without them. Acutely aware that a dislike of military service and opposition to the current organization of the army were a far cry from the open contempt for patriotism that was the essence of Hervéism, Jaurès had worked hard to check Hervé's influence within the party.[2]

But while Hervéists in attendance at the Nîmes Congress recognized that their influence was waning within the Socialist Party, they and everyone else present also appreciated the considerable strength that *enragé* element wielded in other organizations—indeed, within the very sinews of the French left, including specific unions and federations of unions affiliated with the *CGT*, including the Union of Seine Unions. Militants were also quite well represented in auxiliaries such as the *Jeunesses Socialistes Révolutionnaires* (Revolutionary Socialist Youth) of particular Parisian *arrondissements*, and in a newly formed organization called the *Liberés des Bagnes Militaires* (Former Military Prisoners).

When Jaurès's associate Pierre Renaudel announced Rousset's conviction to the Nîmes Congress, the entirety of it accepted his proposal for a campaign of opposition. Yet even then, its moderate and militant factions must have wondered just what role the other would play in the agitation to come—and whether the campaign would benefit or suffer from the participation of people who so fundamentally misconstrued the military question, both theoretically and tactically.

Outside the halls of the congress, one militant organization would contend strongly for leadership of the Aernoult-Rousset Affair: the *Comité de la Défense Sociale* (Committee for Social Defense) or *CDS*. The *CDS* was a significant but shadowy organization formed in 1905–1906 during a period of intense labor agitation around the question of the eight-hour day. The struggle had been marked by violence and a great many arrests, which had led a set of radical lawyers, labor activists, and journalists to found an organization that would fight for militants who ran afoul of the law for what they understood to be political rather than criminal acts. Indeed, one of the war cries of the *CDS* was that "political" offenses should be adjudicated before juries in a *cour d'assises* (superior criminal court) rather than before panels of judges in one or another *tribunel correctionnel* (magistrates' tribunal). It was envisioned by its leaders as a sort of proletarian counterpart to the League for the Defense of the Rights of Man, a free-floating body dedicated to "the defense of individual or collective victims who, falling into the clutches of military or civilian justice thanks to the infamies of the police and the hatred of the gold-braided class, have no other means of defending themselves."[3]

Critics looked askance at the *CDS*'s claim to stand "outside and above any political party, any revolutionary or nonrevolutionary grouping, any sect or philosophical clique." That claim, in the view of some reformers, simply confirmed the organization's lack of a tangible mandate, or real roots in the working-class world. One disillusioned former member would dismiss it as a collection of radical dilettantes: "lawyers, affiliates of the Socialist Party, a couple of bosses . . . who happen to be enamored of anarchist propaganda."[4] Yet even its critics could hardly fault the *CDS*'s fervor.

The organization took particular interest in cases that revealed the class biases of police and judicial authorities and the general perfidy of republican justice. It displayed a definite flair for headline-generating acts (e.g., automobile parades outside ministry offices, or attempts to break into the office of the interior minister).[5] At the time of Rousset's conviction, the committee was heavily involved in the case of an accused pimp, Liabeuf, facing the death penalty for killing a member of the *police des moeurs* (morals police). The *CDS* considered the morals police a wholly corrupt body that existed mainly to extort money from minor miscreants; and Liabeuf, by their reckoning, had been driven to his deed by harassment, including multiple unjust imprisonments. What lent Liabeuf's case special piquancy in *CDS* representations was the contrast with that of another killer, Graby, who had thrown a woman to her death from an omnibus after robbing her. Unlike Liabeuf, Graby would not be guillotined—but then, Graby was a soldier and the son of a police lieutenant.[6]

Naturally, the Aernoult-Rousset matter in particular was sheer catnip to the *CDS*. In fact, the breadth and scale of the entire agitation would owe much to the aggressiveness of this particular organization. For the loose coalition of antimilitarist forces that would be assembled to shed light on what had happened in Djennan-ed-Dar would move well beyond those particular events, exposing wide swaths of military justice to public scrutiny. Indeed, the public agitation surrounding these cases would eventually constitute an open, multifront assault on the entirety of the system, including its investigatory procedures, its courts and judicial processes, and its penal practices. Public pressure would be deployed—often quite effectively—to forcibly reverse what antimilitarists held to be all too typical miscarriages of justice within the full manifold of the military jurisdiction's operations. It was to be the worst nightmare of the jurisdiction's designers, as well as those individuals who had beaten back parliamentary reformers' attempts to reconfigure it in 1907 and 1909. It was an organized, sustained invasion of the system by political forces, a willful intervention in its operations on behalf of specific political constituencies for overtly political purposes.

What renders this invasion particularly striking is that it occurred at what might have seemed the least propitious historical moment. For the multifront assault on military justice that was the essence of the Aernoult-Rousset Affair would gather steam precisely when the nation as a whole was experiencing a tangible nationalistic revival, steeling itself for war in response to the markedly more aggressive tone of German foreign policy and tending to the needs of its army more carefully than it had in decades. How to explain the scale and force of the assault on military justice, and its surprising outcome, in a fundamentally conservative, pro-military era? The explanation lies in the complex political synergy between the antimilitarist movement and the government, as well as the multileveled calculations in each camp.

First of all, there was the peculiar dynamic linking radical and reformist elements within the attacking forces—a dynamic that would call forth the most effective tactics from each. They shared some common goals—punishing Aernoult's killers, liberating Rousset, terminating Biribi. Beyond that, however, their visions diverged. *Enragés* saw the Aernoult-Rousset matter as a means to aggressively advance a broadly antimilitarist agenda; while reformists, more attuned to the temper of the times, worried about the possibilities of political overreach and the risk of nationalist backlash in that project. Each element knew that the other was only a provisional, temporary ally. Each hoped always to maximize its own general influence on the left at the other's expense. Neither could therefore afford to be outdone by the other. In moments of apparent stalemate, then, each element was anxious to seize the mantle of leadership and take the cause further down the path it knew best—to achieve what the other, with its dubious vision and tactics, had not.

Each side had a distinctive political *modus operandi*, reflecting both ideological and temperamental differences. Moderates, committed to the efficacy of the state and respectful of institutionalized channels for the public expression of social grievances, pursued a rules-based, focused activism. Their favored tactics were the parliamentary interpellation, the public oration, the courteous letter to a cabinet minister (subsequently published), even the invocation of personal relationships with particular political leaders. Radicals scorned all these as the machinations of insiders, a gentlemen's game played for no stakes beyond the electoral advantage of the gentlemen playing it. They favored the direct, sensational gesture over the chess moves of parliamentarians: the inflammatory, barely legal placard; the defiant publication of classified materials; the pugnacious, public confrontation. The mistrust and rancor between and even within these groupings would repeatedly bubble to the surface over the course of the Aernoult-Rousset Affair (in fact, individual personalities and personal relationships would play a significant role in the direction the entire business would take). But these divisions, which might have crippled the movement's efficacy, actually had the opposite effect. The competition between radicals and reformists repeatedly generated new energies, opened new fronts in the struggle, and forced the government into defensive postures.

The calculations on the government's side were exquisitely Machiavellian. As in the Dreyfus Affair, everything would ultimately depend on cabinet ministers' determination to defend the institutions of military justice: the trustworthiness of *parquet* investigations; the irrevocability of *conseil de guerre* decisions; the basic fairness, for all its hardness, of the army's penal regime. But the government's position in 1910–1912 was more delicate than it had been in 1898–1899. No one knew with precision just how powerful antimilitarist sentiment in society really was, but it was certainly taken seriously enough. One measure of the importance the government accorded the matter was the decision taken in February 1910 by Interior Minister Aristide Briand to endorse and update a secret project of the Clemenceau government—the notorious *Carnet B* (Memorandum B), a designation of known antimilitarists who were to be arrested immediately in the event of war.[7] Indeed, the last thing any cabinet minister could want, at a time of rising tensions with Germany, was a public, visible revelation of the strength of antimilitarism in France. Accordingly, the question for the government was always how to abort, or at least muffle, that revelation (that is, how to avoid mass public demonstrations) at an acceptable political cost. Given the circumstances, it was perhaps inevitable that ministers would elect to shift that cost to the spokesmen and defenders of military justice. Faced with a choice, cabinet ministers would decide that the public image of a united and patriotic France was more important than the integrity of the military jurisdiction.

Supporters of military justice had successfully resisted parliamentary reformers' efforts to remake their system. They would now have to contend with "politics" in a very different key: not reasoned debate on legislative proposals for new rules of military justice but, rather, pressure exerted on ministers to directly intervene in the application of existing rules—precisely the sort of "politicization" of military justice through street-level agitation and interest-group lobbying that the system had been explicitly designed to preclude. In fact, the very success the jurisdiction's champions had enjoyed in the parliamentary arena was precisely what conjured this new, more difficult political challenge. Systemic reform, which might have encompassed a cautious, calibrated opening to the political order, had been thwarted. But in blocking that route, the jurisdiction's supporters had channeled their foes into a far more threatening brand of politics. For the mercurial, fractious coalition that assembled around the causes of Aernoult and Rousset would prove oddly more formidable than the sober, painstaking reformers who had considered the issue in parliament from 1906 to 1909. Indeed, the Aernoult-Rousset agitators would actually force a wider range of reversals from the jurisdiction than even their models, the Dreyfusards, had: reversals not only of *conseil de guerre* decisions but also of investigative practices, penal policies, even entire penal institutions.

The campaign began in earnest following the Nîmes Congress, with the delegates' public declaration of engagement. At that stage, and under that leadership, its stated goals were actually rather modest: revelation of the truth about Aernoult's death and Rousset's conviction; justice for both men; and, more distantly, the end of Biribi. Initially, in fact, activists were focused less on the operations of the military *parquet* of Oran than on those of the civilian administration of Algeria—and of its masters in Paris.

At the urgings of M. Leroy, municipal councilor of Romainville and secretary of the twenty-second section of the Socialist Party, Aernoult's father had earlier submitted two petitions to governmental officials.[8] One, addressed to the Captain-Mayor of Beni-Ounif, requested that he authorize the exhumation of Aernoult's body. The other, addressed to the interior minister, asked him to authorize transfer of the remains back to France. Action on the petitions had been delayed while the *parquet* of Oran conducted its initial inquiry into Aernoult's death, on the grounds that further examination of the body might be necessary.[9] But with the completion of that initial investigation, there seemed no grounds for further delay.

The return of a soldier's body to his grieving parents was both eminently reasonable and perfectly legal under a ministerial decree of April 27, 1889, and the Socialists who took up the cause in the winter of 1910 had every reason to expect that the necessary permissions would be forthcoming—especially in light of the publicity that *L'Humanité* and other left-leaning journals were providing. *L'Humanité* proceeded to open a public subscription drive for funds to cover all expenses involved in the exhumation and transport of the corpse, inaugurating the process with a hundred francs from its own coffers. Throughout the winter and spring of 1910 the journal published the small amounts pledged by various unions, youth groups, and other labor/leftist bodies representing the core of the Socialist Party.

Of course, those groups and their Socialist sponsors had much more in mind than a quiet reinterment of Aernoult's body in Romainville. What they planned was a sort of funerary agitprop: anti-Biribi demonstrations to be held at each stop on the route taken by the train bearing the body back Paris, with the most imposing of all to mark its arrival in the capital. At each location Socialist orators' denunciations of Biribi would be dramatically framed by Aernoult's casket and grieving cortege—a public spectacle no reputable French newspaper could possibly ignore.[10] Republican France had a long tradition of mounting elaborate funerary rituals to mark the death of individuals held to embody republican ideals (including solemn transfer to the Pantheon of the remains of the most illustrious exemplars of republican virtue).[11] Aernoult's final journey home would provide Socialists and others on the left an opportunity to partake of this tradition and share in its emotional power, even while inverting its meaning. Most state obsequies congratulated the republic for the human achievements it inspired; these would chastise it for the human degradation it countenanced, in Biribi.

The target of those demonstrations would be Biribi, but even while they were being planned some Socialists in parliament were growing interested in another aspect of the military jurisdiction: its investigatory procedures. Adrien Veber and Francis de Pressensé persisted in questioning the quality of the inquiry thus far conducted into Aernoult's death and urged War Minister Brun to provide a fuller public accounting. In March Pressensé would write Brun to complain that the investigation to which the minister had referred in dismissing Allemane's concerns on November 12 was hardly worthy of the name, consisting of little more than the unchallenged accounts of Sabatier, Beignier, and Casanova themselves.

Pressensé explicitly contrasted the inquiry conducted by military personnel at Djennan-ed-Dar with the investigatory procedures that would be expected within any civilian jurisdiction. At Djennan-ed-Dar, he charged, prisoners and native auxiliaries with contrasting versions of events had not been formally deposed, and the officers themselves had not been submitted to the rigorous cross-examination that civilian investigators possessed the training and independence to conduct.[12] Further, claimed Pressensé, those prisoners who supported the authorities' version had testified with no guarantees of their security, leaving open the possibility that their testimony had been forced (Rousset, in fact, specifically alleged that prisoners had exchanged favorable testimony for reduced sentences).[13] Insisting that Brun order a new investigation, Pressensé could note that the *CJM* had explicitly incorporated specific provisions of the civilian Code of Criminal Investigation precisely in order to hold military investigators to the same standard of care and rigor as civilian ones—although critics of the military jurisdiction had long alleged that few officers serving in it actually understood this.[14] As both officials understood, Pressensé was also directing Brun to do something any war minister would have been both loath, and scarcely able, to do: directly intervene in the operations of a military *parquet*. Naturally, Brun would resist that, as well as Veber's requests that the full version of Dorange's autopsy be read aloud to the Chamber of Deputies and entered into the public record. Just as naturally, demands for a more thorough and public investigation of the Aernoult-Rousset matter would widen.

Indeed, the February 23, 1910, issue of *La Guerre Sociale* specifically called for using the Aernoult-Rousset matter as a springboard for a broader attack on military justice itself. But militants outside parliament were highly dubious that this would happen so long as parliamentary Socialists were directing the agitation. Actually, they were highly dubious about Socialists' real level of commitment even to justice for Rousset. In his letter to War Minister Brun, Pressensé, a rather aggressive Socialist, specifically included the Rousset case alongside Aernoult's death as items that merited further investigation. But it was true that many of his fellow Socialists were not yet persuaded that Rousset was a worthy object of their attentions.

Members of the Executive Commission of the Union of Seine Unions noted that Rousset had been dispatched to a *Bat d'Af* for common-law offenses, not labor militancy, and that intervention on his behalf was a "very delicate" matter.[15] On March 9 *La Guerre Sociale* complained about the inadequacies of *L'Humanité*'s fund-raising, which it attributed to the desire by a number of sections of the Socialist Party to retain funds for the upcoming electoral season. Pointedly entitled "Let's Save Rousset," the article implicitly raised the question of who and what was to be prioritized in the campaign. Funds were limited, and from militants' point of view the legal travails of the living Émile Rousset clearly merited as many resources as the transport of Albert Aernoult's corpse and ensuing political theater—however useful that occasion might be to the practiced orators of the Socialist Party.

The leaders of the *CDS*, observing developments from a distance, would conclude that the Socialist tactic of supplicating administrators and organizing obsequies as platforms for yet another rhetorical display represented a waste of the opportunity at hand. The Aernoult-Rousset matter might provide a wonderful vehicle for an aggressive, frontal attack on the entirety of military justice and, beyond that, on militarism itself. In March 1910 the *enragés* of the *CDS* made a fateful decision, one with which they would place themselves at the center of the Aernoult-Rousset agitation. Turning from Aernoult to Rousset and from funeral arrangements to legal strategy, they decided to invite prosecution by blanketing working-class quarters of Paris and other cities with a deliberately provocative poster entitled *A Bas Biribi* (Down with Biribi).

The poster recounted the story of Aernoult's death and specifically named Sabatier, Beignier, and Casanova as his killers. It then added an indictment of the *conseils de guerre* to its denunciation of Biribi, describing Rousset's crucifixion at the hands of military judges determined to silence him. Finally, it accused War Minister Brun of covering up these crimes, and the entire parliamentary system of complicity in the despotism of the ministry. Biribi, the poster pointedly noted, continued to exist despite repeated expressions of the people's will to reform it. It concluded with some deliberately incendiary language: "Soldiers! If you feel yourself threatened, menaced by Biribi, do not hesitate, desert! . . . Remember that the military crimes already committed legitimate all reprisals against the head murderers. . . . [Y]ou have bayonets; make use of them!"[16] The *CDS* proudly identified itself as the poster's source, and sixteen individual members affixed their names to it.

The poster was a calculated risk, based on antimilitarists' considerable experience testing the limits of the country's press laws. On the surface, those laws seemed daunting. An 1881 statute had ensured freedom of the press, but it had been revised by laws of 1893 and 1894: the notorious *lois scélérates* (villainous laws) enacted amid the anarchist outrages of the 1890s. In an attempt to stem anarchist terrorism, those laws had criminalized not just violent "propaganda by the deed" but public endorsement of it—even post facto support. These laws had remained in force long after the emergency of the mid-1890s had passed and could be applied to any utterance or social movement the government could plausibly associate with anarchism. They had already been applied to antimilitarists on several occasions. The most notable was the famous *affiche rouge* (red poster) trial of 1905, when Hervé and other militants of the International Antimilitarist Association of Workers had been successfully prosecuted for posting a placard that called on soldiers to fire on officers when ordered to shoot strikers, and to strike if mobilized for war. For all his opposition to Hervéism in general, Jaurès had dutifully testified for the defense on grounds of free speech: "If the poster was wrong to place governmental responsibilities on the heads of individual officers, it has the merit of putting the question before society."[17] Jaurès, however, may have shared the government's mixed feelings over the outcome of the trial. Despite the jury's verdict, the five days of well-publicized court proceedings provided a wider showcase for Hervé's views than he had ever had (and his four-year sentence was eventually reduced to one).

As the *CDS* knew full well, the government's overall record in prosecuting antimilitarists for verbal excesses was mixed, especially in cases tried before juries rather than before panels of judges. Prior to the passage of the *lois scélérates*, it had failed to convict antimilitarist author Lucien Descaves (Non-Coms) in a celebrated trial of 1889, a failure that may have owed something to a petition signed by a number of writers (including Maurice Barrès) defending liberty of expression.[18] The 1893–1894 legislation had provided new juridical firepower, but it had not proven infallible. Its first test case, an 1894 show trial involving thirty noted militants accused of criminal association, had ended in acquittal for twenty-seven. In 1899 the government had failed to convict Urbain Gohier, author of the antimilitarist tract *L'Armée contre la nation* (*The Army against the Nation*). To be sure, there had been successful prosecutions, including those of the 1905 *affiche rouge* trial. But the convictions the government secured had often been eclipsed by the propaganda opportunity antimilitarists had been afforded, a dilemma never more evident than in 1905. And in 1907 a jury had acquitted members of the International Antimilitarist Association of Workers and the Union of Seine Unions for posting a placard that had called on soldiers to defy any order to fire on strikers (although not to shoot officers). On that occasion attorney Jacques Bonzon had been quite effective in arguing for "a France where one can say anything, where one can discuss anything." He had certainly been helped by the fact that the trial had occurred just after the outbreak of violence in the Midi. At least one juror had expressed explicit sympathy for antimilitarists' interest in preventing precisely the sort of civilian deaths that had occurred there.[19]

As late as May 1910 it was not clear that the government would actually prosecute the signers of the "Down with Biribi!" poster at all. It first had to decide on the charge: whether to indict them for libeling Sabatier, Beignier, and Casanova specifically; or to instead invoke the *lois scélérates* and indict them for general provocation to military desertion and violence against officers, as reflections of anarchist ideology. Each strategy carried both promise and risks. If the prosecution were for libel, the defense's argument would be that the poster had spoken no more than the truth; it would bring its own evidence against the officers into court and, in addition, invite public scrutiny into the inquiry by means of which those officers had been officially exonerated. A conviction could not be assumed. The provocation charge, on the other hand, was narrower, seemingly easier to prove, and likelier to lead to conviction. But the problem with this course was that success in court might carry a disproportionate political cost. The defendants, accused of being enemies of the state, would take full advantage of the opportunity to respond to that charge, by articulating at great length their grievances against the entire sociopolitical order.

The *CDS* hoped the government would calculate that, on the whole, prosecution for provocation was the best alternative before it (in fact, committee members were already contemplating posting another, more violent placard if Justice Minister Barthou should decide to forgo that prosecution for the "Down with Biribi!" poster).[20] In the end they got their wish, and the trial of the sixteen signers was scheduled for July. The committee hoped to raise tempers there, plus something more—more, even, than raising awareness of the horrors of Biribi, or of the depredations of military justice in general. In fact, their interest in the legal subsystem in which Aernoult and Rousset had been ensnared was itself subordinate to their larger interest in the class structure that legal subsystem so perniciously served.

To the *CDS* the political value of the case as a whole related to the symbolic identity of its protagonists: Aernoult and Rousset stood for the proletariat at large, its activism thwarted, the lives of its righteously rebellious young finally snuffed out by uniformed thugs whose entire *raison d'être* rested on manufactured national rivalries and the grand fraud of patriotism. By *CDS* lights, the direction the Affair should take was toward an ever-broadening range of targets rather than a focused and narrow one: first Djennan-ed-Dar, then Biribi as a whole, then the entire idea of military justice, then the social pathology of militarism, then the capitalist order that militarism propped up.

With that agenda, the *CDS* never bothered to acknowledge legislation of April 11 declaring the government's intent to repatriate most military penal camps to metropolitan France.[21] Even if that promise was fulfilled, a relocated Biribi was hardly the committee's endgame. In fact, *CDS* thinking on the whole Aernoult-Rousset matter was nicely encapsulated by its representatives' oratorical contributions to an edgy protest meeting organized by the Revolutionary Socialist Youth of Paris's fourth *arrondissement* on April 19, with Aernoult's parents on the dais. After hearing ex-prisoner Allaire's account of Aernoult's death, some three hundred attendees listened as speaker after speaker represented the events at Djennan-ed-Dar as mere symptoms of broader pathologies within the bourgeois order. It was Louis-Jean Thuillier, cofounder of the *CDS* and secretary of the Union of Seine Unions, who most clearly incorporated the Aernoult-Rousset matter into the Hervéist worldview, reminding his audience of the army's role in crushing labor disturbances and asserting that Aernoult had been killed not because he was a disciplinary problem but because he was a "revolutionary." Thuillier was followed by antimilitarist songwriter and performer Gaston Montéhus, who raised passions to a fever pitch by urging Aernoult's parents to hunt down their son's assassins themselves. The *conseils de guerre* would never disappear through legislative action, averred Montéhus, all the while displaying his own gun.[22]

L'Humanité and the Socialists remained decidedly more restrained, in both goals and methods. They remained focused on the return of Aernoult's body, which *L'Humanité*'s editors had determined would cost around eighteen hundred francs in all. By April 1910 they had raised about half that sum, and hoping for the rest by June, they had begun assembling a delegation to go to Marseilles to retrieve the remains. It was to include Léon Jouhaux, representing the *CGT*. But if that was intended as a friendly gesture toward labor militants, the radicals of the *CDS* would have none of it. In fact, they had already decided to undertake their own initiative in Algeria rather than associate themselves with that of the Socialists. In April the committee and *La Guerre Sociale* dispatched René de Marmande, a *CDS* member and one of *La Guerre Sociale*'s editors, to Douerà to interview Rousset, organize protest meetings on his behalf in Algeria and southern France, and generally assist in any way possible in the prisoner's defense.

"Marmande" was actually the Vicomte de Rorthays de Saint-Hilaire, a journalist of some repute in anarchist circles and something of a leftist *bon vivant*. Emma Goldman once described him as a "revolutionary and true bohemian, jovial, full of spirit," the kind of radical who "refuses to see in the Mother of Freedom—Revolution—a black-robed nun walking about in penitence for the sins of mankind." Rather, wrote Goldman with approval, "Revolution to him is the great liberator, the joy-bearer."[23] Before the Aernoult-Rousset Affair had concluded, René de Marmande would find much less joy in revolutionary ranks; and he would certainly be viewed very differently there. But in the spring of 1910, most of those relationships were intact, and few associates suspected that Marmande's decision to tarry in Marseilles before departing for Algeria involved anything other than what he claimed—assisting the young naval reservists there with the strike action they had undertaken.[24] Indeed, at the time his colleagues at *La Guerre Sociale* and friends at the *CDS* could only have been delighted by the vivid reportage he provided upon finally reaching Douerà in May. For upon meeting and personally interviewing Rousset, René de Marmande would find himself utterly captivated.

By Rousset's own account, the personal transformation that had begun at Djennan-ed-Dar reached fruition at Douerà. He would claim to have been irrevocably affected by the murder of yet another prisoner there (a fellow Lyonnais named Serres, shot by a native auxiliary on the orders of a Sergeant Paris in the prison chapel during an escape attempt). In particular, he would describe at length a violent, exploitive homosexual subculture at Douerà—in its depravity, a function of the casual sadism and amorality of Biribi's masters, who, Rousset charged, deliberately ignored it. Rousset submitted that his encounter with that repellent quarter of Biribi, in particular, left him more determined than ever to raise himself above the moral rot in which he had spent his entire life to date.[25] Marmande believed him and was deeply affected by Rousset's apparent passage to an honorable manhood.[26]

The worldly anarchist and the nervy *apache* clearly did see something special in one another, for the rapport they established at Douerà was not simply that of journalist and subject. It was deeply personal, and intense. One of their meetings at Douerà was so emotionally charged that, according to Marmande, the two men simply "clasped hands and gazed for long minutes into each other's eyes."[27] For his part, Rousset would fill his letters to Marmande with expressions of deep affection, in highly emotive language. "I can't wait to be near you, to clasp you in my arms and tell you that you have found a devoted friend," he wrote in one, promising Marmande that "henceforth I will abandon this agitated life and go to work seriously, with the sole purpose of rehabilitating myself and helping through my labor my poor mother, who has sacrificed so much for me."[28] To Marmande, Émile Rousset was an example of what happened to a man in whom base passions finally yielded to a passion for justice. He never tired of pointing out that Rousset had incurred not a single disciplinary action at Douerà, that he had remained stoic even in the face of harassment by camp authorities and deteriorating physical health (Rousset suffered from an inguinal hernia). Above all, beamed Marmande, the prisoner kept himself far removed from the violence and deviant sexuality that marked Douerà. Rousset, Marmande wrote, was "neither a god nor a hero but a very brave man who wants to be very loyal"—loyal to his new ideals; loyal to those on the outside who shared them and believed in him; loyal, above all, to René de Marmande.[29]

Certainly, no one would agitate more indefatigably on Rousset's behalf than he—within and, eventually, outside the parameters set by the Committee for Social Defense. Marmande immediately proposed that the committee retain the celebrated Jacques Bonzon as Rousset's attorney (who, as it happened, was also attorney for Aernoult's old union).[30] He next set up a conference on the Rousset case at the Bourse du Travail (Labor Exchange) of Algiers and began arranging additional meetings and public demonstrations in Oran, Marseilles, Toulon, Toulouse, Lyons, and a variety of other cities where either the *CDS* or the *CGT* was able and willing to host them. All this marked only the beginning of Marmande's engagement in the Aernoult-Rousset Affair, an engagement that would decisively affect its eventual resolution.

Meanwhile, the Socialists continued on their own track, unaware of the obstacles they were about to encounter. In early June, *L'Humanité*'s subscription fund having reached its goal, the journal dispatched Alfred Kurz to Algeria to arrange for the transport of Aernoult's body. The Socialists' intention was to have the remains in Paris by June 25 and then, after the grandest demonstration of all, to reinter them in Romainville the following day. That would be the date of the *Grand Prix*, when much of Paris would be on holiday. Permission to exhume and transport the body had already been granted, so Kurz expected no problems with Algerian officialdom. What he didn't know was that the government in Paris—mindful of "all the red and black flags and antimilitarist speeches" that would mark the "promenade of the cadaver" to its final resting place—had changed its mind.[31]

On June 7 the governor-general of Algeria received a telegram from the *Sûreté Générale*, the national criminal investigative force under the authority of the interior minister, recommending the use of "dilatory measures so that Aernoult's body could not arrive in Paris before June 28."[32] By June 19 the governor-general was able to reply that "all dispositions useful to the observance of your instructions would be observed." General Alix, acting in his administrative capacity as commandant of the military division of Ain-Sefra, had ruled that no exhumation could be performed between June 1 and September 10 on the grounds that seasonal heat elevated health risks to an unacceptable level. Captain Pariel, the mayor of Beni-Ounif, informed Kurz of the general's decision, which *L'Humanité*'s representative believed was "surely taken by superior order" since he had previously considered this contingency and confirmed, with Pariel and his consulting physician, that the exhumation could be done safely.[33]

Algeria's governor-general, for his part, recorded an official denial that the ruling was in any way arbitrary. On June 19 he informed the interior ministry's secretary-general that transport of the remains of soldiers killed in Morocco had been deferred during the hot season for similar reasons; typhus, he reported, had made an appearance in the vicinity.[34] Privately, however, he was uncomfortable with the decision. On June 21 he wrote the secretary-general again to explain that if Kurz chose to appeal the ruling it would be difficult to sustain it. The journalist, after all, had arrived in Algeria as legal agent of the Aernoult family and had sufficient funds to pay for both the requisite zinc-lined coffin and whatever legal assistance he might require. The secretary-general replied that in the event of an appeal, the governor-general was to take no action before consulting the ministry.

In the meantime, Kurz was treated to what he interpreted as a contrived bureaucratic roundelay, with one official deferring responsibility to another while valuable time was wasted. General Alix himself "amiably" invited the journalist to appeal the general's own ruling to the governor-general, going so far as to promise to support the appeal himself once his safety concerns were effectively met. Kurz fully expected both Alix and the governor-general to protect themselves in the event of an appeal by jointly deferring the entire matter to Pariel's judgment—secure in the knowledge that Pariel would find or invent circumstances in Beni-Ounif to block the exhumation for as long as the ministry ordered. Aernoult's body couldn't be kept in Beni-Ounif indefinitely; but it could certainly be kept there for *Grand Prix* day—and probably far beyond that date. The interior minister may even have hoped that the entire Aernoult-Rousset matter—still a low-level affair of interest mainly to a few leftist journals and organizations—would die down if the planned funeral march and demonstrations were simply deferred long enough.

Kurz, for his part, saw political capital for activists in that very delay, arguing that the government's action should not be appealed but exposed. "I believe it preferable to establish the bad faith of all," he telegraphed the office of *L'Humanité,* since "demonstrations will be more imposing after publication" of the government's malfeasance.[35] Kurz understood that the attempt to deny or muffle public awareness of the crimes at Djennan-ed-Dar could now be tracked beyond War Minister Brun to the very heart of the government since Interior Minister Briand was, at the time, prime minister as well. Briand was a special *bête noire* of the left, and especially of antimilitarists. A former Socialist, he had been expelled from the party in 1906 for agreeing to accept a ministerial portfolio in a Radical government, where he proceeded to break a railway workers' strike by abruptly conscripting strikers into active military service. Indeed, the "Jesuitism" of Briand in the summer of 1910 and beyond would become one of the established journalistic tropes of the Aernoult-Rousset Affair among militants. Antimilitarists had just been granted valuable ammunition with which to flay this renegade, plus the time to make it hurt.[36]

Yet, for all their disdain of Briand and the Radical government in general, Socialists could perceive risks in widening the range of political targets and intensifying the attack on them. That, after all, was a strategy more consistent with the sensibility and agenda of Hervéists than those of Socialist parliamentarians, and adoption of it might grant the *enragés* an unwelcome prominence among the still small band of Aernoult-Rousset partisans. The ideological divide between militants and parliamentarians had already manifested itself there. In June the Union of Seine Unions had curtly rebuffed Socialists' invitation to join them in the demonstrations they were planning around Aernoult's Paris obsequies, heeding the advice of Secretary Thuillier that militants must have "nothing to do" with Socialists in this matter. Thuillier urged unions affiliated with the organization to arrange their own demonstration, physically removed from those of the Socialists. There was even talk of a separate, breakaway demonstration at Romainville, from which Socialists would be excluded.[37]

Socialists had been angered by the rejection.[38] But their own failure to bring Aernoult's body home strengthened militants' hand, and they knew it. Their response was to suggest a "mixed commission" in which representatives of the Union of Seine Unions and the *CDS* would sit alongside Socialists to organize and direct "the violent campaign of protest against the attitude of the government" that the minister's actions had invited.[39] Better to keep the militants in view—and hopefully in check—while planning the demonstrations Socialists now expected to occur in October, when the government would presumably have to lift its ban on the exhumation of Aernoult's body.

But Socialists did not reckon on the results of the dramatic "Down with Biribi!" trial before the superior criminal court of Paris on July 4 and 5—certainly the high point of the Aernoult-Rousset Affair to date. The trial was galvanizing the militant left and propelling the *CDS* itself to the forefront of the agitation. Indeed, in militants' representations of the situation it was unclear who the worst villains were: the minions of military justice, or their alleged enablers among parliamentarians. The *CGT*'s weekly journal, *La Voix du Peuple* (*The Voice of the People*) devoted nearly the entirety of its June 26–July 3 issue to the Aernoult-Rousset matter, seamlessly merging a hostility to the military jurisdiction with contempt for that "multitude of Three-Points and business yids" (i.e., Radicals and Dreyfusards) who had marched so enthusiastically when the system had claimed a well-to-do captain but showed little interest when it victimized proletarians.

Yet the most consequential overviews of what the historical moment required with respect to French military justice were probably occurring far from leftist quarters. They were occurring, rather, in the minds of government ministers. For the "Down with Biribi!" trial would force the government to carefully consider which it valued more: the political insularity of military justice or the political neutralization of the antimilitarist movement. After the trial, it would become increasingly clear that one could be achieved only at the expense of the other.

Triumph of the Political

The sixteen signers of the offending poster were represented by three attorneys (Jacques Bonzon, Jean Robin, Joseph Hild), whose strategy was to openly politicize the case.[1] Their clients were to be seen not as criminals but as activists who were unashamedly using the courtroom as a political rostrum: "To make ourselves accusers," explained one signer, the sociologist Charles Albert, "we first had to get accused."[2] The signers themselves had committed no crime; no effective "provocation to desertion and violence" could be taken from a poster that actual denizens of Biribi had never even seen. Rather, the poster's signers had reasserted the natural right of self-defense for the unfortunates of that hellish netherworld. For it was those hapless prisoners, not their officers, whose lives were truly threatened. To confirm that threat, the defense would present to jurors precisely what had happened at Djennan-ed-Dar—including its source, scale, and typicality. That is, these heirs of Zola intended not only to exonerate themselves but to put a great many other people on trial in their stead, starting with Djennan-ed-Dar's officers. It was a high-risk strategy, but the potential payoff was considerable: an acquittal could be taken "only as the moral condemnation of Aernoult's murderers."[3]

The most consequential phase of the trial may well have been the pretrial rulings on the defense's witness list, which included three sets of witnesses. The first included actual participants in the events at Djennan-ed-Dar: Rousset, Debon, Allaire, Cott, Captain Finot, Lieutenant Sabatier, Sergeant Beignier, Sergeant Casanova, and Captain Alix. The defense also wanted testimony from longtime critics of military justice: Georges Lhermitte, Jacques Dhur, Urbain Gohier, René de Marmande, Gustave Rouannet, and others. Finally, it wanted representatives of the political world: War Minister Brun, former War Minister André, Adrien Veber, Jean Allemane, Pierre Renaudel, Francis de Pressensé, even Jean Jaurès. All this testimony was necessary, argued defense attorneys, to demonstrate that the defendants had spoken nothing but the truth. The first set of witnesses would establish the real circumstances surrounding Aernoult's death and Rousset's defiance. The second set would reveal broader truths about Biribi and military justice in general. The third set would reveal the government's obfuscation of these truths and complicity in those crimes.

The prosecution naturally fought to keep many of these witnesses out of court, with partial success. Most of the first set of witnesses were ruled out for the legally compelling reason that any crime committed at Djennan-ed-Dar must be adjudicated before the *conseil de guerre* of Oran rather than the *cour d'assises* of Paris. However, the court did not extend this invocation of the *rationae personae* principle to Allaire and Cott, who were by then civilians. The defense would use them not only to denounce Sabatier, Beignier, and Casanova but War Minister Brun as well, who, defense attorneys claimed, had submitted the most vapid sort of whitewash to the chamber.

The jury also heard a parade of witnesses denounce Biribi in extremely graphic terms. Aernoult's parents came forward to describe their son's grief, followed by a parade of witnesses who enlarged on his case. An old Communard, Jean-Constant Breton, showed the scars he carried from his own time in an African prison. Jacques Dhur described conditions at Djennan-ed-Dar in particular. Georges Lhermitte displayed thumbscrews he claimed were still in use. Deputy Allemane argued that Biribi "has made more antimilitarists than all the theories you can condemn," then decried the hypocrisy of "patriots" who looked away while Arab auxiliaries, "insensitive to pity" and driven by "the bitterness of a vanquished race against its invaders," satiated their "racial hate on French prisoners confined to their care."[4]

Turning to the formally legalistic side of the defense's case, attorney Robin submitted that Biribi in its entirety was a fundamentally illegal undertaking. Unlike the *Bats d'Af*, Robin argued, the *compagnies de*

Gustave Rouanet, at the "Down with Biribi!" trial. *La Guerre Sociale*, July 6–12, 1910.

discipline operated without explicit statutory authorization. What was criminal was the army's maintenance of its own, autonomous prison system, not the defendants' (entirely verbal) assault on it.[5] The government itself, then, should be in the docket.

It was attacked by Pressensé, who recalled Dreyfusards' unfulfilled promises to end Biribi; by Gohier, who recalled equally "violent" language used by Briand during his Socialist period, when he supported a general strike; by Kurz, who recounted the government's attempt to stall the return of Aernoult's body; and by Veber, who described the difficulty he had experienced in prying Dr. Dorange's autopsy report from the hands of War Minister Brun for presentation to the public: "They always condemn with these secret dossiers!" shouted Bonzon.[6] When weighed against the grotesque physical violence of Biribi and the blatant deceptions of the government, jurors were asked, could a few intemperate words of protest on a poster really be considered a crime against society?

The prosecution proved curiously desultory (even *L'Humanité* remarked on prosecutor Servin's failure to object to Marmande's insistence on reading his own account of Rousset's first trial into the record).[7] Its basic claim was that the defendants were dangerous revolutionaries whose acquittal could only encourage violence and disorder. Pressensé, Jaurès, Bonzon, and many others answered this charge by insisting that being "revolutionary" simply meant being willing to challenge unjust laws and to defy authority when it acted unjustly. The prosecution argued that the letter of the law must be observed; that the events at Djennan-ed-Dar were not relevant to the case at hand; and that, in any event, the defense was presenting unproven allegations about them, which had been publicly disputed by the war minister himself.[8] Jaurès deftly countered that invocation of ministerial authority. The minister's judgment, he argued, was only as good as the information on which it was based, and "there are so many veils between the facts that play out in the military prisons and the war minister that he can't have an exact perception of them."[9]

It was Attorney Hild, however, who provided the broadest rejoinder to the prosecutors' arguments, by turning them against their framers in his summation. The prosecution wanted jurors to consider only one bare fact, argued Hild—one phrase of the poster, taken out of context, divorced from the realities that had inspired it, and measured against the specific wording of the law. But a truly juridical approach required a full consideration of context, circumstance, and motive. The purpose of law was justice, Hild insisted, and justice must never be sacrificed to a literal reading of law. Only military courts, those caricatures of real courts, endorsed the sort of crabbed, cruel legalism the prosecutor wanted jurors to adopt. "The attorney general asks you to judge this trial as a bad *conseil de guerre* would have," Hild told them. "He requires, in effect, condemnation for the crime . . . without concern for motives."[10] In rejecting that blinkered reasoning, they would be rejecting more than the prosecution's case against the signers, more even than Biribi. They would be rejecting the essence of military justice itself.

The jury took only a few minutes to acquit all signers of all charges. An elated *CDS* could claim victory for its brand of activism: a direct, rude, public confrontation had secured a victory where the respectful parliamentary petitions of Socialists had yielded only frustration. The defendants had persuaded a jury that what seemed like a crime was a political act—in fact, an entirely commendable one. They had advanced the Aernoult-Rousset cause further in two days than Socialists had in seven months. Ideological brethren at *La Guerre Sociale* now set forth their minimum demand: the *compagnies de discipline* to be transferred from Africa to France were also to be opened to public inspection and submitted to "the control of public opinion." "When is the government going to execute the order of the jury?" demanded *La Guerre Sociale*—as if a *cour d'assises* jury, now, were politically sovereign.[11]

The trial had lasted a scant two days and generated precious little coverage outside leftist journals. Indeed, if the perfunctory quality of the prosecution was intentional, this might have been the desired result. But if the government had limited the political fallout from the "Down with Biribi!" trial, it had hardly escaped the summer unscathed. This was, in fact, the last of three trials of antimilitarists prosecuted for verbal violence against military justice, and jurors had acquitted each time. Those judgments would be pointedly recalled in subsequent interpellations of the war minister on the Aernoult-Rousset matter, but the government needed no reminder of its own vulnerability in the court of public opinion.[12] Public wrath against the jurisdiction could be mobilized rather easily, which in turn meant that large-scale demonstrations on behalf of Aernoult and Rousset were not only possible but likely if steps weren't taken to forestall them.

What changed after the "Down with Biribi!" trial was the government's preferred method of forestalling. Prior to the trial, it had simply stonewalled activists. Henceforward it would make strategic concessions to them—at the expense of the integrity of the military jurisdiction itself. For throughout this first part of the Aernoult-Rousset Affair, the government's actions demonstrated that its main priority was avoiding the series of large-scale public events that antimilitarists envisioned taking place around the return of Aernoult's body.

What followed were a series of contests over the procedures of the military *parquet* of Oran: Who was to be investigated and/or prosecuted, and by whom? Who was to be pardoned, and why? When and under what circumstances were prisoners to gain access to their attorneys and the latter to gain access to military dossiers? Some were relatively small matters. All, however, were matters over which military authorities had always maintained exclusive control. The sacrifice of that procedural control to politicians, whose calculations ranged far beyond the preservation of unit discipline, was a very large matter indeed. If these procedures could be politicized, why not *conseil de guerre* actions or, for that matter, the tone and content of the *CJM*? The system's guardians didn't know it yet, but military control of the jurisdiction's procedures had become expendable political capital that the government was prepared to sacrifice if this was what was required to preclude a public flexing of antimilitarists' political muscles. To preserve the world's image of France as a nation that trusted and respected its army, military justice would have to be compromised—reluctantly, grudgingly, but definitely.

The contests began with the conclusion of arrangements for the "mixed commission," proposed earlier, to coordinate efforts by the various elements that had taken an interest in the Aernoult-Rousset matter to bring Aernoult's body home and organize the dramatic demonstrations that were to mark its progress. The Socialist Party, the *CDS*, and the Union of Seine Unions were to be equally represented on the commission, which was to dissolve after the attainment of its specified end. But awareness that their marriage of convenience was temporary didn't dispel the tension between moderates and militants. The *CDS*'s Tissier (Vincent Meo) put it bluntly: "There are two clans in the commission, the one that wants legality and calm and the one that wants some racket. The first is the Socialist Party, the second is us and the Union of [Seine] Unions." Tissier's tactical prescription was equally clear: "We're the ones who are more numerous, we should decide" the tactics to be used.[13] Yet militants could not afford to antagonize their Socialist partners too openly.

The *CDS*, in particular, was chronically short of money and hoped that the subscription fund raised by *L'Humanité* to support the return of Aernoult's body could be spent with spillover benefits for itself (e.g., the organization of protest meetings foregrounding *CDS* speakers, the printing of pamphlets written by *CDS* authors and expressing *CDS* positions).[14] In the eyes of one police agent observing the mixed commission's internal dynamics, the Socialist Party, the Union of Seine Unions, and the *CDS* all sought to bring "'the blanket over to its side,' that is, to draw all the benefits from the proposed demonstration" that was to occur in Paris upon the return of Aernoult's body.[15] The *CDS*'s Thuillier certainly had misgivings about the Socialist Renaudel's control of *L'Humanité*'s subscription funds. In fact, he suggested that Kurz's subsequent trips to Algeria should be financed not through the general fund, compiled from numerous organizations' small contributions, but rather, by *L'Humanité* alone.[16] Financial tensions may have sharpened chronic bickering within the commission over such questions as who was to represent the Aernoult family, whether Aernoult should be reinterred in Romainville or incinerated at Père-Lachaise in Paris, whether demonstrations should be arranged in such a way as to minimize the possibility of violence, and who would be dispatched to Algeria.[17]

Yet, if the commission was a cockpit of divergent tactics, it was also an incubator of productive politico-legal strategies. The first was announced in placards posted on July 23. The placards reprinted a letter sent to the justice minister by Aernoult's parents, who had retained Bonzon's legal services. They were publicly petitioning the minister to initiate criminal proceedings against their son's assassins. Sabatier, Beignier, and Casanova, they proposed, had already been indicted by the Paris *cour d'assises*, which in acquitting the signers of the "Down with Biribi!" poster had formally validated the accusations of witnesses Allaire and Cott. In effect, jurors had delivered the functional equivalent of a judgment by a *chambre des mises en accusation* (indictment court). If the government were genuinely democratic, claimed the petitioners, it must act on the considered judgment of the people, formally impaneled and publicly apprised of the facts.[18]

Justice Minister Louis Barthou obviously could not act on that petition without colliding with the *rationae personae* principle: any prosecution of the individuals in question would have to be initiated within the military jurisdiction, as the *CDS* and other commission members certainly understood. Ministers could prod the *parquet* of Oran to take action, but this meant breaching the *cordon sanitaire* insulating military *parquets* from ministerial interventions. And this, of course, was exactly the point. If officers at Djennan-ed-Dar were to be shielded from legal action, the government could expect a great deal more public agitation in the Aernoult-Rousset matter. Yet those officers could not be submitted to legal action without, in effect, rendering military justice accountable to the public. The government would have to choose.[19]

Socialists, with an effective organ in *L'Humanité* and effective representation in parliament, were well placed to tighten the screws—and they were highly anxious to demonstrate their own effectiveness after the militants' triumph in court. Their chosen course was forcing, through parliamentary interpellations, new inquiries into what had really transpired at Djennan-ed-Dar and, more broadly, in the military *parquet* of Oran. Deputy Veber and *L'Humanité* kept the pressure on, denouncing Captain Alix's first inquiry into Aernoult's death as the work of the prisoner's own killers. It was, they insisted, a document contradicted by Finot's own letter to Aernoult's parents, a tissue of lies hurriedly slapped together by Brun in anticipation of Allemane's first interpellation.[20] In a complementary action Louis Rousset, represented by Bonzon, petitioned the war minister for a separate, formal inquiry into the formulation of the "outrage" charge against his brother. War Minister Brun explained that the delay in filing that charge reflected nothing more sinister than a debate within the *parquet* over the juridical weight that could be assigned words uttered by a prisoner behind bars. But *L'Humanité* responded with open derision, likening Brun to General Mercier—and warning that a new campaign to publicly expose the inner workings of military justice was impending if parliamentary pressure didn't yield results.[21]

It did. Brun decided independently to commission a new inquiry into Aernoult's death. It was to be conducted by a certain General Rabier, who would visit Djennan-ed-Dar in October not only to re-interview officers who had been deposed by Captain Alix but to interview a number of other men (prisoners, auxiliaries) whose testimony the military investigator had allegedly slighted (see Appendix B). Formally, Rabier's study would be for the war minister's own use—"informational" only, and entirely "without juridical meaning." The exclusive prerogative of the divisional general to order the collection of legally admissible materials would not be at issue. But of course the war minister might choose to apprise the divisional general of the results of his own inquiry, and any subsequent initiatives the general might elect to undertake with regard to the Aernoult and/or Rousset matters would carry a great deal of juridical weight indeed. More than one officer would express a measure of bitterness over the ploy.[22]

Indeed, the commissioning of the Rabier report was another major turning point in the Aernoult-Rousset matter. At first glance it seems something of an overreaction by the government to the fairly modest degree of pressure activists had thus far exerted on it. The latter, after all, consisted only of a few interpellations; a campaign in the leftist press; a victory in court; scattered, fairly small demonstrations in labor exchanges and small working-class venues; and a somewhat larger one the *CDS* had arranged at Paris's Tivoli Vauxhal, on the eve of the "Down with Biribi!" trial. But there was, it seems, a method to the government's madness. In commissioning the Rabier report, it strengthened its own hand on the front that mattered most to it: the push, formally by Aernoult's parents, for the return of their son's body in November. The government was again able to deny that request—this time on the grounds that additional judicial actions might have to be taken as a result of Rabier's report, and the body must therefore remain in Beni-Ounif in the event that a military court ordered further "medico-legal" testimony requiring its examination.[23]

The government had again staved off the wave of demonstrations still planned by the mixed commission to mark the return of Aernoult's remains. But it did so at considerable cost to the military jurisdiction. The thorough and probing report Rabier delivered in late 1910 would indeed impel the divisional general in Oran to initiate formal investigations and then to approve indictments—not only against Sabatier, Beignier, and Casanova for their roles in Aernoult's death but also against Finestre and Ravot for false testimony against Rousset. What was really significant, of course, was that these would be, in the most literal sense, politically driven prosecutions. Functions of a ministerial decision, taken under political pressure, to reject and supersede the inquiry already conducted by the *parquet* of Oran, they would almost certainly never have occurred if the army's judicial system had been left to its own devices. This was a political victory for which Socialists, exercising conventional parliamentary powers over a government minister, could claim the lion's share of credit.

Rabier scrutinized the testimony of officers for internal inconsistencies and implausibilities, cross-checking their accounts against those of prisoners and auxiliaries. His report, completed in November, called into question the interpretation of Aernoult's death submitted by Captain Alix a year earlier. The general found ample reason to believe that Aernoult had indeed been physically incapable of further exertions after his first couple of hours in the punishment detail. He also found ample reason to doubt that the prisoner had ever represented a physical threat to officers. He went on to criticize Djennan-ed-Dar's officers for their lack of solicitude for the prisoner's health, their excessive use of restraints, and the questionable decision to deposit Aernoult in a remote cell. He did not rule out the possibility that the prisoner had indeed been beaten, and that his death may have been caused or hastened by the treatment officers had accorded him. Those questions were naturally for a military court to decide, but Rabier did not refrain from holding officers responsible for the entire incident in a more general sense, which he ultimately traced back to their refusal to simply arrest Aernoult for his refusal to obey and bring him to the judgment of a *conseil de guerre*.[24]

The Rabier report would provide considerable leverage—in particular, for activists anxious to ease Rousset's situation. They had actually begun pressuring the war minister to personally monitor the prisoner's well-being as early as the conclusion of the "Down with Biribi!" trial, when Bonzon, Marmande, and Louis Rousset had met personally with Brun to press Rousset's complaint that, while hospitalized for a hernia, officers had intercepted his mail and spoken ominously to him ("Rousset, take care, this has to end"). A grateful Rousset had confirmed that the intervention had worked, and he had been left alone to recover comfortably. He also expressed appreciation for the money his supporters had been sending (although, he explained, he was not permitted to touch it until his last set of legal expenses were paid and was therefore obliged to request more).[25]

In October, after Bonzon had joined Gandolphe as Rousset's attorney, another initiative was launched. The two attorneys were contemplating appealing his conviction to the civilian High Court of Appeals and requested dossiers the *parquet* of Oran chose to deny them (presumably containing all or part of the testimony Rabier was then collecting). An angry Francis de Pressensé shot off a stern letter to War Minister Brun. "By what title and in the name of what right does the minister of war consitute himself the exclusive holder of judicial dossiers in his department?" Pressensé asked, adding that "this exorbitant claim to keep judicial dossiers secret . . . exists nowhere but in the department of war." Pressensé, in fact, had long been concerned by the military jurisdiction's preference for classified documents, closed hearings, and the like. In his October 10 letter to Brun, he argued that this inclination toward investigative and prosecutorial secrecy was further evidence of "a regrettable antinomy between military justice and justice without epithet," an antinomy that was "inadmissible under a Republic, in a modern State."[26] The lawyers got their dossier—even though, technically, the Rabier report was an administrative rather than a judicial document until such time that prosecutions were actually initiated.

That didn't occur until December 1910, when General Alix decided that Rabier's findings mandated formal proceedings against Sabatier, Beignier, and Casanova.[27] It was those indictments that provided the most effective ammunition for Rousset's defenders. At the time, he was in Douerà because Article 96 of the *CJM* prescribed severe punishment for detainees who made ill-founded charges against officers. But thanks to Rabier, his allegations could no longer be described as ill-founded. Veber, Marmande, and other supporters naturally began lobbying the new war minister, Maurice Berteaux, for a pardon or at least a significant reduction in Rousset's sentence. Berteaux was hardly enthusiastic about that, and not without reason.

The minister recognized that any action connoting a withdrawal, or at least softening, of his office's commitment to the case against Rousset could carry implications for the cases pending against Sabatier, Beinier, and Casanova. The Oran *conseil de guerre* had conflated Rousset's two charges, outrage to a superior and refusal to obey, in fixing his five-year sentence. If that sentence were now reduced, it might be seen as a ministerial acknowledgment that there had been some merit to Rousset's claim of extenuating circumstances for his refusal to obey, which in turn could be taken as *ipso facto* support for his charges against Djennan-ed-Dar's officers. When Veber raised the possibility of reducing Rousset's sentence during his interpellation of March 16, 1911, Berteaux promised to "see if it's possible to take some measure of kindness" toward the now celebrated prisoner. But the minister pointedly added that "whatever measure is interposed, it cannot be prejudicial to the persons against whom a judicial investigation is pursued. If Rousset obtains a pardon, it can only be pronounced for his conduct and not because of the thesis that is put forth here."[28]

René de Marmande, in particular, was incensed that Rousset should be further scrutinized when it was the government that had actually committed all the crimes in the affair.[29] For the moment, however, Brun's juridical sensibility prevailed over Marmande's political/moral one, and Douerà's Captain Bocquillon was duly consulted. Bocquillon was not one of Rousset's admirers (he would later describe the prisoner as "a cagey fellow and a man capable of anything"); but he did confirm that, at least at Douerà, Rousset had more or less behaved himself.[30] That was license enough for Berteaux, and on April 13, 1911, the prisoner was pardoned (a ministerial action that may or may not have been hastened by a demonstration in Lyons that turned somewhat violent).[31]

To Rousset's horror, however, he was to be transferred not to a regular infantry unit to finish his active military service, as he had hoped, but to another *compagnie de discipline*, this one at Djelfa. Rousset had always understood the massive gap between his standing in France (where since the "Down with Biribi!" trial circumstances had favored him) and his standing in the *bled*—where his celebrity status enraged his superiors and rendered his own position increasingly perilous. In fact, an ongoing reorganization of the *compagnies de discipline* remaining in Africa raised the disquieting possibility that some of Djennan-ed-Dar's officers might be waiting at Djelfa to greet their accuser. "This is to put me back in the hornets' nest," he wrote Marmande. "They'll never forgive me for having revealed their cowardice, and everything will start up again."[32] An even more immediate concern was the twelve-day journey on foot from Douerà to Djelfa under native *spahi* escort—an arduous trek through barren territory, where anything might happen. Indeed, that trek would evoke some of the most bitter passages in Rousset's memoirs. His inguinal hernia rendered it torturous until a physician finally confirmed his inability to walk any further and ordered that transport be provided for the final leg of the journey. Upon his arrival in Djelfa, Rousset later claimed, he was greeted with an ominous sneer by the commanding officer, a Captain Chalzibi ("little slime of a malingerer").[33]

Rousset and his supporters argued that this posting flew in the face of a 1907 ministerial circular holding that prisoners who completed their sentences were to be reassigned to their old units.[34] They might have noted another circular of July 1908, which proposed that anyone pardoned after a conviction for refusal to obey, outrages, or assault against an officer must be sent to a unit where he would not be serving under the officers he had allegedly defied or attacked.[35] But in fact, military law was not so clear-cut on the subject, because the *CJM* said something else on the specific subject of pardons.

Ultimate responsibility for the execution of all juridical decisions fell to the divisional commander; and in the case of pardons he could, depending on conditions on the ground, conditionally delay that execution and even delay informing the minister of his decision.[36] That power belonged in this case to General Drude, now the (interim) divisional commander, and he could claim at least some legal authority for failing to promptly deliver to Rousset the full benefits of the pardon he had been granted. The entire matter of pardons was, in fact, contested terrain, with both the political order (the war ministry) and the juridical (the military jurisdiction) claiming final authority. Indeed, the pardoning of Dreyfus shortly after his second conviction had actually been one of the few times that the decision of a *conseil de guerre* had been countermanded—and that had come from the president of the republic himself, not the minister of war.

Once again the political order won out. Both the *CDS* and *L'Humanité* vigorously protested Rousset's posting to Djelfa, bluntly reminding the war minister that Rousset's well-being was now a matter of public interest and would be continuously monitored.[37] In May a ministerial decree (No. 24.482) reassigned him to the Third *Bat d'Af* Company, garrisoned at Médéa. He would arrive there in early June.

Yet even while the Aernoult-Rousset coalition was successfully pressuring these ministerial interventions on Rousset's behalf, it was encountering obstinate opposition to its plans for the return of Aernoult's body. War Minister Berteaux had disclaimed responsibility for that matter, insisting that it lay with the Algerian authorities and the interior minister. So in late November 1910, Deputy Veber was asked by the mixed commission to make a personal appeal to Interior Minister Aristide Briand. The deputy submitted his request in writing, but the minister was maddeningly slow to answer (after eighteen days, Veber had to ask the president of the chamber to remind the minister of the procedural rule requiring ministers to respond to written questions within eight days). In April 1911 a Dr. Crespin was commissioned to detach and examine Aernoult's head for evidence of fatal blows; he would take until late May to conclude that none could be detected.[38] By June, of course, both civilian and military officials in Algeria were reiterating their concern about exhumation amid summer heat. The project was deferred yet again—to the considerable annoyance of the mixed commission.

The commission had been no less annoyed to learn that the investigations (and, if it came to that, indictments) of Sabatier, Beignier, and Casanova on the one hand and Ravot and Finestre on the other were in the hands of the much excoriated Captain Alix, who remained *rapporteur* of the second *conseil de guerre* of Oran. How, asked Rousset's supporters, could anything resembling objectivity be expected of an investigator who had already concluded in two official inquiries that Rousset's allegations against both sets of individuals were false? This was the same investigator who, Rousset's defenders believed, had actually tried to extort a disavowal of those allegations by bringing a false charge of his own. The question had emerged as early as January 1911, and Veber raised it forcefully in his March 16 interpellation of War Minister Berteaux.[39]

At that time the minister had properly insisted that the staffing of the *parquet* of Oran lay within the legal competence of General Alix as divisional commander. But he had also sympathized with Veber's position—and certainly recognized its political utility to activists. Berteaux acknowledged that the situation was indeed "abnormal." Even while defending Captain Alix from what he considered unproven charges of malfeasance, he expressed the wish that the *rapporteur* had voluntarily recused himself, and he explained that he had already asked the general whether a substitute might be found for these particular investigations. The minister had gone so far as to promise Veber to look into possible legal means of either removing Captain Alix from the cases or perhaps even remanding him to another military *parquet* (*dessaisissement*).

The civilian High Court of Appeals could, in fact, order such removals. But arguments for them were treated with great care, and complaints could come only from specified, official quarters—from the public minister of the jurisdiction involved, or from the ministry of justice itself, in the person of the solicitor-general (who represented the general interests of the government before the High Court). Accordingly, Berteaux took the entire matter to that ministry, and the solicitor-general requested that General Alix deliver the relevant dossiers for his consideration.[40] General Alix would dutifully, if reluctantly, comply with that request, taking pains to describe Captain Alix as an officer of the highest integrity.[41] As it turned out, the solicitor-general's view of the matter was all that both General Alix and Captain Alix could have hoped for.

Article 24 of the *CJM*, the solicitor-general explained, did indeed preclude any *rapporteur* who had served as judge or administrator of a tribunal hearing a given case from subsequent investigation of that or related cases. Technically, however, Captain Alix had pursued his investigations as an officer of the *parquet*, not the tribunal; according to the solicitor-general's reading, Article 24 was never intended to "include the *rapporteur* who, in the course of a prior procedure, receives declarations of testimony on the occasion of which a second prosecution is intended." Captain Alix, then, was not legally debarred from serving as investigator on the current cases simply because he had previously investigated one to which they were related. Regarding the Ravot/Finestre case, the solicitor-general argued that French jurisprudence "has always admitted that magistrates before whom false testimony has been produced are competent to rule on prosecutions directed against the false witnesses."[42] Logically, the same norm would apply to investigators. As for the trial of Aernoult's alleged assassins, "There isn't any reason of law for the cases of Sabatier and Sgts. Casanova and Beignier to be examined in another military court."[43] The solicitor-general simply refused even to bring the request to the High Court. This time the letter of the law would be observed.

In fact, the decision to resist pressure to force Captain Alix off the cases marked another turning point in the evolution of the Aernoult-Rousset Affair—this time, toward a period of ascendance by the defenders of the military jurisdiction over its foes, and over politicians who would placate those foes at the jurisdiction's expense. In mid-August Ravot and Finestre were duly indicted and tried before the first *conseil de guerre* of Oran. But they were acquitted, despite the testimony of Rousset, his fellow prisoners Marcel and Maurice Moreau, and Lieutenant Jeannin, his sole supporter among Djennan-ed-Dar's officers.

L'Humanité was outraged that the defendants hadn't even been held in custody, and that Rousset's testimony had been repeatedly interrupted and cut short by the tribunal's president, Colonel Vittemin.[44] *La Bataille Syndicaliste*, the *CGT*'s new daily organ, took a more sanguine view, adopting the conventional militant position that these were show trials and should be assessed for their political benefits rather than their juridical outcomes. "The army dreads only one thing: public censure," asserted the journal confidently. "The public has been enlightened on the African prisons, on Biribi and on the military tribunals. Right now the people know. And that's enough for our personal satisfaction."[45]

But no antimilitarist, whether radical or reformist, could be sanguine about the acquittal of Sabatier, Beignier, and Casanova by the second *conseil de guerre* of Oran on September 12, 1911. Certainly no defender of Émile Rousset—once again the trial's star witness—could feel quite as certain about either his moral transformation or his political utility. For when Rousset testified at that trial, he did so under a much darker cloud than any that had hovered over him in his notably stormy life.

Only a week earlier he had been accused of the murder of a fellow soldier at Médéa.

The Rousset Murder Case

In 1902 General Jules Bourelly had countered the argument that military officers were unqualified to perform judicial functions with the claim that those officers, however unschooled in the fine points of juridical argumentation, were nonetheless far more attuned than any civilian jurist to the specific subculture that military courts were designed to regulate, as well as to the requirements of discipline within it.[1] They knew their men, Bourelly insisted, and they knew what it took to make soldiers of them. The entire system of military justice was geared to those realities, which military men understood far better than any civilian lawyer, judge, or even warden possibly could. Yet politicians simply couldn't resist inserting themselves and their civilian agendas into the operations of the jurisdiction. Politicians simply didn't understand the truth on the ground.

Like-minded conservatives especially lamented legislation of 1889, when the politicians in their wisdom had decided that the army must incorporate even the nation's criminals and moral degenerates—its *apaches*. Politicians hoped these men could be either redeemed or safely stored for a few years. But the military professionals to whom those tasks had been consigned generally saw things very differently. By their lights, these were men whose chronic hostility toward authority was more often exacerbated than attenuated in the barracks—only a few were redeemable, and the incorrigible majority would corrupt the healthy body of the army if carelessly dispersed through it. The army had struggled for years to build units where the salvageable few could be identified and helped, while the irredeemable many were kept safely segregated. Hence, the *Bats d'Af.* Yet even those units were insufficiently punitive for much of the detritus the politicians had decided to honor with a soldier's uniform. Hence, Biribi.

Then, complained the guardians of military justice, the same politicians who had created the conditions calling forth those penal institutions in the first place proceeded to meddle in their operations. In the wake of the Dreyfus Affair, with its supposed revelations of the arbitrariness of military *parquets,* reformers with scant understanding of military realities had decided to press for more lenient treatment of the criminal element the jurisdiction was struggling to contain. In 1905 the politicians decided that those with relatively modest criminal records were to be spared the rigors of the *Bats d'Af* and assigned to regular units in France, at least for their reserve duty.[2] But civilians soon learned what military professionals had known for some time: wherever these men went, thievery and violence followed. In 1910 the politicians changed course again and reasserted the exclusion of incorrigibles from regular units, even while (with characteristic inconstancy) bending to the demands of humanitarians for repatriation of the disciplinary companies to metropolitan France.[3]

The interventions of reformers in other areas of military justice made it difficult for the military jurisdiction to do this penal work well. The reforms of 1897 (extending access to legal counsel), 1901 (granting defendants the right to claim extenuating circumstances), and 1904 (expanding the incidence of suspended sentences) had, according to even knowledgeable critics of the system, "softened discipline without bringing true justice."[4] Enlisted men were losing that fear of a *conseil de guerre,* which had once served as the beginning of soldierly wisdom. Nowhere were the consequences more difficult than in the special sections, the public works units, the various *compagnies de discipline.* Politicians, of course, showed little interest in the dangers and difficulties faced by the officers and enlisted men attempting to maintain order in those institutions, or in the endless problems they presented to the war ministry.

Above all, there was the expensive, time-consuming stream of *conseil de guerre* cases the camps generated. That concern was grave enough at

By Bernard Naudin, from *L'Assiette au Beurre,* August 5, 1905.

one point to spur discussion of whether to simply remove all serving corporals from them on the grounds that those corporals were usually ex-prisoners themselves, tied to their old comrades by complex, often adversarial, relationships that generated hosts of accusations and counter-accusations.[5] That particular idea hadn't been adopted, nor was any other measure found to thin the flow of court actions. The war ministry was essentially compelled to accept this as a fact of military life under the Third Republic. It tried to compensate for the expense by seeking out efficiencies in the configuration of the camps themselves: moving or combining them, rearranging their functions and staffing, reshuffling their inmates. These sorts of administrative measures, however, couldn't address the problem that camp personnel faced each day: applying the level of force necessary for managing a highly volatile prison subculture without drawing the attention of Parisian dilettantes.

Émile Rousset would claim that the "bourgeois militarists" who staffed the Oran *parquet* secretly yearned to "purge" the army once and for all of the "vermin" in its penal camps—especially himself.[6] He believed he had been targeted for defying the homicidal madness that was Biribi; indeed, that the only thing keeping him alive was the political influence of his newfound sponsors in France. But to nearly all the officers who knew him, Rousset was a highly skilled dissimulator, a moral pathogen whose malign influence they could not neutralize because of the protective bubble that a cabal of venal politicians had cast around him. His pardon, his posting to Médéa, and not least, the funds that his admirers periodically relayed to him all demonstrated the strength of that bubble—and its creators' utter obliviousness to the truth about Rousset, and about so much more.

At Médéa one officer's concern to reveal that truth, to expose the real man inside that bubble, would prove particularly consequential. That officer was twenty-four-year-old Lieutenant Charles-Louis Pan-Lacroix, commander of the garrison's *subsistants* ("full-rations" unit). Pan-Lacroix duly noted the apparent correctness of Rousset's behavior at Médéa; the former prisoner was indeed every inch the good soldier—when under observation. But the accounts the lieutenant was receiving from fellow officers who had known Rousset at Djennan-ed-Dar, Douerà, and Djelfa painted a very different picture of the man when officers' eyes were averted. That Rousset was not just a chronic malingerer and petty thief. He was also a notorious *malabar,* a violent sexual predator who reduced victims to the status of *tapettes,* or passive receptacles of his lust.

On July 11, just about a week after arriving at the garrison, Rousset had surgery for his hernia, remaining in camp while most of the company was deployed to combat duty in Morocco. By August, he was looking forward to the month's convalescent leave in France he had been granted, which he was to begin as soon as he finished testifying at the upcoming trial of Sabatier, Beignier, and Casanova. But Rousset was never to take that leave. On the evening of August 27 he was to be involved in a criminal act that, to an observer like Lieutenant Pan-Lacroix, had been inevitable for some time.

At around 9:30 p.m., after evening roll call, another soldier under Pan-Lacroix's command, the cook Augustin Brancoli, was holding forth to a small assemblage of soldiers at the far end of a narrow barracks corridor leading from a courtyard to stairways ascending to sleeping quarters. The grouping included the cook's friends Robert-Georges Sauval and Émile Bintein; another soldier, Denis-François Bordessoulle; and Émile Rousset. Brancoli, a Corsican, had been drinking, and the conversation grew loud and argumentative, with much talk of "buggers" and "buggering." It reached a kind of crescendo, whereupon Brancoli was abruptly stabbed in the stomach.

The severity of the wound wasn't immediately apparent, but Bintein and Sauval immediately went to Brancoli's aid while Rousset and Bordessoulle hurried upstairs. Several soldiers standing around the courtyard entryway saw or heard various portions of what transpired, but they scattered upon the arrival of Corporal Despax, who had hurried from the courtyard to the stairwell upon hearing the sounds of argument and arrived almost immediately after the attack. Despax summoned some other *sous-offs*, who joined him in trying to calm Brancoli as he seized a rifle and staggered about with it for a bit. When it became apparent that his wound did require medical attention, they improvised a stretcher for him. They also made inquiries into who had been present at the scene, eventually taking Bintein, Bordessoulle, Rousset, and Sauval into protective custody.

Captain Giacomoni, the camp commander, arrived at the barracks shortly afterward and accompanied the *sous-offs* as they took Brancoli to the hospital. Giacomoni asked him who had attacked him, but Brancoli said he didn't know. The captain had taken on his duties at Médéa only a few days earlier. Upon leaving the hospital, he decided to assign Lieutenant Pan-Lacroix the task of conducting a preliminary inquiry into what had actually happened. This would prove an important decision.

By the terms of the *CJM*, the responsibilities of police judicial officer automatically fell to Giacomoni by virtue of his rank as commanding officer of the company. It was his job, then, to submit to the divisional general the first report on the incident, which was to either provisionally ascribe or deny criminal responsibility. Military law discouraged delegating this responsibility. It was understood that circumstances might occasionally require corps commanders facing crimes within their units to ask subordinates to conduct the investigation. However, those commanders were strongly advised to delegate that power with care, and lower ranks were granted much less leeway (captains and battalion chiefs were strongly urged not to delegate their own police duties without formal authorization by their own commanding officers).[7] By involving Pan-Lacroix, Captain Giacomoni may have expected the lieutenant simply to report the facts, leaving the determination of culpability to himself. But Pan-Lacroix would go well beyond that. Now a sort of second-tier operative of military justice, he would foray deeply into that netherworld of criminality, dissimulation, and sexual passion so well-known to personnel of the Oran *parquet*. In the end, all strands of his investigation led directly to Émile Rousset (see Appendix C).

Pan-Lacroix could reconstruct events only through direct testimony, but the interviews he conducted on August 28 with Bintein, Bordessoulle, Rousset, and Sauval, as well as with Despax and the other *sous-offs*, yielded little of use. The investigator understood the difficulties he would face in reaching the truth, difficulties that extended beyond the empirical reliability of testimony on a sudden, confused event in a dimly lit corridor. Pan-Lacroix recognized that none of the soldiers he was questioning would want to inform on a comrade—particularly if the comrade was a dangerous man or allied with other dangerous men. The men of the *Bats d'Af* spoke of a "soldier's code," but to Pan-Lacroix that code had little to do with real honor. In his view it was nothing but an expression of hostility toward military authority and a preference for private vengeance. How was he to extract testimony from men so powerfully disinclined to give it?

On the morning of August 29 the lieutenant went to the hospital to interview Brancoli, accompanied by a Corporal Laloo (who had known Rousset at Boussâda, where both had served brief sentences for disciplinary infractions in 1908).[8] The attending physician, Dr. Legrand, would permit only a brief amount of time with the victim, but Pan-Lacroix was able to ask Brancoli several times who had stabbed him. Brancoli repeated what he had already said to Giacomoni and would repeat to Legrand and several orderlies: it was dark, he didn't know—but he would have his vengeance.

Pan-Lacroix suspected that the Corsican knew exactly who had stabbed him but had no intention of delivering the assailant to military justice and forfeiting the pleasure of personal revenge. The investigator wasn't yet sure who had wielded the knife, but he was struck by Despax's observation that Bintein had loudly denied Rousset's guilt before the corporal or anyone else had even accused him.[9]

Returning to the holding cells, the lieutenant hit upon the idea of stationing Corporals Laloo and Michée in cells near those of the four detainees to eavesdrop on their conversations. None of the prisoners yet knew that Brancoli's condition was very serious. Pan-Lacroix's spies would report a conversation in which Rousset urged Bordessoulle to admit to the attack, suggesting that the punishment for assault was tolerable and would be mitigated by a confession. Rousset, said Laloo, actually promised that while on convalescent leave he would telegraph Pan-Lacroix, take the blame upon himself, then "disappear."[10] A shaken Bordessoulle seemed willing to take Rousset's counsel, but to Pan-Lacroix that hardly denoted guilt. The core truth of the *Bats d'Af* was that the weak were ordinarily used and discarded by the strong; and Rousset was clearly the stronger man.

On August 30 the lieutenant returned to re-interview a worsening Brancoli. This time Brancoli heatedly insisted that Rousset was not his assailant before lapsing into semiconsciousness. He would later repeat this to Dr. Legrand and to several orderlies. But to Pan-Lacroix, the very passion and frequency of Brancoli's insistence that Rousset had not attacked him were highly suspicious. Indeed, they further suggested that Émile Rousset—darling of the antimilitarists, the reformed *apache* of leftist myth—was, in fact, the attacker.

Pan-Lacroix decided to summon Bordessoulle for another interview, casually dropping the information that the Corsican's wounds might well prove fatal, amid questions about the detainee's dealings with Rousset. As intended, Bordessoulle returned to the cells and shared that information with the others, confiding to Rousset his own impression that the latter was emerging as the object of Pan-Lacroix's suspicions. An alarmed Rousset immediately demanded to be interviewed again, and the opportunity to personally confront Brancoli in the presence of witnesses.[11] Pan-Lacroix denied this, calmly explaining that he had not yet arrived at any conclusions.

Brancoli died around 4 p.m. on August 30. Shortly afterward, Bordessoulle, Sauval, and Bintein all came forward to announce that Rousset was indeed the killer. They had not accused him earlier, they said, out of fear of reprisals by Rousset or his friends. The possibility that any of them might now be accused of murder had forced the truth from them.

According to their complementary accounts, the seeds of the crime of August 27 lay in the relationship between Rousset, Brancoli, and Sauval. Sauval and Bintein had only arrived in Médéa on the morning of August 26, after completing prison terms elsewhere. Previously the "weak and small" Sauval had been sexually terrorized by, among others, a prisoner named Chabot, who happened to be a friend and accomplice of Rousset's.[12] Sauval had finally turned to prison authorities for protection, whereupon Chabot and several others were formally charged and jailed. Rousset had sworn to avenge them. When Sauval and Bintein arrived at Médéa, the *mouchard* (informer) was greeted warmly by Brancoli, who had known him in Morocco and assumed the role of protector. But Rousset bluntly advised Brancoli to abandon Sauval to his fate—which was to include replacing another soldier, Leprêtre, as Rousset's personal whore.

That afternoon Brancoli had gone into town with Sauval and Bintein, while Rousset sauntered through its streets with a couple of fellow soldiers, Pierlot and Lelarge. The two groups met at a tavern, where Rousset told Brancoli he had letters from friends confirming that Sauval was a paid informant. Brancoli agreed to read those letters and to drop Sauval if they proved persuasive. They shook hands in the street and seemed to part amicably enough.

But that night a drunken Brancoli incurred Rousset's wrath by again vowing to protect Sauval ("I'll shit on anyone who does you harm," he allegedly told Sauval), then launching into a violent diatribe against the men of the company. "I'll bugger all those Parisians and Marseillais!" he had allegedly shouted. The Lyonnais Rousset, now seething, asked if any of those remarks had been directed at him. Brancoli replied, "At you and all the others," whereupon Rousset responded with the impulsive violence and skill with a knife that had marked his entire history.

This, at any rate, was Pan-Lacroix's reconstruction of events. It was undergirded by the impression the lieutenant had formed of Rousset's capabilities. He was a "sly, hypocritical, violent" poseur who had exerted a baleful influence on camp morale and discipline since his arrival.[13] In fact, Pan-Lacroix had concluded that Rousset was the deeply feared leader of a criminal gang, the tendrils of which extended into several camps. The investigator decided to incorporate into the report he was preparing for Giacomoni ancillary testimony he collected on a plan hatched by Rousset and a confederate, Deliat-Besson, to rob the garrison's commissary on

August 26. They had missed their opportunity on that day, but Rousset had recast the plan for the next. He spent much of August 27 socializing with Lelarge, the commissary's guard—disarming the guard's wariness toward the Rousset circle, while Deliat-Besson was to conduct the actual break-in. When the latter lost his nerve, an enraged Rousset would loudly assert, in Lelarge's presence, that the boots on Deliat-Besson's feet had in fact been lifted from the commissary. Lelarge punished Deliat-Besson with a beating, while the real miscreant posed as the guard's conscientious ally. The incident, Pan-Lacroix felt, was Émile Rousset in a nutshell: cunning, manipulative, unscrupulous.

On August 31 Pan-Lacroix submitted a report to Captain Giacomoni attributing the murder to Rousset and describing the motive as his conflict with Brancoli over Sauval. To flesh out his portrait of Rousset's character, he included his findings on the planned theft of the commissary. He also included a detailed listing of Rousset's long record of offenses, both civil and military, which he felt bore indirectly on the plausibility of the accusations Rousset's fellow detainees had made against him.[14] Pan-Lacroix did not, however, describe his own interviews with Brancoli, or his deployment of Laloo and Michée. The former, after all, had yielded no tangible information, and the latter he presumably considered extraneous to the main purpose of the report.

Giacomoni would add little to what Pan-Lacroix had already presented. On September 1–2 he conducted interviews with Bintein, Bordessoulle, Deliat-Besson, Lelarge, Sauval, and Antoine-Jules Sappa. The first five simply repeated to Giacomoni what they had earlier told Pan-Lacroix. Sappa, also located as a witness by Pan-Lacroix, would describe an incriminating encounter with Rousset on the stairs immediately after the stabbing. Sappa said that Rousset told him to misdirect investigators looking for the knife to a locked box, in order to give him time to dispose of the knife elsewhere.[15]

Giacomoni also briefly interviewed Rousset, who admitted advising Brancoli against an association with Sauval but insisted that the sole reason was Sauval's history as an informer. Rousset claimed that he had been returning from a trip to the latrine with Bordessoulle when he found Brancoli volubly denouncing the mores of the company at the foot of the stairs and threatening to desert. According to Rousset, he had tried to calm Brancoli and lead him upstairs when the stabbing occurred. He claimed he did not know who struck the blow—but he did observe in the interview that Sauval had handed one of the *sous-offs* a bloodied knife (Brancoli's own, in fact). Rousset disclaimed any ascendancy over his comrades, any intent to rob the commissary, any conflict involving Deliat-Besson and Lelarge.[16] But his disclaimers did not convince Giacomoni. On September 2 the police judicial officer finished his report, appended transcripts of the interviews he had conducted, and sent it off to General Oudard in Algiers. It included his recommendation that Rousset be formally arraigned and investigated for both murder and attempted theft (see Appendix C).

Someone had already leaked the news of events at Médéa to the conservative Parisian newspaper *Le Journal*, which ran an article entitled "The Accuser Rousset Kills a Contradictor" on September 5. The next day Battalion Chief Salagnac reported that Rousset had tried to commit suicide by banging his head against the wall of his cell (although his wounds were described as light).[17]

The Sabatier/Beignier/Casanova trial was to begin on September 8 at Oran. Rousset arrived under armed guard and was kept in protective custody while awaiting his turn to testify. His protective bubble, he knew, was collapsing as supporters in France absorbed the "stupefying news" that the heroic Rousset stood accused of murder. *L'Humanité* struggled to reserve judgment while at the same time acknowledging that a number of its journalists had already accepted Rousset's guilt.[18] Indeed, no less zealous an advocate than Francis de Pressensé couldn't help wondering "whether it wasn't possible, psychologically explicable, that Rousset, finding himself in this environment, had succumbed to certain temptations and committed the crime."[19] In fact, the trial of Sabatier and others afforded a dramatic opportunity for the defenders of military justice to strike back at those who had constructed that bubble: the activists and politicians whose interventions had elevated to heroic status a calumniator of responsible officers and forced this totally illegitimate, wholly politicized prosecution.

The trial featured plenty of impassioned testimony. Sabatier himself began with a vigorous denunciation of "entrepreneurs of extortion" in France who aimed to exploit Aernoult's death in their ongoing struggle with military justice. General Rabier had been dispatched to Djennan-ed-Dar to do their bidding; he "saw and heard only what pleased him."[20] Witness after witness followed with claims that the testimony Rabier had collected against the officers was tainted. The most effective of these was certainly the ex-prisoner Marcheval—one of the original signatories of the letter that Deputy Veber had used in his first interpellation of War Minister Brun. Now weeping, Marcheval insisted that his earlier declarations had been obtained through terror (Sabatier congratulated him on his courage in telling the truth at last and asked the judge to reassign him in order to protect him from the ordeal that fellow prisoners would surely inflict on him now).[21] Commandant Pinoteau of Beni-Ounif expressed bitterness that Rabier had never bothered to interview him, while Beignier actually asserted that many of the accusations credited by Rabier were, in fact, the result of *CGT* bribes. Casanova's defense attorney, Garnier, noted that Rabier was a longtime critic of the army of Africa in general, and particularly of the quality of its officers. Sabatier's attorney, Pourtabourde, charged that for all practical purposes the general "had been sent on his mission by the *CGT* and not by the minister."[22]

Portabourde went further. The contaminating touch of politics, he argued, had been carried by the Rabier report directly into the Oran *parquet* itself. It had reached *rapporteur* Alix, who understood the chronic mendacity of prisoners perfectly well yet had inserted their lies into the report by which the defendants stood falsely charged. In fact, defense attorneys charged that Captain Alix and the public minister, Bichemin, might themselves be prosecutable, having possibly violated regulations distinguishing administrative documents from juridical ones by incorporating portions of the Rabier report directly into the dossier they had submitted to General Alix.[23] On the final day of the trial, Beignier and his attorney, Montbrun, spent hours denouncing Captain Alix as "a true public danger for society and for military justice."[24] Alix himself was so enraged by the traducing that he subsequently returned from France to physically confront Montbrun (the shaken attorney would ask the divisional general for sanctions against Captain Alix and, when none were taken, organize a strike by Oran's attorneys against the military *parquet*).[25]

Indeed, wrote *L'Humanité*'s reporter Bremond, "the only trial that has been going on, for three days, before the *conseil de guerre* of Oran [is] the one against General Rabier and the [accusing] prisoners."[26] The issue of the politicization of the Oran *parquet* through the Rabier report certainly seemed far more gripping to the panel of military judges than the actual case against the defendants. That case was not, however, a negligible one. Dr. Lafeuille, who had examined Aernoult's remains in February, testified that Aernoult had indeed been denied proper medical care, and that his death could have been prevented had a physician been summoned when the prisoner showed himself unable to carry out his punishment. Dr. Dorange offered the view that some of the punishments inflicted on prisoners at the camp were indeed excessive (while at the same time declining to blame the defendants for not recognizing the gravity of Aernoult's illness). Testimony from Rousset and other prisoners on what had been done to Aernoult was supplemented with depositions from Debon (Aernoult's companion in the punishment detail, then serving another sentence at the Santé prison in Paris) and from the ex-prisoner Allaire.

Rousset, among others, found it decidedly odd that the least impeachable witnesses—for instance, Sabatier's own orderly, Save, who had testified against the lieutenant to Rabier—were not available to testify at Oran. They either couldn't be found, like Save, or had somehow recently died, like one of the accusing auxiliaries. In fact, the prosecution seemed suspiciously dependent on witnesses with shady pasts and charges outstanding—specifically, himself and Debon.[27] Bichemin's summation was notably wan.[28] The charges against Casanova were dropped completely, and the acquittals of Sabatier and Beignier were greeted with cheers by most of the trial's spectators.

Rousset's testimony indeed had been a great gift to the defense, and he knew it.[29] From the first day of the trial, defense attorneys had devoured it as the self-serving lies of a murderer, prompting a vigorous rejoinder from Rousset but only the most half-hearted reproof from Colonel Le Ray, the president of the tribunal. In fact, Rousset believed that the dossier currently being compiled on the murder at Médéa had been sent to Le Ray for private examination by himself and the other military judges.[30] He wanted to consult with his attorney, Gandolphe, about the legality of this, and about other aspects of his own defense. But the meeting was barred. Gandolphe protested to the war minister himself and secured a favorable dispatch from the minister to General Alix. But the general was emboldened to resist this particular intervention from the political world on behalf of the notorious Émile Rousset. He had not yet ordered a *mise en jugement* for Brancoli's murder, and according to his reading of the law of 1897 Rousset was not entitled to professional legal counsel until he did. Gandolphe disputed that reading of the law. By that reckoning, he argued, Rousset could theoretically be prevented from communicating with his attorney indefinitely, since the timing of the decision on the *mise en jugement* was one of the many prerogatives assigned the general in military justice. For all practical purposes, Gandolphe insisted, Rousset was arraigned and under investigation already; if not, Sabatier's lawyers should never have been permitted to raise the question of his alleged involvement in Brancoli's murder in court. Nevertheless the general's decision held.[31]

Rousset's and his advocate's positions were certainly weakened in the eyes of the court, the public, and possibly the war minister by sensational accounts of the Médéa incident—and the deviant sexual dynamics that apparently underlay it—in the Algerian press. On the eve of the Oran trial, *L'Écho d'Oran* and other Algerian journals had published open allegations by attorneys Montbrun and Pourtauborde that Brancoli had incurred Rousset's wrath by attempting to protect Sauval from the *malabar*'s perverted lust. This, the public was informed, was the individual the politicians had been protecting—and this was just the tip of the iceberg. Djennan-ed-Dar itself was a notorious hotbed of sexual perversity, claimed the attorneys; it was a camp where prisoners "have the same influence over auxiliaries that women have over men, and they try to make use of this influence by getting rid of the officers they loathe."[32] These were the conditions that were allowed to fester in the *Bats d'Af* because meddling politicians thwarted the proper operations of military justice and the proper cleansing the camps required.

It was a powerful charge, and a difficult one to counter, for the evolving narrative that the *parquet* of Oran was developing regarding what had happened at Médéa would be detailed, coherent, and well attested by witnesses and participants. The full-scale investigation of Brancoli's murder that General Oudard of Algiers ordered his *parquet* to undertake was assigned to a Captain Godiot. But Godiot would rely heavily on the work of Lieutenant Pan-Lacroix, who remained vitally interested in the case (see Appendix C). Pan-Lacroix would deliver to Godiot important evidence, including new information about the disposition of the murder weapon. In fact, Pan-Lacroix would take the initiative to conduct a number of interviews with various witnesses in mid-September, which he delivered to police judicial officer Giacomoni, who in turn passed them on *to rapporteur* Godiot.

Sappa had described a Rousset frantic to dispose of his knife before investigators arrived on the scene. But Pan-Lacroix determined that he had not had time for that and had actually taken the knife with him into protective custody (the lieutenant would claim that the *sous-offs* who conducted the detainees to their cells had neglected to search them carefully). According to the lieutenant's later account, he himself was approached by a soldier named Blé with an offer to help find Rousset's knife during the latter's period of detention. Blé, Pan-Lacroix would explain, claimed to know the weapon well—he had personally stopped Rousset from using it against a Sergeant Nardy the preceding week.[33] When Bordessoulle was released, he would join Blé in the search; and the two would locate the knife buried in a shallow well beneath the door to the cell where Rousset had originally been held. Bordessoulle claimed that Rousset believed this was the last place officers were likely to look for it.[34] The bloody knife was identified by several witnesses as Rousset's.

During his mid-September inquiries, Pan-Lacroix also unearthed two additional witnesses willing to come forward and accuse Rousset. The testimony of the soldier Pierlot was both surprising and especially damaging since he appeared to be a confidant of Rousset's. "I was always rather good to him," an indignant Rousset would later remark.[35] Pierlot told Pan-Lacroix that he had arrived on the scene just as Rousset had drawn his knife, had tried to hold him back, but had been brushed off and left to watch helplessly as Rousset killed Brancoli. Yet another soldier, Vigouroux, came forward to echo Pierlot's account, claiming that he had witnessed the entire scene unfold while walking down the corridor to the stairway.[36] After speaking to Pan-Lacroix, Pierlot and Vigouroux officially confirmed their accounts in formal depositions taken by Captain Godiot, who compiled additional testimony throughout September and October.[37] Pierlot and Vigouroux brought the total number of eyewitnesses positively identifying Rousset as the murderer to five.

Godiot enlarged the dossier he was assembling with testimony regarding Rousset's character and social relations, none of which was favorable. The most important was that of a Lieutenant Maitrot, to whom the *rapporteur* was specifically referred by Pan-Lacroix. Maitrot had commanded the *dépot des isolés* at Algiers, where Rousset and other conscripts destined for the *Bats d'Af* had been held upon arriving in Algeria in 1908. Maitrot described Rousset as one of the worst *malabars* he had ever known, extremely dangerous to anyone standing between himself and his chosen victims. He claimed to have seen letters from Leprêtre to Chabot confirming that Rousset had raped the former repeatedly; and others from Chabot to Rousset asking him to leave Leprêtre, with whom Chabot had fallen in love, to himself.[38] That, concluded Godiot, explained why Rousset had turned from Leprêtre to Sauval, who Chabot informed him would be arriving at Médéa shortly. Sauval, according to this testimony, was basically a sexual plaything, incapable of defending himself; while Brancoli was a well-known protector of the helpless.[39]

On September 17, however, Godiot received a document that challenged an important component of the case he was assembling against Rousset. It came from Dr. Legrand, who took the initiative to write the *rapporteur* and prefaced his letter with an expression of concern that his own and his orderlies' observations of Brancoli during his last days might not be officially recorded—for some reason, neither he nor his orderlies had ever been formally deposed.[40] Legrand thought the authorities should know that, in fact, Brancoli's denial that Rousset was his assailant had *not* been unprompted, nor suspiciously spontaneous. Rather, it had been in direct response to specific questions posed at least twice by Pan-Lacroix during his interviews. Legrand also thought the authorities should know that the dying man had specifically requested that Pan-Lacroix bring Rousset to the hospital, insisting that no telltale signs of guilt would issue from the encounter; and that Brancoli's denials had been consistent and numerous, delivered to Legrand himself and to several orderlies. Several of those present shared Pan-Lacroix's belief that Brancoli knew who his attacker was.[41] Yet there was a big difference between their accounts of Brancoli's demeanor as he faced death and that of Pan-Lacroix.

The issue was an important one. Pan-Lacroix would repeatedly maintain that Brancoli had exculpated Rousset spontaneously and with no prompting from himself.[42] To him, the unbidden quality of those disavowals was precisely what rendered them so revealing. Shortly after Godiot received Legrand's letter, Pan-Lacroix stepped forward to give his own deposition—accompanied by a supporting affidavit from Laloo. According to the lieutenant, on August 28 he had asked Brancoli how he could insist that he didn't know who his attacker was while simultaneously swearing vengeance against him. At that point, said Pan-Lacroix, Brancoli had abruptly blurted out that it wasn't Rousset. On August 29, Pan-Lacroix testified, he had told Brancoli that he thought he knew the assailant but wanted to hear it from the victim's own lips. Again, said Pan-Lacroix, Brancoli spontaneously avowed that it wasn't Rousset. According to Laloo as well as the lieutenant, it was only then that the investigator had begun putting the names of each of the detainees before Brancoli for specific responses. But, they claimed, Pan-Lacroix had been able to ask only whether it was Rousset or Sauval before Brancoli began to weaken and the interview had to be terminated.

Pan-Lacroix was, of course, acting exactly as General Bourelly and other defenders of the procedures of military justice had always argued its investigators and judges must and should act: with an awareness of how real soldiers act, rather than in deference to the procedural norms of civilian jurisdictions. In a civilian jurisdiction Brancoli's actual words (as well as those of Doctor Legrand and his orderlies) would be weighty, perhaps even dispositive. Here, that would be disastrous. Rousset's own behavior, Pan-Lacroix felt, confirmed his guilt—at least to anyone who knew how to interpret the demeanor of men such as these. Pan-Lacroix explained to Godiot that in his August 28 interview with Rousset the latter had first tried to shift blame onto Sauval, who, according to Rousset, had been holding a bloody knife (Pan-Lacroix had concluded from the testimony of the other detainees that the knife was Brancoli's own, bloodied when the victim unsheathed it and passed it across his wounded torso to Sauval). Rousset had then offered the preposterous notion that Brancoli might have accidentally wounded himself in the fury that had gripped him just prior to the stabbing. Rousset was clearly clutching at straws, his desperation the clearest indicator of his guilt. As to the lieutenant's own investigatory procedures, Pan-Lacroix explained to Godiot that he had indeed denied the confrontation with Brancoli that Rousset had requested on August 29 because he felt it would be meaningless. Brancoli had no intention of identifying his attacker. In any event, Rousset had enough "force of character" to remain impassive before the dying man. If one understood these men, one knew these things.

The case against Rousset was indeed hardening. Five eyewitnesses had accused him. His bloody knife had been located. Extensive testimony had been gathered concerning his motive, supplemented by broader accounts of his unsavory character. What did Rousset have to say in his own defense? What counternarrative would he put forward? What dismayed his supporters in France and rendered the entire case so difficult to assess was that until October 7—nearly six weeks after the crime—Rousset offered no such counternarrative: no alternative explanation of events, nothing except fervent but unsupported claims that he was innocent and had been accused in order to undermine his testimony at the Sabatier/Beignier/Casanova trial.[43] In fact, in his first interview with Captain Godiot on September 23, Rousset seemed to reinforce the case against himself. Godiot asked how, if he had really taken Brancoli by the arm and attempted to lead him upstairs to bed, he could possibly have failed to see the assailant. At that point, Godiot's secretary recorded, Rousset "hesitates, seems embarrassed and doesn't respond."[44]

Only in his next interview, a very dramatic one on October 7, would Rousset begin offering an alternative to the account that Godiot, with vital help from Pan-Lacroix, was compiling. This was when he first accused Bordessoulle of murdering Brancoli. He had seen it, Rousset said, and he had corroborating testimony. At that point his attorney, Montès, handed a surprised Godiot a letter from one Robert Dérieux, a fellow inmate of Rousset's at the military prison of Algiers. In it Dérieux explained that he had been in the barracks corridor on the evening of August 27, that he had witnessed the attack, and that he was prepared to testify that Bordessoulle, not Rousset, was the assailant.

Rousset went on to offer his own description of the whispered conversations he had had with Bordessoulle while in protective custody. Bordessoulle, he said, had confided that he intended to confess to Pan-Lacroix, only not out of remorse. He was frightened of the vengeance of Brancoli or his friends and actually intended to physically attack Pan-Lacroix in order to make sure he would remain in protective custody for an extended period, pending a *conseil de guerre* trial. Rousset explained that despite their short acquaintance he knew Bordessoulle to be an unstable character and fully capable of executing so bizarre a plan. He also suspected that Bordessoulle had stolen his knife several days earlier and feared that if it were used on Pan-Lacroix he would somehow be accused of having instigated and abetted the act. He therefore persuaded Bordessoulle to pass him the knife, claiming that he had found a window bar that could be cut and intended to escape. He promised to return the knife, and after some coaxing Bordessoulle complied. A relieved Rousset had then hidden the knife. To support this story, Rousset asked Godiot to interrogate Sergeant Fleury, who had brought the prisoners their morning soup. Rousset claimed that it was Fleury who, at Bordessoulle's request, had retrieved the knife from Bordessoulle's own pack, where the real killer had hidden it immediately after the murder. According to Rousset, Bordessoulle had hoped to find an opportunity to incriminate him with it.

In this and subsequent interviews with Godiot, Rousset went on to challenge various other aspects of the Godiot/Pan-Lacroix narrative. For example, he insisted that he had indeed been searched by Sergeant Lemaitre, who had found no knife on him for the simple reason that he was carrying none. Bordessoulle had testified that he and Rousset had been in their sleeping quarters when Brancoli arrived, and that Rousset had demanded that Bordessoulle accompany him downstairs to confront the Corsican. In fact, said Rousset, he had gone to the latrine alone, had chanced to meet Bordessoulle on his way back to the barracks, and had unexpectedly found Brancoli at the stairwell. Above all, he denied the accusations of homosexuality. Leprêtre had been a friend, nothing more, and Rousset had dropped him when he realized the association might become unsavory. There had been no sexual motive behind his warnings to Brancoli regarding Sauval; his exclusive concern had been Sauval's reputation as an informer. Godiot brandished before Rousset other letters he had seized suggesting either long-standing homosexual relationships or the desire for one. Rousset dismissed them as the fantasies of men he barely knew, insisting "I'm just not interested in things like that."[45]

But why hadn't Rousset come forward with his allegation against Bordessoulle earlier? There were two possible explanations for the delay. One was Rousset's claim that he had been torn between the desire to tell the truth and reluctance to inform on a *Bat d'Af* comrade—even one he scarcely knew. He had hoped that Bordessoulle would have the integrity to come forward and accept responsibility on his own. Further, although Dérieux had not penned his letter until September 29, Rousset said he had known it was forthcoming and therefore didn't think he would have to implicate Bordessoulle himself.[46]

The other explanation was the one on which Godiot would settle: it had simply taken Rousset this much time to concoct his story and to extort the kind of testimony he knew he would need to support it. His minions had tried threatening his accusers with grave harm if they didn't retract their stories—Bordessoulle had, in fact, written to General Oudard to request reassignment, claiming he feared for his life, while Vigoroux was absent without leave, allegedly fleeing Rousset's minions.[47] When that tactic hadn't worked, the ever-resourceful Rousset had turned to the hapless Dérieux.

Godiot himself aggressively interviewed Dérieux on October 9. He noted that no one else had mentioned his being on the scene; posed complicated questions about exactly where the witness was positioned and what he could have seen; demanded an explanation for Dérieux's delay in writing his letter; and pointedly observed that the accusation he was bringing against Bordessoulle was a very grave matter, and that the penalties for false testimony were severe. Godiot asked him whether Rousset had intimidated him into writing the letter—whereupon Dérieux broke down. "I'll tell you the truth," he sobbed. "I was stupid enough to do what he said. Today I feel my heart sink at the thought of condemning an innocent man, and I swear to you honestly that I wasn't at the scene. I was in bed and saw absolutely nothing."[48]

But this wouldn't be the last time Robert Dérieux would change his story. Indeed, retractions of testimony and substitutions of new accounts would be recurring features of the investigations and judicial processes around Brancoli's death (and, for that matter, around Aernoult's). To determine who was telling the truth, and when, Godiot was authorized as *rapporteur* to arrange "confrontations" between witnesses presenting divergent accounts of the same events.[49] On October 14 he arranged one between Rousset and

Dérieux. Dérieux now retracted a portion of his prior retraction. He now said that Rousset had not extorted or in any way solicited the letter. Rather, he had heard Rousset speak of his case in prison and offered to write the letter of his own accord, prompted by loneliness and a need for attention.[50]

Dérieux's twists and turns would become genuinely dizzying. On November 3 Rousset requested another audience with Godiot in the presence of attorney Montès, during which he claimed that Dérieux had confessed to him that he had denied the truth of his original testimony only because the *rapporteur* had frightened him with the suggestion that Brancoli's friend Bintein had sworn to avenge the murdered Corsican—a vow that, Dérieux knew, would encompass all of Rousset's defenders, especially if Rousset himself somehow managed to escape punishment at the hands of the *conseil de guerre*. But in another interview that Godiot held with Dérieux on November 6, the prisoner recanted that alleged recantation of his prior recantation: "What I declared in that confrontation with Rousset is false; it's the deposition I made before you [Godiot] on October 9 [i.e., his denial that he had witnessed Brancoli's death] that is the truth."[51]

Dérieux's case, extreme as it was, was simply the *reductio ad absurdum* of the key problem in the investigation. The only way to determine the truth was through the testimony of witnesses—but these were witnesses in peculiarly vulnerable positions. They were men of the *Bats d'Af*, former or current prisoners. They might indeed be bullied by predatory comrades. Or they might be bullied or bribed by representatives of military justice anxious to make a case against one of those comrades. The case would entirely depend on the credibility of those witnesses. Were they telling the truth?

It was difficult enough to answer that question, let alone the larger ones that were arguably even more significant. What was the truth about Émile Rousset? Was he the reformed reprobate he claimed to be? Or was he the dissimulating criminal most of his officers and at least some of his comrades saw?

What was the truth about French military justice itself? Was it a harsh but honest system that attempted to maintain order and discipline among some of the most dangerous and unreliable elements in French society? Or was it the all-devouring monstrosity of antimilitarist rhetoric—Rouannet's "judicial minotaur"?

Breaking Codes

Captain Godiot didn't submit his report to General Oudard in Algiers until November 29, 1911. He quietly dropped the attempted theft charge that Pan-Lacroix had suggested be added to the indictment, since after all, no theft had ever been attempted. But he was much less circumspect regarding the murder charge. Godiot recommended to General Oudard that Rousset be prosecuted for voluntary homicide, the weightiest of charges. General Oudard decided to convene the *conseil de guerre* with surprising swiftness. Rousset's trial would begin on December 8. If convicted, he would theoretically be liable for the death penalty.[1]

Would the various types of antimilitarists who had sought to outdo one another in supporting Rousset prior to the incident at Médéa be willing to fight on for him now? What were the stakes of sallying forth against military justice one more time under the banner of Émile Rousset, proletarian martyr?

Certainly any pragmatic assessment of the general political climate would leave doubts about the prospect of success—that climate continued to shift quite palpably in militarists' favor. Tensions with Germany had spiked with the dramatic arrival of a German gunboat at the Moroccan port of Agadir in July 1911, a deliberately provocative intervention by the Kaiser into what had been regarded as a French sphere of interest. Such was the temper of the times that Premier Caillaux's effort to lower temperatures by bartering a portion of France's African holdings for German acceptance of her Moroccan protectorate would be met with howls of outrage and lead to the fall of his government in January 1912. Under the circumstances, it was hardly surprising that both the cabinet and the legislature were prioritizing military strength and preparedness.

Regarding military justice specifically, this could be expected to translate into a hardening of basic institutions and practices, and abrupt dismissal of reformists' initiatives. The idea would be to act even more resolutely against elements subverting discipline, including those unruly *apaches* who so demoralized and even corrupted the honest recruits with whom they came in contact in the ranks. On November 30, Georges Berry submitted a proposal to the Chamber of Deputies intended to widen the barriers against those contaminants by extending the cachement pool for the *Bats d'Af* beyond the categories stipulated in the 1905 legislation. Berry's proposal would reduce the prison term involving a *Bat d'Af* posting, from three months to one, and add vagabondage and graft to the criminal acts covered. *Apaches*, however, were not the only threats to discipline against which military justice could be directed. Antimilitarist propagandists and leftist radicals were targeted as well. Rumors that the war ministry would seek to supplement Berry's proposal—by adding to his list of offenses triggering a *Bat d'Af* posting actions such as "outrages to the army, provocation to disobedience, desertion, and insubordination," as well as strike-related sabotage—would prove true.[2] The measures were first considered by interim War Minister Adolphe Messimy and, after January, by War Minister Alexandre Millerand (like Briand, a heretical Socialist). To the left, the Berry-Millerand Law announced in February 1912 was frightening on two levels: for what it directly portended and for the apparent ease with which it was passed. The national mood was clearly changing, and the antimilitarists knew it.

What was to be done? Were propaganda and agitation on behalf of Émile Rousset appropriate countermeasures against this new threat, and against the nationalist/militarist tide on which it advanced? Or would such actions strengthen militarists' position? Pragmatists within the Aernoult-Rousset coalition could see the risks. If Rousset were indeed guilty, the new measures would be politically fortified. Not only would the jurisdiction's harshness toward real and suspected *apaches* seem justified, but its critics would stand revealed as naïve, or worse.[3] What was needed was, at the very least, a reasonable argument for Rousset's innocence. But this argument would be hard to mount. There were, after all, five eyewitnesses alleging his guilt. There was the seeming implausibility of his explanation of how his bloody knife had found its way to his cell. Above all, there was his delay in accusing Bordessoulle and the weakness of that allegation, including the absence of any apparent motive.[4] Not surprisingly, Socialists on the mixed commission charged with arranging demonstrations to accompany the return of Aernoult's body were unenthusiastic about incorporating manifestations of support for Rousset into Aernoult's obsequies.[5] When the possibility of a separate rally in support of Rousset was proposed, Socialist leaders let it be known that the party "is not looking to press this matter," having "received, from several correspondents in Africa, some information not very favorable to Rousset."[6]

Militants, of course, were delighted to rush in where moderates feared to tread. As early as September 20, the *CDS* had posted placards denouncing the "odious machinations" that had been undertaken against Rousset, announcing that it had taken the beleaguered prisoner under its own protection and informing the war minister that he "will answer to us" for Rousset's life.[7] There was little agonizing in militant circles about whether Rousset was innocent or not. After all, there were bigger matters involved than justice for Augustin Brancoli—bigger things, for that matter, than justice for Émile Rousset.

To militants, Rousset had always been an instrumentality, a symbol. Their gaze was fixed beyond him, toward the larger vision of a France without *conseils de guerre*, a Europe without armies, a world without war and oppression. The militant perspective may have been best articulated by CGT secretary Leon Jouhaux. Privately Jouhaux conceded that "Rousset is no pearl," even that "it would be better to have another, somewhat less tarnished victim."[8] Publicly, however, it was vital that the prisoner be presented as "popular courage and workers' probity personified!" Rousset's value lay in the public outrage that could be generated through perceptions of his victimhood—and, if anything, that value had increased with his latest arrest. Jouhaux was quite prepared to assert, with blithe disregard for the complexities of the actual case, that "Rousset was punished because he had revealed the killers of Aernoult, and this would be easy to explain to the public—*our* public."[9]

Militants never lost sight of the big picture and never viewed Rousset and his legal travails outside that context. "We want to save Rousset," Jouhaux wrote, "but we also want, with the help of his case, to strike a fatal blow against the *conseils de guerre* and the *compagnies de discipline.*" Indeed, Jouhaux was thinking beyond even those institutions. "For us revolutionary syndicalists," he proclaimed, "it's not just a question of shedding light on the falsehoods of the beribboned hyenas" but of exposing "the real, deep causes of these crimes." For, as Jouhaux put it, "It's not only the Pan-Lacroixes or the Beigniers or the Casanovas who make the army bad; on the contrary, it's the habits of idiotic discipline, the anti-natural mores and customs constituting the life of the barracks, that form these mentalities."[10] *CDS* leader Charles-Ange Laisant had a similarly grand view of the stakes: "The Rousset Affair is a lot more important than the Dreyfus Affair," he opined, in that it would lead more directly than the latter to "the exposure of a phony patriotism, a military caste that can no longer even evoke the health of the country as an excuse." Rousset himself was a "symbol" incarnating "the sufferings, the rages of a people victimized by the most atrocious oppression."[11]

As to Socialist concerns over whether further involvement in Rousset's case would advance or retard the "reform" of military justice, what could be more myopic? After all, wrote Rousset admirer M. Pierrot in the anarchist journal *Les Temps Nouveaux* (*The New Times*), "Reforms do nothing but temporarily mask the deep vices that come to light incessantly . . . propping up a system that is collapsing." Pierrot elaborated:

> We really need to get rid of the military prisons of Africa, but we'll have military prisons installed on a little Channel island or in the ocean. . . . Civil tribunals will replace the *conseils de guerre*. But professional judges are known for their insensitivity. After a certain time, it will be seen that the benefits acquired boil down to almost nothing. . . . The army is founded on discipline and passive obedience. It defends and maintains the social order of the country. How can the most profound reforms change those conditions? . . . All the abuses of authority develop there and will continue to develop there despite the good intentions of humanitarians. We thwart one abuse, ten others appear.

Radicals were called to hasten, not delay, the system's collapse. Their goal was "not keeping militarism and looking for ways to improve it but getting rid of it in all ways and by all means." The Rousset case provided an excellent opportunity "to show the masses all the ignominies that are committed in the name of patriotism."[12]

This, then, was the agenda militants brought to this new phase of the

Aernoult-Rousset Affair (or, rather, to "the New Rousset Affair," as they preferred to call it). It was nothing if not ambitious, and in the autumn of 1911 it appeared as though those ambitions would be unqualified by the qualms of moderates. Confused and uncertain, moderates seemed inclined to divorce themselves from the Rousset murder case entirely and to concentrate their energies on the return of Aernoult's body—that is, until they were rallied by an unlikely defector from militant ranks.

René de Marmande had developed a special personal relationship with Émile Rousset and felt a far keener interest in his personal fate than some colleagues on the militant left might have felt. To him, Rousset was very much a man, not a symbol: "neither a god nor a hero, but a very brave man."[13] The man had to be saved, not used; and saving him meant moving from rhetorical denunciations of military justice to full and effective engagement with it. Marmande would have to enter that arena and play to win, not stand apart and demand new rules. His focus would have to shift from the global to the specific, from the historic to the immediate, from the visionary to the pragmatic, from the moral to the legal. Simply in opting for that path, the path of real participation, Marmande began loosening his ties to the *enragé* world—conceptually and morally, if not yet socially and politically. Slowly but inexorably he would disencumber himself of that world's code.

What was urgent now was examining the Rousset case in detail, revealing its weak points, and attacking them in terms that might compel attention—not just in the labor exchanges and workers' meeting halls, where militants conducted their rallies, but in the military jurisdiction itself. It had been Marmande who had recommended Montès as Rousset's attorney. Now Montès apprised him of the evidence assembled by Rousset's prosecutors as it became available to him. Both men found serious weaknesses in it, and especially in the investigative methods used to collect it.

There was, first of all, the quality of the testimony against Rousset. Neither Sauval nor Bintein was a disinterested or unimpeachable witness: Sauval because of the personal hatred he bore Rousset, as a friend of Chabot; Bintein because of the contradiction between his urgent exculpation of Rousset at the actual scene of the crime and his equally confident accusation three days later. As for Bordessoulle, Pan-Lacroix and Giacomoni had been aware of the contradiction between that witness's account of earlier events (in which Rousset had demanded that Bordessoulle join him in confronting Brancoli) and Rousset's own account (in which the two men had met by chance while returning from the latrine). Why had other soldiers not been queried on this point, to determine which of the two accounts was more reliable? A competent investigator, Marmande would argue, would have "impartially researched the moral value of the witnesses . . . submitting them to the most scrupulous analysis by employing the elementary procedure of comparison and rational critique."[14] Instead, Pan-Lacroix had simply accepted all anti-Rousset testimony uncritically, while both Giacomoni and Godiot had done little more than adumbrate his initial report. In fact, Pan-Lacroix may have done worse. There were suspicious similarities between the exact phrasing of Pan-Lacroix's report of August 31 and the phrasing that witnesses used in their subsequent interviews with both Giacomoni and Godiot. Had Pan-Lacroix coached them?[15]

Rousset himself would always reserve special odium for Pan-Lacroix, describing him as "simian" in appearance and as an undistinguished officer determined to please his superiors by destroying the man who had revealed their iniquities at Djennan-ed-Dar.[16] Marmande found this indictment fully confirmed by the way Pan-Lacroix had assembled his report. Why had the lieutenant declined to include in it any of the testimony that tended to cast doubt on his claim that Rousset bore a deep animus against Brancoli (such as the fact that the two men had concluded their final discussion on the subject of Sauval with a handshake, later confirmed to Godiot by both Bintein and Lelarge)? On the other hand, why had he included unverifiable allegations of a plot hatched by Rousset to rob the camp commissary, allegations that even Captain Godiot had declined to take seriously?

Moreover, why had Pan-Lacroix failed to include in his report what Brancoli had actually said when queried at the hospital? This information would never have come to light at all had Dr. Legrand not taken the initiative to contact Captain Godiot himself. Pan-Lacroix might excuse his failure to formally transcribe any statements by Brancoli, the doctor, or any of the hospital orderlies on the grounds that only the police judicial officer—or, later, the *rapporteur* of the *parquet*—was officially authorized to take actual depositions. But then why had he taken Corporal Laloo to the hospital with him at all? What need of a secretary, unless Pan-Lacroix had fully intended to record Brancoli's statement (only to change his mind when Brancoli refused to indict Rousset)? Then there was the matter of Pan-Lacroix's actions after Dr. Legrand communicated his own concerns to Captain Godiot. The lieutenant had hardly behaved like a man content with the modest role he had been assigned in the matter. His official duties already discharged, Pan-Lacroix had nonetheless taken it upon himself to conduct no less than sixteen nonofficial interviews. Each of them buttressed his own account of events. All of them were passed on to Captain Godiot.

Marmande, like Montès, was appalled by Pan-Lacroix's conviction that every denial by a witness that Rousset was the assailant represented further evidence that he was. Marmande would describe this as a form of "reasoning by dereasoning"—and a peculiar failing of military justice. The same willful blindness led the lieutenant to interpret the very respect that Rousset had earned from Médéa's officers and noncoms as evidence of his skill at dissimulation. "Are we having a nightmare?" Marmande asked rhetorically. "No, the inquiries of Lieutenant Pan-Lacroix and of Captain Giacomoni are only too real."[17]

All this, of course, could be traced back to a larger failing long decried by critics of the military jurisdiction: entrusting investigations to men who lacked the training, temperament, and institutional independence needed for unbiased, competent work. Only a *Bat d'Af* officer would have seen Brancoli's exculpation of Rousset as insincere; any civilian investigator would have understood that men facing death have no more use for such charades. Only a subaltern trained to see and expect the worst in his charges could have failed to see the illogic of Rousset's risking, in one impulsive act, everything he stood poised to gain: a desperately needed convalescent leave, impending discharge from active service, the spotless soldier's record he had compiled since Djennan-ed-Dar, the respect of his new friends and supporters in France. Only an ambitious, underachieving lieutenant would have been so determined to deliver Rousset's judicial corpse to his superiors that he was willing to ignore or conceal evidence, skew testimony, and violate standard procedures to reach that goal. Only a functionary of military justice could have been so secure in the knowledge that no one outside the jurisdiction could hold him accountable for those errors, and no one within it would fail to applaud him for the trophy he was delivering.

Marmande knew that, in the end, political pressure would probably be required to reverse what the military jurisdiction was doing to Émile Rousset. But he was losing confidence that the methods or vision of his associates on the militant left were the most promising ones in this instance. In the current political climate, associating Rousset's case with the cause of radical antimilitarism could prove toxic: the closer that association, the firmer the government's likely resistance to interventions of the sort that had once resulted in victories like the Rabier report and Rousset's pardon. In fact, entrusting Rousset's fate to the powers of Marmande's old radical colleagues might be a potentially fatal error. There was, however, an alternative.

Moderates, reformists, legalists—"the intellectual and lettered public" whose support for Dreyfus had proven decisive in the end—were people who still might influence events.[18] Many were Socialists. Marmande understood their reluctance to engage: they, too, had agendas that reached beyond Émile Rousset, agendas that might be compromised if he were found guilty. But surely those concerns would be outweighed by their commitment to the maintenance of proper juridical forms and procedures. Those forms and procedures, Montès and Marmande both felt, were blatantly violated at Rousset's trial for murder before the *conseil de guerre* of Algiers, and that "intellectual and lettered public" must be made to recognize how.[19]

It began with the denial of Montès's request for a delay, occasioned, in part, by testimony Captain Godiot had acquired only at the end of November. At that time Godiot had learned about another prisoner, named Deleu, who claimed to have valuable information to offer about the case. Deleu, then serving his own sentence at Djelfa, had been a patient at the garrison hospital at Médéa when Brancoli was brought in. He claimed that Brancoli had confided to him that Rousset had indeed been his assailant. Deleu was the only witness claiming to have heard this from the victim, and he had come forth with this information only months later. Montès had therefore wanted additional time to personally query hospital personnel regarding Deleu's actual access to Brancoli and the plausibility of his depiction of the dying man's final hours. The attorney also wanted time to depose additional witnesses who, he said, would support Rousset's version of how Robert Dérieux had come to write his original letter to Godiot. Above all, he wanted to depose Sauval once again. The latter had been discharged from the service, ostensibly for medical reasons, and was residing at Creil in France. He agreed to submit a written deposition, but Montès wanted the opportunity to challenge it, plus the genuineness of his purported disability, before the tribunal.

The attorney argued that the December 8 trial date was precipitous and highly prejudicial to the defense. He submitted that the CJM was basically silent regarding trial delays. In a situation like this, proposed Montès, Article 1033 of the Code of Civil Procedure should be consulted, and this article should be read as an expression of regard for the rights of the defense. But military justice quite consciously set celerity above other considerations and conferred on the divisional commander responsibility for seeing to it. General

Oudard respectfully reminded Montès that the investigation of this murder had already lasted nearly three months; that Captain Godiot's adherence to proper procedures had been punctilious, duly providing advance notice to the defense of every witness he was to interview and every question he intended to pose; that Montès's own list of witnesses had not included those he now sought to question. The trial would proceed as scheduled.[20]

Montès would next protest the absence of any definitive official transcript of Brancoli's statements at the hospital. He protested Pan-Lacroix's refusal to arrange the confrontation between Rousset and Brancoli that both men had, in fact, requested. In particular, he protested the inclusion, in the official dossier of the investigation, of those statements that Pan-Lacroix had collected on his own initiative from various witnesses after Dr. Legrand had volunteered his information to Godiot. Formally, the statements carried no juridical weight, and Montès had not been apprised of them. But they had been important to Godiot, providing direction for the authorized depositions the *rapporteur* took later. Montès described Pan-Lacroix's statements as the equivalent of a separate, confidential, illegally assembled dossier. But Colonel Ungerer, president of the Algiers *conseil de guerre,* found nothing particularly offensive in that. "If this is irregular, a jurisdiction superior to ours will decide on it," Ungerer concluded. "I hope so!" snapped Montès.[21]

During the trial Montès concentrated on exposing contradictions and inconsistencies in the various witness's accounts of the events of August 27, with some success. Bintein, for instance, had no response when Montès asked him why, if he had been standing in front of Brancoli at the time of the stabbing, as he had testified, he had been unable to prevent it. Sappa was forced to acknowledge that he had not exchanged words with Rousset on the stairs, as he had originally testified, but rather in the bedchamber. "This is the kind of testimony that could lead somebody to an execution!" Montès exclaimed. Montès also challenged the contention that Rousset had brought the murder weapon into his cell when taken into custody, pointedly noting that if the *sous-offs* really had failed to carefully search the detainees, as they and Pan-Lacroix claimed, then the most elementary procedures had, for some reason, been cavalierly ignored. ("I'd like to see you go finding things in the places where they hide them," muttered Laloo.) But none of this shook the prosecution's case very much.

In fact, Rousset was his own most effective advocate. The killer, he openly insisted, was Bordessoulle. He reiterated that Bordessoulle had confided to him his intention to "ventilate" Pan-Lacroix, repeated his explanation of how he had coaxed the knife away, and attributed Laloo's false account of their furtive conversations to a grudge the corporal had held against him since their days together at Boussâda, where Laloo had wrongly accused him of stealing a knife. Fleury, who denied that Bordessoulle had asked him to retrieve any knife, was lying. Dérieux, who repeated his claim that Rousset had dictated the letter he had submitted to Godiot, was lying. Bintein, who insisted that Rousset had been waiting at the foot of the stairs when he and Brancoli arrived at the end of the corridor, was lying. But Rousset went further.

Those and other lies, he suggested, had been suborned by the investigating officers. They had circulated to soldiers the story that it was Rousset who had broken the "soldier's code" by attempting to deliver first Sauval and then Bordessoulle to the authorities simply to protect himself. The reality was that he had delayed telling the truth, risking even his own life, out of his profound respect for the code. Pierlot's, Sappa's, and Deleu's hostile testimony, Rousset proposed, had actually been teased from them by Pan-Lacroix, who knew perfectly well how to manipulate to his own advantage prisoners' loathing for a presumed collaborator. "Everything that's been said is a warped plot against me," insisted the defendant, "because it was thought that I had denounced a comrade."[22] As for the repeated allegations that Rousset was a fearsome figure, a *malabar* who had established a reign of terror over his comrades—all lies. "Where is the proof of my pederasty?" Rousset asked plaintively. On the contrary, he had been a model soldier for the last thirty months, incurring not a single disciplinary infraction.

At one point in the trial President Ungerer raised his arms and blurted out: "There is no way of shedding light on this debate."[23] But in the end the court endorsed the argument of public minister Domenech de Cellès. Too many eyewitnesses asserted Rousset's guilt. Too many comrades and superiors confirmed the depravity of his character (especially Sauval, who spoke tearfully of "the bad treatment that men like Rousset and his band force young guys to submit to").[24] He was found guilty, although the court decided to reduce the charge from voluntary to involuntary homicide. His sentence was twenty years of forced labor. He wrote his brother Louis that "twenty years in prison isn't too dear since I won't be doing it. I'll be dead first."[25]

But Montès and Marmande were determined to make sure he lived, and that the questions he had raised about the quality of the case against him, and about the procedures of the tribunal, would not fade from view. Their method contrasted rather vividly with that of the *CDS*, which was already considering posting another "very violent placard, signed by all its members, to draw attention to the prosecution."[26] Instead, Marmande and Montès quietly filed a formal appeal to the High Court of Appeals to quash the Algiers court's verdict.

In addition, they lobbied the leadership of the Socialist Party for active engagement in support of Rousset. Misgivings about Rousset's innocence had not dissipated in those circles; Pierre Renaudel, one of Rousset's earliest champions, would remain conflicted for months over the murder charge, despite several sections' demands for a full commitment to his cause.[27] That's why the party had not responded to the *CDS*'s invitation to send representatives to a massive protest meeting it was planning for December 23.[28] Marmande and Montès tried to raise disquiet regarding the trial procedures, reminding Socialists of their obligations—if not toward Émile Rousset, then toward defendants in *conseils de guerre* in general. Renaudel was receptive to that idea at least and proposed that *L'Humanité* undertake its own investigation into the facts surrounding Brancoli's murder.[29] It was to begin with a careful study of portions of the dossier provided him by Montès.[30]

The idea that testimony in military courts might have been deliberately manipulated by officers was indeed troubling to Socialists, especially when contemplating the possible scale of the practice. By January 3, 1912, *L'Humanité* was sharing with its readers "information acquired from a good source" that cast doubt on the honesty of the crucial testimony that witness Marchevel had so tremulously delivered at the trial of Sabatier, Beignier, and Casanova in early September. Marcheval's recantation of his prior accusation of those officers had been a vital factor in their acquittal. But the journal had learned that theft charges the witness himself had been facing at the time of that trial had mysteriously been dropped, and Marcheval had been whisked from the *compagnie de discipline* where he was serving his prior sentence to a Tunisian *Bat d'Af*. Gradually, Renaudel and other Socialists abandoned their opposition to the linkage of Rousset's case to Aernoult's funeral obsequies, which the mixed commission was still working to arrange. By February 6 *L'Humanité* would specifically advertise the demonstration to take place in Paris on February 11 as "necessary to make governments understand that the entire working class protests against the iniquitous condemnation pronounced against the courageous Rousset by military judges."[31]

Marmande, however, knew that Socialist moderates weren't the only ones concerned with the integrity of military courts' procedures—or even necessarily the most effective monitors of it. The League for the Defense of the Rights of Man represented a particularly valuable source of support for Rousset, if only it could be brought to recognize the stakes involved. Almost since its inception at the height of the Dreyfus Affair, the league had been divided between legalists, who wanted its commitment to justice to be a strictly nonpartisan one, and leftists, who felt that a commitment to justice necessarily placed the league on the side of the workers.[32] Something like the Rousset trial was actually appealing to both sides, and Marmande began an assiduous courtship of the organization. On January 7, 1912, the league, under the direction of Paul-Hyacinthe Loyson, dispatched an "Open Letter to the Magistrates of the High Court of Appeals" demanding that "bourgeois justice be equitable toward a worker-soldier." By February 5 a special "Rousset Affair Committee" had been formed by such league notables as Louis Havet (president), Paul Painlevè (vice president), Wilfred Monod, Georges Russacq, Loyson, and others.[33] Its secretary-treasurer was René de Marmande.

The following month the Rousset Affair Committee secured an appointment with the war minister's chief of staff to bring to his personal attention some complaints Rousset had tendered about the conditions of his incarceration pending his appeal.[34] This was precisely the sort of influence in the halls of power Marmande had wanted—a brand of influence, direct and effective, that could never have been wielded by his old militant colleagues. But he would not be able to remove himself from that old world, or detach Rousset's case from it, painlessly.

The *CDS* reacted with real fury to Marmande's overtures to the old Dreyfusards of the league, especially to Havet's summary rejection of any involvement by *CDS* members at the meeting in the war ministry.[35] That reaction could hardly have surprised anyone. The *CDS*'s own devotion to Rousset's cause had been unflagging, especially when others had doubted. The committee had even assumed Rousset's legal expenses, enlisting one of its own attorneys, Berthon, to represent Rousset's interests in Paris while Montès tended to them in Algeria. *CDS* was already organizing a host of public demonstrations despite its own chronic financial weakness.[36] Its members certainly felt themselves entitled to assume the direction of any new agitation on his behalf. Yet Marmande was creating a parallel organization of "intellectuals" to take control of the movement, elements that would certainly deflect it from its properly revolutionary goals. The *CDS* went so far as to direct a written protest to Louis Havet, scoring him for co-opting "our Dreyfus Affair."[37] Havet responded by insisting that the Rousset matter didn't "belong" to anyone. Marmande, for his part, protested that the new Rousset Affair Committee and the *CDS* would simply use different means to the same end. But the *CDS* would have none of it, charging that he was delivering the working classes into the treasonous hands of celebrity liberals and "millionaire" progressives simply to get himself near their funds. Marmande had to acknowledge, sadly, that "war was declared" against him by his old comrades.[38]

Yet those militants also redoubled their efforts on Rousset's behalf—perhaps precisely in order to maintain primacy of place in the agitation. The rallies and demonstrations the *CDS* either organized or co-organized (with, among others, the Union of Seine Unions) picked up steam in January 1912. Marmande may have winced at the language used at some of these events. At a rally in Bordeaux on January 12 one speaker endorsed sabotage, while another expressed sympathy for any soldier who killed a brutalizing officer. The *CDS*'s Thuillier called the Third Republic "the great whore" and insisted that Rousset owed his initial liberation to the "Down with Biribi!" trial the *CDS* had provoked.[39] The very reformers and parliamentarians with whom Marmande now consorted were excoriated with particular vehemence at another meeting, this one featuring Rousset's friend Marcel Moreau (one speaker, scorning the "reform" route, claimed that no worker would have objected if Aernoult's mother had personally confronted Sabatier with "the necessary gesture").[40] But Marmande still hoped for *CDS* cooperation on a particular project that was assuming real salience in his mind.

Portions of the Algiers trial dossier, including all documents assembled by the *parquet* in its investigation of Brancoli's murder, had already been selectively leaked to leaders of the Socialist Party and the League for the Defense of the Rights of Man, and interest in it was widening. "Let's scour the dossier!" urged the leftist journal *La Libertaire* (*The Libertarian*) in a report on benefits that seemed to fall with suspicious regularity on witnesses who had testified against Rousset.[41] Marmande decided that the dossier should indeed be scoured—by the entire French reading public, alongside those politicians and activists who had long argued for more transparency in military justice. "The dossier never left my mind," he would later write. "I really felt that [publishing it] could be and was the key to the military and judicial machinations."[42] Marmande's thinking may have reflected the influence of his new associates. Figures in the League for the Defense of the Rights of Man, especially Francis de Pressensé, had long protested the military jurisdiction's "exorbitant claim to keep dossiers secret."[43] He obviously knew that actually publishing one, especially this one, would be an audacious move sure to enrage defenders of military justice and possibly open to prosecution. Even if a journal were willing to run that risk, other obstacles had to be surmounted—not the least of which were the printing costs, given the enormity of the dossier. Officially, only Montès and Berthon had access to it, and both were formally affiliated with the *CDS*. Would either go so far as to release the entirety of the dossier to the public? Would the *CDS* allow it?

When Marmande proposed publication to the *CDS* leadership, they put him off with "puerile pretexts." Their reluctance to cooperate may have reflected nothing more than a preference for publication arrangements providing more financial and political benefits to themselves (probably with *La Bataille Syndicaliste*) than to groupings they viewed as rivals within the movement.[44] But Marmande, for his part, had established cordial relations with *Les Temps Nouveaux*, a sophisticated, artistically influential anarchist journal edited by the venerable Jean Grave, who bore no love for the *CDS*.[45] It was Berthon, in the end, who placed the full dossier into Marmande's hands. On February 8, 1912, *Les Temps Nouveaux* published the whole thing.

The publication of an entire dossier assembled by military investigators was a significant act: basically, a well-shielded quarter of the military jurisdiction had been raided for intelligence that would prove enormously valuable in the larger struggle to come. The timing was especially significant. The hope was that publication of the dossier, followed immediately by *L'Humanité*'s publication of the full stenographic record of Rousset's trial on February 10, would enlarge and energize the crowd that activists hoped would assemble to solemnlymark the cremation of Aernoult's remains at the Père-Lachaise cemetery in Paris. This event was scheduled, at long last, for February 11, 1912.

The "mixed commission," which had been working toward this end since the summer of 1910, had finally managed to prevail—more or less. Various sorts of rulings had delayed the event for a year and a half (the latest requiring Aernoult's reluctant parents to take up residence in Paris in order to qualify their son for cremation at the city's municipal cemetery).[46] At last, the red tape had been cut, but the prospects for a large and enthusiastic turnout seemed dim. The main problem was the commission's internal divisions, which had never healed—elements on each side remained suspicious of the other and reluctant to participate fully. The internal squabbling extended to finances, most of which had been raised by *L'Humanité*'s subscription drive. *CDS* members questioned whether Renaudel and other moderates on the commission were more concerned with protecting the Socialist journal's investment than in expediting the return of Aernoult's body.[47] There certainly seemed little likelihood that the demonstration would be sufficiently grand to impress the judges of the High Court of Appeals prior to their February 21 consideration of Rousset's case.[48] That goal was particularly dear to Thuillier and other *CDS* members, who had hoped to schedule the obsequies as close to that date as possible.[49]

But the scale and effectiveness of the Aernoult funeral demonstration in Paris would put the lie to those expectations, astonishing its own organizers no less than the police observers who had confidently predicted a fairly paltry crowd of perhaps twenty thousand. It was the single most dramatic public moment in the entire Aernoult-Rousset Affair, a ringing affirmation of the impact the agitation had made in at least certain quarters of French society—and a pointed reminder of the continuing strength of the antimilitarist movement in France.

"Glory to Rousset"

The government had precluded Marseilles as a point of disembarkation for the small delegation that brought Aernoult's body from Algiers to France. Instead, they made port at the small Pyrenean fishing village of Port-Vendres. Demonstrations held between February 8 and 10 in Toulon, Rochefort, Nancy, Chalons, Lyons, Bordeaux, and elsewhere drew crowds numbering only in the hundreds.[1] But one reason for the poor turnout may have been that many of the people who had been moved by the Aernoult-Rousset story and wanted to register their feelings had elected to travel to Paris, to participate in the final commemoration at the columbarium of Père-Lachaise.

When the body arrived at Paris's Gare de Lyon station, it was met by some fifty representatives of various trade unions and Socialist Party sections, who (under the watchful eye of Police Prefect Lepine) organized the cortège that was to escort the coffin to Père-Lachaise. At about 2:15 p.m. the procession got under way, with the marching band "Socialist Harmony of the 12th *Arrondissement*" at its head. The coffin and its pallbearers followed directly behind the musicians, trailed by Aernoult's parents in an automobile and finally by delegates of various unions, party sections, anarchist and youth groups, each identified by a banner. The entire procession probably numbered only about a thousand at first, many singing or humming along with the band's renditions of the "*Internationale,*" the "*Carmagnole,*" Chopin's "Funeral March," and a new anthem—"Glory to Rousset." But as the procession snaked its way up the boulevard Diderot to the Place de la Nation and then along avenue Philippe-Auguste to the cemetery, something remarkable happened.

The ranks of marchers swelled into the thousands, then tens of thousands, as newcomers joined in at various points along the route. As the assemblage grew larger, it also grew louder. Weeping, and cries of "Down with the army!" and "Death to Sabatier!" punctuated the air. There was pronounced hissing as the procession passed by the barracks at rue Reuilly. There were, as yet, no incidents. But the procession's increasing size constituted an event in itself, one anticipated by neither the police nor the procession's own organizers.[2] *L'Humanité*'s observers would initially estimate it as around 120,000, later raising that count to 200,000.[3]

Whatever the final figure, there was no question that a very impressive expression of solidarity with both the martyred Aernoult and the heroic Rousset had been mounted. Only around 20,000 of the marchers were able to fit into the columbarium, but those who did heard a series of impassioned speeches by Renaudel, Maurice Sembat, and others representing the Socialist Party; Jouhaux for the CGT; Thuilier and Bodechon for the *CDS*; plus other antimilitarist activists. There was frequent mention of Rousset and his torment. There were cries for vengeance against Sabatier, Beignier, and Casanova. There were denunciations of the Berry-Millerand Law, the *conseils de guerre*, the penal camps.

Scattered incidents of violence occurred as demonstrators began to filter out of the cemetery and stream through the city. Some resisted police attempts to seize an anarchist banner at the cemetery's gates. Later, at Place Gambetta and elsewhere, mounted police would charge rock-throwing crowds. By the end of the day roughly twenty demonstrators had been arrested and fifteen policemen wounded, some "rather seriously."[4] That violence was foregrounded in reportage by the militant *Bataille Syndicaliste* on the one hand and by the conservative papers *Le Journal*, *L'Éclair*, and *Le Petit Parisien* on the other. In leftist accounts, it was provoked by the police, who discharged their fear of The People with brutal attacks on proletarian women and children. In conservative accounts it was the work of the foreigners and *apaches*, who actually made up most of the crowd and were far more interested in petty theft and property damage than in solidarity with the victims of Biribi.[5]

But other, less polemical journals recognized that most of the day had been entirely peaceful, and they devoted more space to measured reflections on what the composition and behavior of the crowd actually portended. The generally conservative journal *Le Temps* offered a particularly intriguing observation. "So many bad things have been said about the *compagnies de discipline*," its commentator acknowledged, that "the people honestly believe that there is torture and murder in these African battalions." All the same, he continued, the events of the day needed to be assessed coolly. Paris had not given itself over to a Hervéist bacchanale. "The majority of yesterday's demonstrators have not been conquered by antimilitarist ideas," *Le Temps* insisted. In fact, "Tomorrow, these same men will follow in the streets the military tattoos [parades] that M. Millerand has just reestablished."[6]

War Minister Millerand must also have observed the day's events with interest and pondered their import. From the government's point of view, the broadest political requirement of the moment was national solidarity, expressed as visibly and as frequently as possible. By that reckoning, the Aernoult obsequies were a disaster—precisely the expression of antimilitarist strength the government had wanted neither France nor Germany to witness. Already, in the leftist press, militants now boasted about their ability to derail the war machine should the reactionary state dare activate it.[7] Yes Millerand may well have wondered: was it really a committed antimilitarism that had impelled those thousands into the streets? Or was it mainly something else, something other than what radicals wanted and the government feared?

As *Le Temps* suggested, it was by no means clear that the throngs who wept in the streets at a presumed miscarriage of military justice were entirely lost to the larger call of patriotism, or even to the allure of the military. The Aernoult and Rousset cases alone were at issue. It was military justice, not "militarism," that had brought those tens of thousands into the streets, as all objective observers must surely have recognized. Indeed, Millerand might have considered the possibility that political gain might actually accrue to the government if it were to express a carefully calibrated measure of concern for the fairness of the juridical and penal treatment accorded Rousset. Certain modest interventions on his behalf might even be in order, simply to belie antimilitarists' contention that the Third Republic would never quench its thirst for proletarian blood. That, after all, had been how the Aernoult-Rousset agitation of 1910–1911 had been countered—with selected modifications of actions taken within the military jurisdiction, in an attempt to gratify moderate elements and split them from the intransigents while denying the latter the ammunition they needed to stoke public outrage. Theoretically, this was a strategy that might well work again. The problem was that it was not one to which Millerand was naturally inclined.

He had only recently taken over the war ministry, but he had been aware for some time of German military capabilities—and of the need to enhance the French army's capacity for rapid, imaginative action to compensate for its numerical and material shortcomings. The general mission Millerand set himself in the ministry was to fortify the prerogatives of the army's top leadership and to protect them from any sort of political interference. To that end he would advance further down a path opened by his predecessor, Adolphe Messimy: strengthening the powers of the General Staff and especially those of its new chief General Joseph Joffre. In fact, Millerand generally conceived his own job as minister to involve not the assertion of civilian prerogatives over the army but, rather, service as the military's "political chief, its defender against attack and arbiter in controversial issues."[8] The new minister's preference for consolidating and disencumbering military authority carried over into his thinking on military justice as well. The Berry-Millerand Law already indicated Millerand's concern with eliminating even the occasion of indiscipline.[9] He would also lend his support to the efforts of Senator Flandin to harden various provisions of the *CJM* (e.g., eliminating the offense of "illegal absence" entirely, in favor of the more serious and harshly punishable one of "desertion").[10]

Solicitude for the treatment accorded Émile Rousset by the institutions of military justice, then, would run entirely counter to the general pattern of Millerand's thinking on military matters. He was disposed to lighten political oversight, not exercise it; to strengthen the authority of military courts, not undermine it by intervening to reverse their actions. Millerand was both a skilled politician and an estimable attorney capable of seeing both the political logic and legal means of intervening on behalf of Rousset. Yet his understanding of the nation's security interests left him less inclined than his predecessors to trifle with military justice. Indeed, he might well have hoped he would be spared the need to consider the Rousset matter much further at all. With a conviction secured at Algiers and Aernoult's Paris obsequies finally over, the entire affair might reasonably be expected to recede from public consciousness. But on February 22, the High Court of Appeals rendered that hope an idle one with its ruling on Rousset's case.[11]

The court chose to quash that verdict on the grounds that proper legal form had been egregiously violated. But its determination of where the error lay was almost as significant as its basic decision to overturn. The court found nothing particularly problematic in the Algiers tribunal's refusal of Montès's request for a trial delay. It found no serious trespass in Pan-Lacroix's failure to formally transcribe (or even, initially, mention) Brancoli's statements; nor in his failure to accede to either Brancoli's or Rousset's request for a formal confrontation; nor in his deployment of spies; nor in his collection of witnesses' statements when he lacked the formal authority to do so. Based on the court's reading of the relevant articles of the *CJM*, none of these acts tainted the deliberations of the Algiers tribunal "to the point of nullity," as was required before a court verdict could be overturned. The failure to properly swear in Dr. Legrand and collect his testimony under oath, however, did.

This, concluded the court, violated Article 44 of the Code of Criminal Investigation, binding on military *parquets* as well as civilian ones. From this point on, ruled the court, the investigation had been tainted—which meant that none of the testimony collected by Captain Godiot after September 15, when Legrand had submitted his unsolicited statement, was admissible. A few days later, the court referred the Rousset case to General Leguay, the (interim) commander of the division of Constantine, who was to decide whether to order the Constantine *parquet* to initiate another investigation. If he did, the new *rapporteur*'s point of departure could only be the reports of Pan-Lacroix and Giacomoni, plus the few statements by witnesses taken prior to September 15. The rest of the investigation would have to be entirely redone.

The decision of the High Court of Appeals created an entirely new situation, replete with both pitfalls and opportunities for the government, for Rousset's partisans, and for the broader antimilitarist movement. To Millerand, the obvious problem was the ruling's timing. Coming right on the heels of the Aernoult funeral demonstration, it could be taken as confirmation of the proposition that French military justice could be undone by street demonstrations of sufficient magnitude. Naturally, the *CDS* shouted that claim from the rooftops. "The powerful push of indignation made by the proletariat and all honest men has obliged the judges of the High Court to quash the verdict," exulted one speaker, adding with relish, "for a futile motive by which no one was duped."[12] Yet legalists within the antimilitarist camp were nonplussed. True, Rousset would be afforded another chance to prove investigative and prosecutorial malfeasance. But how could that be done in Algeria? They had hoped that his case would be remanded to a venue in metropolitan France. They were further disquieted by the court's apparent invitation to the Constantine *parquet* to build a new and better edifice on the basic foundation of Pan-Lacroix's early findings.[13]

The new Rousset Affair Committee that Marmande had organized immediately announced a major meeting at the hall of the Grand Orient in Paris and, at the same time, outlined the priorities that would guide its own actions. "The Rousset Affair Committee," read the announcement, "has since its formation indicated, and precisely delimited, the spirit in which it wants to act, the terrain on which it intended to place itself, the questions toward which it would direct its efforts: Spirit of Justice, Terrain of Law, Research of the Truth."[14] In other words, procedural concerns were to be elevated, with no *a priori* assumption of the innocence of Rousset. This focus would prove quite effective at generating interest among old Dreyfusards, many of whom would speak at meetings organized by the committee and the League for the Defense of the Rights of Man throughout the winter and spring of 1912. Alfred Dreyfus himself offered a qualified statement of support, but on purely procedural grounds.[15]

The increasingly Dreyfusard tinge of the entire agitation infuriated the militants who had been involved in it from the beginning and whose interests were considerably broader than the formal correctness of military court procedures. They were organizing their own meetings and posting their own placards throughout that winter and spring and palpably sharpening their rhetorical tone. On March 2, 1912, War Minister Millerand issued an official communiqué to interior minister (and fellow former Dreyfusard) Théodore Steeg, in which he called the latter's attention to placarding, which might qualify as seditious. Perhaps recalling the "Down with Biribi!" trial, Millerand explained that he had apprised the interior minister rather than the justice minister because he understood "the difficulty of establishing before a jury the culpability of the authors of these texts."[16]

The public agitation was indeed heating up, but it was also—as in the earlier phase—bifurcating. At one meeting organized by the editors of *Les Temps Nouveaux* several *CDS* members walked out when Marmande rose to speak.[17] What would this widening fissure within the movement mean for Rousset's fate? Might the government find a way to neutralize the agitation by widening it further?

On March 15 General Leguay presented his order to reopen the investigation to Public Minister Darblade, who named Captain Guillaud *rapporteur* for the new investigation. The latter would proceed with great alacrity, possibly occasioned by the realization that the longer his investigation took, the more political pressure he and the Constantine tribunal could expect to encounter. With the assistance of the Rousset Affair Committee, Louis Rousset had immediately written War Minister Millerand to formally request an official investigation into the conduct of Lieutenant Pan-Lacroix during the Algiers investigation, stressing the mysterious absence of any formal transcript or even notation of Brancoli's exculpatory statements in Pan-Lacroix's initial report. Pan-Lacroix's errors (or, possibly, crimes) had to be acknowledged and corrected, Louis argued, before Guillaud could be allowed to formally depose him as a witness.[18]

Millerand, aware that the High Court of Appeals had pointedly declined to declare Pan-Lacroix's report inadmissible, responded with a polite promise to remind the (newly installed) General Oudard that the rights of the defense must be fully respected in the new investigation. This challenge deflected, Guillaud promptly interviewed Pan-Lacroix, who offered both a lengthy, detailed theory of the crime and a spirited defense of his own actions.[19] Guillaud was impressed. In his view, Pan-Lacroix had been unfairly maligned by people who didn't understand the duties he had assumed or failed to credit the zeal he had shown in tracking down a crafty murderer. Guillaud was entirely persuaded that Rousset had indeed murdered Brancoli.[20]

But Guillaud also knew he would have to act quickly to prove it. Demonstrations in France were multiplying and growing more vehement; far less formal and correct attempts to intervene in the investigation than Louis Rousset's polite letter would surely follow if Rousset's more raucous supporters were granted the time to mobilize. By early April, in fact, *CDS* representatives had already arrived in Constantine, placarding city walls with assertions of Rousset's innocence, slipping into the barracks and even under the door of the military prison a pamphlet entitled "Justice for Rousset." The pamphlet explicitly described the February 21 decision of the High Court of Appeals as "the first victory [in the case] for the working class" and warned that "the new *conseil de guerre* must not ignore the fact that we will rise up against a new condemnation, if by the spirit of caste they dare to commit a second iniquity."[21]

Rousset and his attorneys (Montès had been joined in Algeria by an associate, Toretta) were concentrating their efforts on discrediting the credibility of the defendant's accusers and suggesting, where possible, that

Captain Guillaud, as depicted by Raieter in *La Bataille Syndicaliste*, December 2, 1912.

their testimony had been manipulated or coerced. Sauval, recently returned to civilian life, seemed especially vulnerable. He was currently awaiting trial for a stabbing in Creil, where he had taken up pimping and apparently attacked a nonpaying customer. That recent history called into question both his earlier representation as a passive victim and perhaps even the army's explanation that he was physically unfit for active duty.[22] In addition, Rousset and Montès were canvassing prisoners who had served with Bintein and Bordessoulle for evidence that it was they, not Rousset, who were enmeshed in the homosexual underworld with its explosive and often violent passions. The head of the *Sûreté Départementale* of Constantine delivered to General Oudard two letters addressed to Hippolyte Chabot, which he said were unknowingly pressed into the hand of an agent by one of a group of detainees—presumably Rousset—with a request for direct mailing. The letters, from Montès and Rousset, asked Chabot to confirm that Bintein and Bordessoulle had sexually brutalized a prisoner named Christ, and to attest to Rousset's own sexual probity.[23]

What Rousset and his defenders really wanted was the opportunity to confront Rousset's accusers—Bintein, Pierlot, Deleu, and Vigorouroux (returned to duty and awaiting trial for theft committed while illegally absent)—directly. They especially wanted to confront Bordessoulle, also recently discharged from active duty and returned to his hometown of Lichères, in the canton of Chablis, Yonne. But most of all they wanted to confront Pan-Lacroix. The defense considered these confrontations absolutely essential, a matter of elemental fairness. But whether they would be countenanced in the military jurisdiction of Constantine was to become a pivotal procedural—and eventually, political—question.

Decisions regarding the necessity of such confrontations were ordinarily left to the discretion of the investigator, and Guillaud was disinclined to permit them in this case. Rousset, after all, had been afforded the opportunity to confront most of those witnesses in Captain Godiot's earlier investigation. And there could be no doubt that Rousset was an intelligent, commanding figure, fully capable of overwhelming weaker men in personal encounters—especially Bordessoulle. The latter, Guillaud concluded on the basis of testimony compiled at Algiers, was simply "a being of weak character . . . a laughingstock to his comrades" rather than the violent near lunatic Rousset made him out to be.[24] But Bordessoulle, again formally accused of the crime by Rousset, would certainly have to be reinterviewed at the very least. Guillaud duly subpoenaed him, and on April 12 Bordessoulle began the journey from Lichères back to Constantine.

By any reckoning, he was the key witness: Rousset's own account of the murder had left only two possible assailants, Bordessoulle and himself. One problem with attributing the crime to Bordessoulle rather than Rousset had always been motive. Bordessoulle seemed to lack any grievance against Brancoli, whom, by all accounts, he had barely known. Initially, Rousset himself had been able to suggest nothing more substantial than that Bordessoulle had been enraged by some of the disparaging comments Brancoli was making against the men of the company.[25] More recently, he had tried to collect evidence indicating that Bordessoulle was mentally unstable and had secured a letter from his friend Marcel Moreau lending support to that characterization. Moreau described an incident he claimed to have witnessed at the infirmary at Médéa in which Bordessoulle had become unaccountably enraged at orderlies, attacking them with a cobbler's knife and then tearing up the courtyard garden.[26] Guillaud countered this by gathering statements from commanding officers at the military prisons of both Teboursouk, where Bordessoulle had originally been confined, and Aïn-Beida, where he had been transferred. The former described his conduct as "good," his morality as "passable."[27] The latter said his conduct "was always very good" and his "character calm and mild"—although he did admit that Bordessoulle had been "exceptionally, and in the interest of his own well-being, removed from the company of the other detainees coming from the African Battalions of Tunisia." No reason for that removal was given.[28]

Bordessoulle's testimony was vital to both sides, but particularly to Rousset. He had already confronted Bordessoulle in the presence of Captain Godiot, but much had changed since then. Bordessoulle's discharge, in particular, raised new questions, and a personal confrontation might well yield impeachable answers to them. But no one would have the opportunity to interrogate Bordessoulle further: he simply never arrived in Constantine. On April 24 Guillaud issued a warrant for his arrest. The *Sûreté* continued to search for him in the Yonne, in Marseilles, in Algeria; but they found no trace. His father telegraphed Guillaud that he had no idea where either his son or the seventy francs the *rapporteur* had forwarded to underwrite the journey to Constantine might be. François, he allowed, had never been entirely normal.[29]

Bordessoulle's disappearance might have left Rousset and Montès all the more anxious for confrontations with the other witnesses. But Guillaud was hurrying to officially close his investigation and deliver his report to the *commissaire du gouvernement*. Guillaud may have been worried about the intensifying public pressure on the war minister, and how Millerand might respond to it. In April Louis Rousset, with the backing of the Rousset Affair Committee, had again written the war minister, this time not simply requesting an official investigation of Pan-Lacroix but demanding that the lieutenant be formally charged with malfeasance.[30] At the same time, Marmande was arranging the sorts of publications that would help retain interest in Rousset's case on the left: a tract (*Émile Rousset et l'enquête du lieutenant Pan-Lacroix*) and in *Les Temps Nouveaux* a set of Rousset's letters. Most notably, protest meetings continued to multiply, with the new Rousset Affair Committee and the League for the Defense of the Rights of Man adding their resources and organizational skills to those of the *CDS*, the various labor federations, and the sections of the Socialist Party that had been arranging demonstrations on the Aernoult-Rousset matter since 1910.

Guillaud officially closed his investigation on May 17, 1912, without confrontations. But the kind of closure he wanted could not be so easily achieved. Rousset immediately appealed the decision, and on May 20 Millerand decided to personally receive the delegates of the Rousset Affair Committee, who had petitioned to meet with him. Louis Havet articulated for the minister several requests the committee had formulated. Its members wanted the Rousset investigation reopened, to include all confrontations requested by the defense. They also wanted that investigation to be accompanied by a parallel, similarly exhaustive investigation into Bordessoulle's possible involvement in the crime. Last, they wanted the opening of a third investigation into whether Pan-Lacroix had violated articles of the Code of Criminal Investigation in his own inquiry at Médéa.[31] Of course, the minister's ability to carry out these requests was limited. Only the divisional general could order investigations of military personnel under his command; the minister's powers in this regard were mainly persuasive, perhaps augmented by the persuasive powers of the public minister he appointed. Bordessoulle, now a civilian, was currently liable to military justice only for dereliction of the subpoena Guillaud had issued—and it would certainly take more than Rousset's bald accusation to trigger a retroactive murder investigation by the military jurisdiction.[32]

Yet Millerand was not unmoved by the request that he act to influence the military jurisdiction of Constantine. He, too, wanted Guillaud's investigation reopened, with confrontations. General Leguay had no intention of ordering that, and Millerand couldn't directly compel him. What he could do was align his own ministry (and, if possible, others) with Rousset's appeal as it proceeded to the High Court of Appeals. To that end, he officially instructed Public Minister Bonnet of the Constantine *parquet* to initiate his own appeal against the closure of Guillaud's investigation, alongside the defendant's.

This was an extraordinary step, which Millerand did not take lightly. Legally, he felt Guillaud had, in fact, been "guided by a nonjuridical idea" in ruling out the confrontations. The *rapporteur* considered them useless since they had already been done in the Algiers investigation, but he failed to appreciate that everything in Godiot's investigation after September 15, including those confrontations, had been rendered juridically useless by the High Court of Appeals when it overturned Rousset's conviction.[33] Yet Millerand also understood that there were more fundamental issues involved than that. So did Public Minister Bonnet and Solicitor-General Sarrut—both of whom balked at the course Millerand proposed, and for reasons the war minister himself would probably have found persuasive under other circumstances.

According to Sarrut, the act of "putting the *rapporteur* in a position of having to proceed to confrontations... had never been taken." The High Court might consent to hear the appeals; but it would almost certainly reject them. The absence of confrontations in an investigation had never been considered prejudicial to the rights of the defense, because the *conseil de guerre* itself could always order them if it deemed them necessary to the attainment of truth. Sarrut understood perfectly well that what Millerand was proposing was grounded more firmly in political than juridical considerations—and was, in his view, dangerous for that very reason. "It's a serious thing," the Solicitor-General wrote, "to depart from habitual practice, especially when it's a question of a matter of the permanent judicial order, on the occasion of which the press and diverse personalities are intervening."[34] The High Court of Appeals was not likely to lose sight of that truism.

But Millerand, for his part, was less concerned with the decision the High Court would reach concerning the appeals than with forcing it to make one, and clearing the air on the subject of Guillaud's report. Without formal resolution of the matter by the High Court, he feared, Guillaud's report would remain "the object of violent recriminations" by Rousset's partisans—a band that was, unfortunately, growing in number and exhibiting an increasingly disagreeable public face. Indeed, on June 1, at a protest meeting held at the labor exchange of Saint-Étienne, *CDS* member Jean Bonnafous directly attributed the High Court's overturning of Rousset's conviction at Algiers to the pressure exerted by militants and promised that his organization would provoke hundreds of trials like the "Down with Biribi!" trial of June 1910 if the Constantine *conseil de guerre* dared to re-convict Rousset.[35]

Millerand had decided that the Rousset Affair must be terminated—and quickly. Time, after all, served the cause of the prisoner's advocates, who now sought to extend the life of their agitation and broaden its scope by delaying his trial at Constantine as long as possible. Recent requests by Havet to Justice Minister Briand, for instance, would serve that end. If the military jurisdiction could not be induced to investigate Bordessoulle for murder, Havet wrote, then the question should at least be put before a civilian *parquet*. Havet fully understood that once any court took up the question of Bordessoulle's involvement in Brancoli's murder, Rousset could not be taken before the *conseil de guerre* of Constantine until that matter was officially resolved.[36] And Millerand, of course, understood what Havet was up to. But, Millerand also understood, effectively liquidating the Rousset Affair required that the investigation be beyond reproach, and recognized as such. In ruling on the question of confrontations, the High Court of Appeals would either fully legitimate Guillaud's report or impel the creation of a better one. Either way, the report would be "removed from the suspicion that bad faith and ignorance have sought to throw on it."[37] By actively bringing the matter before the court, the government would have shown itself the committed champion of procedural fairness—neither the harsh discipline of the *conseils de guerre,* nor the utopian vision of radical leftists, but justice as France actually knew it. Millerand, in fact, was able to convince the entire council of ministers that this course of action was the best available.[38]

Yet, however well advised, this intervention by political means into the operations of military justice could not have been easy for Millerand to undertake. What explains his willingness to compromise his own established thinking on the subject? Certainly the agitation surrounding Rousset was cresting (on June 30 *La Bataille Syndicaliste* published Guillaud's entire dossier). Moreover, the astute Millerand must have understood that militants would be drawn to ever more provocative measures lest leadership of the Aernoult-Rousset agitation pass entirely to the despised "intellectuals" of the Rousset Affair Committee. In fact, *CDS* members had been in Algeria since April, and by late June reports were surfacing suggesting suspicious activity by them in Médéa.

It was Pan-Lacroix who brought those reports to the attention of his own commanding officer at Médéa, who in turn forwarded them to Guillaud for inclusion in the new Rousset dossier. First, Pan-Lacroix submitted documentation that witnesses who had testified against Rousset were being physically threatened. It included a handwritten note allegedly left on Deleu's bed warning that vengeance was about to fall on "the slut Pierlot, the bugger Fleury, the cow Sappa, the fairy [illegible], and the queen of buggers Deleu."[39] The note was signed "The friends of an innocent man condemned to 20 years by the testimony of 5 sluts." Pan-Lacroix also reported that Deleu, Rouy, and other witnesses still at Médéa had been placed into protective custody after Pierlot was lightly wounded by an unseen assailant on June 21.

The lieutenant's packet of materials also included a letter from the witness Georges-Émile Rouy, who had helped guard the detainees' cells after the violence of August 27, 1911. Rouy testified that Rousset had told him to warn Brancoli to say nothing to the authorities.[40] According to Pan-Lacroix, a troubled Rouy had confided to the lieutenant that two unidentified civilians had approached him while he was convalescing in the garrison hospital and had offered to get his remaining time in the service reduced if he would openly acknowledge that his testimony had been coerced by Pan-Lacroix. By Rouy's own account, he retorted that his testimony was true, whereupon the men offered him some money "for tobacco" and said they would return in a few days after he had had some time to think their proposition over.[41] Pan-Lacroix had seen the men himself and vaguely recalled them from Rousset's trial at Algiers.[42] He also forwarded a letter from Pierlot describing an encounter with unidentified civilians much like the one Rouy reported; plus a letter from a soldier named Collot specifically identifying the visitors as *CDS* representatives. They had approached him, Collot wrote, to gather information on other soldiers, their terms of service and any disciplinary infractions he might know them to have accrued.[43]

There was more. A Colonel Germain, commander of a regiment of spahis, had forwarded to General Murteau (now commanding the Algiers division) a couple of letters that had come into his hands—letters that raised serious concerns about the nature and extent of *CDS* involvement with soldiers at Médéa.[44] One had been sent to "Comrade Rouy" from Thuillier of the *CDS*, dated June 22. In it, Thuillier made reference to some prior communication he had apparently received from Rouy, then went on to promise help with various problems the soldier was evidently having (e.g., securing medical treatment that the medical authorities were reluctant to authorize) if Rouy would agree to "tell the truth" about what he had really witnessed in August 1911.[45] Germain also forwarded a letter that Rouy himself had initially submitted to Dr. Drouineau, the chief medical officer at

Constantine, claiming that he simply had no idea what Thuillier was talking about and protesting that he was being enmeshed in a web of deceit.[46] This letter, passed from Dr. Drouineau to Colonel Germain to General Murteau to Captain Guillaud, corresponded to Pan-Lacroix's statement recounting Rouy's rebuff of his hospital visitors, which included the assertion that Rouy had verbally denied having asked anyone for help with medical treatment, money, family contacts, or any of the things Thuillier had referenced in his own letter.[47]

Rouy's attempt to get into the Constantine hospital and difficulties convincing the authorities that he belonged there were documented.[48] Whether that had occasioned an overture to the *CDS* was not clear, but what was certain was the fact that since April the organization had been attempting to advance Rousset's cause through direct contact with soldiers involved in the case. This initiative and the confidence it bespoke among Rousset's partisans reflected the situation facing Millerand in the summer of 1912, a situation much altered from the one Briand had confronted two years earlier.

At that time, Briand had been forced to decide between intervening in the military jurisdiction and tolerating a public expression of the power of French antimilitarism. He had opted for the former, in order to contain the latter. For Millerand, however, the landscape had changed. The public demonstration of antimilitarists' strength that Briand had hoped to forestall was now ongoing, and rather robust. The *CDS*, in particular, was a wild card. It had always jockeyed for the leading position in the Aernoult-Rousset agitation and had apparently secured it—that is, until the arrival of the Rousset Affair Committee. *CDS* leaders understood that securing retractions from key witnesses would certainly restore their primacy, and the organization's history suggested a ready willingness to travel to the very edge of the law or slightly beyond in pursuit of its ends. The witness-tampering that Pan-Lacroix alleged was by no means beyond its ethical range.

The question, then, was no longer whether "politics" would intrude into the administration of military justice but simply the form that intervention would take. It could be the modest, lawful, almost surgical one formulated by a war minister deeply solicitous of military interests. Or it could be the far cruder and blunter one—possibly overtly illegal—that the jurisdiction's most implacable enemies might have already initiated by the end of June 1912. The political dynamic within the pro-Rousset movement was such that the longer the affair lasted, the likelier some sort of extralegal intervention grew.

But on July 12, the High Court of Appeals dealt a blow to Millerand's effort to head that off by declining to hear Rousset's and Public Minister Bonnet's appeal of the closure of Guillaud's investigation, just as Sarrut had predicted it would. At that point, the war minister had only one option open to him: request that General Leguay order Bonnet to initiate a separate, "supplemental" investigation (i.e., conduct confrontations with either Guillaud or a different *rapporteur* present). In a civil jurisdiction, defense complaints that a given investigation had been incomplete or biased could be brought to an arraignment chamber, which, if convinced, could have ordered them. In the military jurisdiction, the divisional general himself substituted for that chamber. Duly acknowledging that the decision rested with General Leguay, Millerand invoked a ministerial circular dated March 28 1908, which "indicated that if the procedure communicated by the *rapporteur* is incomplete, the general . . . can and should order new inquiries." The confrontations requested by the defense in this case, Millerand wrote, "seem to me indispensable, and I therefore have the honor of asking you to make the necessary requisitions."[49]

Time was now of the essence. Rousset's partisans continued trying to secure more of it by demanding ancillary investigations, of both Bordessoulle (by either military or civil authorities) and Pan-Lacroix (by the Algiers *parquet*).[50] The war minister could check these sallies, but in the end he knew that only settling the larger issue of the investigation's basic fairness could move the affair toward a resolution. For Rousset's partisans were making maximum political capital of the jurisdiction's efforts to hamstring the defense by denying confrontations it considered vital—and, should they learn of the inclusion in the trial dossier of material collected after Guillaud had officially closed his investigation on May 17, their protests would certainly grow louder still.

Yet the decision was not Millerand's but General Leguay's. The latter understood what the High Court of Appeals had confirmed on July 12: Captain Guillaud had acted entirely lawfully when he took it upon himself to determine what the defense did and did not need. Granting the *rapporteur* a sort of veto power over certain defense initiatives was a feature of military justice. Would "politics" neutralize it in this case? If so, what kind of "politics"? Everything seemed to depend on Leguay's decision. But by the time the general announced it, the entire situation had changed dramatically.

On July 29 screaming headlines on the front page of *La Bataille Syndicaliste* announced that four witnesses in the Rousset murder case—Rouy, Sappa, Pierlot, and Deleu—had come forward to retract their testimony against the defendant. All claimed that Lieutenant Pan-Lacroix had extorted their testimony with threats of *conseil de guerre* actions and other forms of pressure. The journal also reported that the irrepressible Robert Dérieux intended to join them.

At that point Dérieux's testimony might have held little value before any military tribunal. For that matter, Rouy's and Sappa's accounts had never really been integral to the case against Rousset. But Deleu's testimony that Brancoli had identified Rousset had carried some weight, and Pierlot's eyewitness identification of him as the killer had carried even more. Above all, five witnesses' public accusation that Pan-Lacroix had coerced testimony would prove utterly devastating if true (and those five would shortly be followed by Fleury, among others).

That same issue of *La Bataille Syndicaliste* also carried specific announcements from the *CDS* taking credit for this surprising turn of events and declaring that the recanting witnesses were officially under its protection. The committee warned that any officers who tried to intimidate or harass these soldiers or any others who chose to follow their brave example would deal with the *CDS* —"and with us, the whole working class." The organization also officially joined Louis Rousset and the Rousset Affair Committee in calling for an official inquiry into the investigative chicanery of Lieutenant Pan-Lacroix.

The next day General Leguay formally ordered Public Minister Bonnet to arrange confrontations among Rousset and Pierlot, Deleu, Vigoroux, Bintein, Denat, Sauval, and Pan-Lacroix. On July 31 a triumphant demonstration organized by the *CDS* took place in the salle Wagram in Paris. With over six thousand participants acclaiming Rousset, it was the largest and most raucous expression of support for him to date—and for the indefatigable activists of the *CDS* who had stood so unwaveringly by his side for so long.[51]

Not surprisingly, the confrontation with Pan-Lacroix was the most emotionally charged moment of the entire investigation—and certainly the most revealing about the cast of mind the lieutenant had brought to his investigation.[52] The encounter was initiated by a blunt question Rousset posed to Pan-Lacroix: "Can you swear on your honor that I'm guilty?" The lieutenant answered, "No, I can't swear it." But Rousset, and his attorneys Montès and Toretta, wanted far more than that. They wanted the lieutenant's admission that he had deliberately framed Rousset. This time Guillaud maintained a studied neutrality as the three peppered the lieutenant with angry questions.

Pan-Lacroix held up fairly well at first, insisting that while he may have been wrong, he had acted in good faith and within established protocols. He had formally recorded no sworn statement from Brancoli because he was not the police judicial officer. Similarly, he had not mentioned the victim's declarations of Rousset's innocence in his initial report because he thought them basically unreliable, dissimulations attributable to the soldier's code. Rousset insisted that "if Brancoli had said, 'Yes, it's Rousset who hit me,' he would have taken written note of that!" But Pan-Lacroix denied it. Culpability, he felt, would have to be determined by the total range of evidence available, not just Brancoli's statements; and that evidence included Despax's testimony, Bintein's premature exculpation of Rousset, and Rousset's own suspicious responses to initial questions, in which he seemed to be trying either to implicate Sauval or suggest that Brancoli had somehow wounded himself. By the time Pan-Lacroix went to see Brancoli, he had already decided that Rousset was the likeliest suspect—and Brancoli's repeated disavowals did nothing but reinforce that belief. Montès then suggested: "But it's hardly admissible that you could believe Rousset guilty precisely because Brancoli told you he wasn't!" Pan-Lacroix replied simply: "But that's just how it is."

Rousset and his attorneys turned to the question of whether Pan-Lacroix had manipulated the accusations against Rousset by Bordessoulle, Sauval, and Bintein, and here the lieutenant was hard-pressed to respond. Corporal Laloo had testified to hearing Bordessoulle tell Rousset that Pan-Lacroix had quoted Brancoli as saying, "That cow! I'll have to croak him, him and all the Parisians and their damned 'Social War.'" That, everyone knew, could have only referred to Rousset—a Lyonnais, but by then a well-known leftist. But there was no record of Brancoli's having ever said that to Pan-Lacroix or anyone else at the hospital. Montès put a stark choice to Pan-Lacroix. Either the lieutenant had deliberately misinformed Bordessoulle in order to delude Rousset into thinking the investigation had already uncovered a motive for his assault on Brancoli, or Laloo had simply lied. Malfeasance was evident in either case—which was it?

Pan-Lacroix responded that he could no longer be sure of his exact words with Bordessoulle, finally muttering, "I leave the responsibility for those allegations to Corporal Laloo." But he was not yet ready to concede error in using Bordessoulle to leak his suspicion of Rousset to the detainees. He was convinced that his initial judgment of Rousset's guilt had, in fact, been correct, and he was aiming for a confession. Indeed, pleaded the lieutenant, his initial judgment had been buttressed by the testimony of Sauval, who had half-accused Rousset in his interview but expressed fear of being the first or only one to make a public charge: "that cost me a lot in Djelfa," Sauval had pleaded. Pan-Lacroix explained that such fears were not confined to Sauval, and that in trying to secure a confession from Rousset he aimed to spare prisoners the need to endanger themselves. Rousset and his allies, Pan-Lacroix insisted, were greatly feared at the camp.

The lieutenant's interrogators then turned to the question of Bintein's and Pierlot's testimonies, as Pan-Lacroix cast about for ways to escape the corner into which he was being backed. Rousset and Montès began with the charge that Bintein hadn't actually accused Rousset until the lieutenant told him that continued silence would result in a *conseil de guerre* action for complicity in murder. Pan-Lacroix had to admit that he had made this threat to Bintein and to Sauval and Bordessoulle as well. How else could he elicit their testimony? The lieutenant insisted that he had never held any personal grudge against Rousset or had any reason to persecute him. He was simply persuaded that Rousset was the most likely suspect of the crime, and he had acted properly in extracting the testimony he needed to bring the case before the military *parquet*. If he were wrong, he knew the truth would be discovered by the *rapporteur*. That, after all, was how the system worked.

But Bintein now asserted: "I was dead drunk at the time, unable to see anything; the lieutenant forced me to accuse Rousset." He also alleged that after the High Court of Appeals had quashed the Algiers tribunal's verdict, Pan-Lacroix had told him that if he didn't stand by his original story in the new investigation he could be prosecuted for false testimony. Pierlot's charge was even more damning. He had resisted accusing Rousset, he said, until around September 11 or 12, when Pan-Lacroix had used a special form of coercion on him. According to Pierlot, Pan-Lacroix had arranged for him to be jailed for attempting to communicate with the detainees, then threatened to increase his sentence from eight to thirty days for lying to an investigator unless he agreed to accuse Rousset. Pan-Lacroix, for his part, denied coercing anyone. He had done no more than inform Pierlot, Bintein, Sappa, and Bordessoulle that concealing information could trigger separate charges against them. Wasn't this acceptable practice?

It may well have been, but this time it would not have the intended effect. On September 24 General Leguay issued a *non-lieu* in the case of Émile Rousset. There would be no second murder trial. The case was over. Military justice and Émile Rousset, it seemed, were finally finished with one another.

"Politics" of a sort had saved him.

Marmande Agonistes

A fair number of successes could, in fact, be claimed by the political groupings that had invaded France's military jurisdiction on behalf of Émile Rousset. The minotaur had not been slain; but it had been checked repeatedly, its aura of invulnerability dissipated. Political pressure, after all, had occasioned the reversal of two separate *conseil de guerre* judgments. Political pressure had forced the system's custodians to indict officers they would otherwise not have indicted, to pardon an individual they were loathe to pardon, to reopen an investigation they had declared closed, and to permit confrontations they had wanted to avoid. Political pressure had forced the jurisdiction's investigative *modus operandi* into the open, with the publication of an entire judicial dossier assembled under the assumption of confidentiality. Political pressure may have affected even the jurisdiction's penal practices. The law of April 11, 1910, which mandated repatriation of most military penal camps to the islands of Oleron, Cézembre, and other sites in metropolitan France, had in fact been fulfilled, perhaps more thoroughly than it otherwise would have been.

"The curtain is raised on the hell of Biribi," *La Bataille Syndicaliste*, October 7, 1912.

Rousset, *Les Temps Nouveaux,* August 24, 1912.

Yet, as War Minister Berteaux had realized during a vigorous interpellation on the Aernoult-Rousset matter by Deputy Veber in March 1911, that hardly sufficed to slake antimilitarists' rage.[1] In fact, in the context of the broad struggle against the multifaceted pathology conjured to leftists by the term *militarism*, these amounted to no more than a set of successful skirmishes with but one of that pathology's many manifestations—the juridical one. Taken together, they comprised nothing more than a satisfying tactical victory. The question now was, would this tactical victory lead to larger, strategic gains for the antimilitarist movement? Would this mark the moment when antimilitarists took the offensive against the massive, extremely dangerous enemy they confronted? The Dreyfus Affair had failed to ignite the sort of sustained, popular outrage against militarism in all its forms that leftists envisioned. Yet one might well emerge now—if the movement's most visionary leaders could seize the moment and fan the flame sparked by the Aernoult-Rousset Affair into a roaring blaze.

Officers of the *CDS* clearly counted themselves among that leadership cadre. They were convinced that it was they who had turned the tide in Rousset's favor by securing recantations of vital testimony against him in Constantine. In their opinion, in fact, victory could not have been secured without the daring they alone had brought to the agitation, from the "Down with Biribi!" trial onward. Whatever political capital that victory conferred was rightly theirs—and that capital properly included Émile Rousset himself.

Rousset was now an iconic figure on the left, where interest in his sufferings, bravery, and moral redemption was deepened by no less than three biographical treatments that emerged in 1912 (he was, in fact, already entertaining competing bids for publication rights to his own memoirs as well).[2] He could be invaluable not only in drawing crowds to the series of large-scale rallies throughout the country that the *CDS* now envisioned itself conducting but also in educating those crowds to the mortal threat militarism really posed to proletarian France. Who better to stoke outrage against the Berry-Millerand Law than this shining hero, whose personal story so compellingly demonstrated that such legislation was "part of a long-gestating plan . . . one simple piece of the war machine forged against the workers' emancipation?"[3] Who better to press the fight on new and multiple fronts than this proletarian Theseus, before whom the minotaur had actually retreated?

But to fully enlist Émile Rousset in the cause, the *CDS* would have to pry him away from his friend, mentor, and champion: the much despised René de Marmande. The resulting controversy would provide a *dénouement* to the Aernoult-Rousset Affair that was alternately poignant, perplexing, and faintly risible.

The intrigue began while Rousset awaited General Leguay's decision regarding the disposition of his case. Rousset was ill, and Marmande and

Louis Havet were trying to secure provisional liberty for him pending what seemed, after the confrontation with Pan-Lacroix, an inevitable *non-lieu*.[4] Before they could attain that goal, however, *CDS* secretary Thuillier arrived in Constantine to inform the prisoner that the committee was in possession of damaging information regarding Marmande—and to advise Marmande to quietly leave Rousset's side lest that information be released. Thuillier urged Rousset to consider the contributions he could now make to the liberation of comrades still trapped within the coils of the military jurisdiction, and to continue the fight alongside the *CDS* worthies who had, in truth, saved him. According to Marmande, a sobbing Rousset had responded that he would rather remain in prison forever than sever relations with Marmande, the man who had shown him an entirely new way to live, to think, to feel. Only that ringing confirmation of the bond between himself and Rousset, said Marmande, could have dissuaded him from simply washing his hands of the entire dirty business and returning alone to France. For he knew that what was to come would be indescribably wrenching for both of them.[5]

What the *CDS* was charging was that René de Marmande was a government agent and had been one for some time. He had defected to the enemy for money at some point well before his formation of the Rousset Affair Committee, the entire point of which had been to dilute militants' influence in the agitation and to channel it into the safe, standard forms of bourgeois protest. He was nothing less than a class traitor, and his offenses were actually reaching new depths of depravity even as he appeared to deliver Rousset from the final phase of his long ordeal.[6]

The moment General Leguay ended the legal proceedings against Rousset, Marmande had set about securing the prisoner's release from active service for reasons of health. This took some doing. Technically, it could be ordered only by the general, who left Constantine shortly after issuing his *non-lieu*. According to Marmande's account, he was repeatedly put off by subordinate officers claiming that they had no legal authority to act on the matter, until he finally brought them to their senses with the magisterial assertion "that it was perhaps preferable, in the Aernoult-Rousset Affair, not to speak of violations of the law."[7] A liberated Rousset was sternly advised by his tireless protector to avoid any large demonstrations until he had fully recovered his strength.

But what Marmande represented as honest solicitude for a beloved friend who had spent the better part of four years in various antechambers of hell was by *CDS* lights a sinister, appallingly cynical undertaking.

CDS executives believed that Marmande had, in fact, secured Rousset's release precisely by promising to keep him away from all antimilitarist demonstrations—depriving the movement of its most charismatic personality, and consciously sapping its political potential.[8] The unholy spell Marmande had cast over Rousset must be broken, lest precious momentum the antimilitarist movement might take from its victory be squandered.

Upon Rousset's release, Marmande promptly booked passage for both of them to Marseilles, where the latter was still held in high regard by the local chapter of the *CDS* on the basis of his role in the maritime strike of 1910. But Thuillier and *CDS* secretary Durand were also hastening to Marseilles, armed with what they considered a devastating brief against their former associate and determined to confront both Rousset and Marmande's remaining admirers in Marseilles with it. There was an awkward scene when the pair arrived from Algeria on September 29. A party of some fifty *CDS* (Marseilles) members were at the quay to welcome Rousset and escort him by automobile to his room at the hotel Deux Mondes. But Marmande was rudely ejected from the car and forced to trudge alone to his own lodgings at a different hotel.[9]

Thuiller and Durand had no time for subtleties. They hoped to present Rousset at a demonstration in Marseilles and had already scheduled a grand one for October 7 at the Cirque de Paris in the capital. The bond between Marmande and Rousset must be definitively ruptured, and Rousset enfolded in the warm clasp of the *CDS* at once. Rousset, however, remained stubbornly loyal to Marmande, and resentful of what he took to be a deliberate smear effort based on incomprehensible, "boutique" quarrels. He vowed he would participate in no demonstrations without Marmande at his side—and went so far as to liken the manner by which the *CDS* rendered judgment on Marmande to that by which the Algiers *conseil de guerre* had rendered judgment on him. Whatever the evidence against him, Rousset insisted, Marmande must be shown all of it and allowed sufficient time to prepare his response.[10]

In a tense meeting at the hotel Deux Mondes, Thuillier and Durand (joined by attorney Berthon and other Parisian *CDS* members) explained to Rousset and members of the Marseilles chapter that they had offered to meet privately with Marmande at the Marseilles labor exchange, but he had refused. They then laid out a series of charges. Marmande, they submitted, had misappropriated *CDS* funds throughout 1910 and 1911. Demonstrations the organization had paid him to arrange had never taken place. He had, in fact, fleeced the *CDS* and other working-class organizations for years by steering business toward attorney Bonzon, from whose inflated fees he had derived handsome commissions. His involvement in the maritime strike at Marseilles in May 1911 had actually consisted mainly of "unnatural relations" with young sailors (one of whom, Ceccoli, he still kept in Paris). He was now attempting to dissuade Rousset from further participation in the antimilitarist movement—keeping entirely to himself this young charge, to whom he was undoubtedly drawn by the same lust that had drawn him to Ceccoli and to so many other proletarian youths.[11]

The meeting grew even tenser when Marmande himself burst in upon it. He "poured invective" on the *CDS*, insisted that he would never march with them, decried their unconscionable attack on him—"he who had made the greatest sacrifices to achieve Rousset's liberation, who had sold his furniture to be able to continue the campaign and had even let his mother die in a trunk." At the conclusion of his tirade, the beleaguered activist had "a violent crisis of nerves." One unsympathetic *CDS* member named Lacourte described that as a standard tactic of Marmande's, entirely simulated.[12]

But Rousset viewed the matter differently. He was simply not to be severed from René de Marmande. In fact, he wired a letter (possibly at Marmande's dictation) to *La Bataille Syndicaliste* vowing he would "always remember what the working class did for me" and committing himself to the continuing fight against Biribi while insisting that credit for his triumph should be shared by "*all* my defenders, children of the people like myself as well as the intellectuals whose souls were elevated enough to defend me." Marmande's contributions, Rousset wrote, had been invaluable—as, for that matter, had been those of Marmande's mother, whose letters had provided so much balm in the darkest days.[13]

The demonstration scheduled for October 1 at the salle Lovy in Marseilles did take place, and in the end both Rousset and Marmande did participate. But its message was oddly mixed, the fissures within the coalition clearly visible. After thanking the assembled workers for their support, a weeping Rousset embraced Marmande and lavished praise on his courage and steadfastness. Anyone familiar with what had been happening behind the scenes, however, would have known exactly what, and whom, subsequent speakers were referring to as they decried "the politicians" who had tried to co-opt the Aernoult-Rousset Affair: "it's not to them that Rousset owes the initiative. . . . The latter honor belongs entirely to the workers, who instead of scrutinizing his past, as the politicians did, saw in him only a comrade in misery."[14]

The Paris demonstration scheduled for October 7 shaped up as a similarly disjointed effort (the *CDS* was engaged in a feverish internal debate over whether to even invite Socialists or any representatives of the moderate camp).[15] But Rousset and Marmande forced an abrupt reconsideration of all future plans when they announced that, rather than traveling to Paris, Rousset now intended to return to his hometown of Lyons. The sudden change of itinerary had been necessitated, Marmande explained, by Interior Minister Théodore Steeg's notification of intent to enforce a penalty that still hovered over Rousset, incurred years earlier through one of his civilian convictions: a legal ban on entry (*interdiction de séjour*) into Paris.[16]

Not surprisingly, the *CDS* was outraged. Steeg was known to be personally close to several members of the Rousset Affair Committee. Was it not clearer than ever that this network of false "progressives" was intent on aborting the grand antimilitarist wave the *CDS* would surely generate with Rousset in hand? Even if the claim were legally authentic, no government would dare arrest Rousset in Paris, where he would be surrounded by tens of thousands of workers. Marmande alone was responsible for keeping Rousset from his destiny, and the antimilitarist movement from its goal.[17]

Marmande agreed that the government was consciously aiming to torpedo the planned demonstrations in Paris but shifted responsibility for Steeg's initiative to the *CDS*. It was their divisiveness, their savage attack on him and on the Rousset Affair Committee, that had fractured the coalition that had liberated Rousset and handed Steeg this opportunity. The worthies of the Rousset Affair Committee might have deployed their influence with Steeg to have the ban rescinded, but they could hardly be expected to abet the *CDS*'s goals after months of vituperation at the hands of that body. As things stood, Rousset couldn't possibly risk arrest in Paris. He was a physical wreck, yet another incarceration might well kill him, Marmande wouldn't hear of it. How dare the *CDS* risk Rousset's freedom, his health, perhaps his very life, simply to fill a meeting hall? What was the *CDS*, anyway? It was an organization without a true mandate from the proletariat. The workers were represented by the *CGT*, by the *Bourses du travail*, by the unions. The *CDS* was a set of political dilettantes who were callously exploiting Émile Rousset and who "didn't represent the workers any more than the Rousset Affair Committee represents the bourgeoisie or radicalism."[18]

Marmande accompanied Rousset to Lyons, where the police awaited them (according to one interpretation, the ban could be extended to metropolitan centers besides Paris if conditions warranted it). Attorneys from the League for the Defense of the Rights of Man were summoned, frantic negotiations were undertaken, and an agreement was finally reached whereby Rousset would be permitted to remain unmolested in the home of his brother Louis and sister-in-law Marie in return for absolute public quiescence. Marmande, for his part, hurried on to Paris, where he managed to reconvene a meeting of the Rousset Affair Committee. The conclave was held in Émile Zola's house in Médan, where the committee drafted a letter to Steeg that Marmande and Paul Painlevé would personally deliver in early November.[19]

While all this was transpiring, the *CDS* went ahead with its October 7 demonstration at the Cirque de Paris despite Rousset's absence. It was a dispiriting setback, poorly attended, its oratory and general energy level disappointingly low.[20] Nonetheless, the organization had already scheduled another one for October 23 at the salle Wagram and had reason to hope for a better turnout and a more rousing display then. Their agents had gone to Lyons to make yet another effort to turn Rousset away from Marmande and toward themselves—and they were, finally, making progress.

A few days before the October 7 demonstration in Paris, the *CDS* held one in Lyons where some fifteen hundred people heard Marmande denounced in the most explicit and vigorous terms.[21] Rousset was not there to hear the attacks, but as October wore on he was clearly growing less certain about things. Just what was the truth about René de Marmande? About the *CDS*? What was the proper course of action now for himself? A police informant reported that "there is the *CDS*, the Rousset [Affair] Committee, and finally there is Rousset. . . . He doesn't know what he wants to do, and he's behaving in quite an oblique manner."[22] Rousset remained skeptical of certain *CDS* members (especially Berthon, whose electoral ambitions and hunger for publicity he found utterly transparent).[23] However, he was coming around to the view that he did owe the *CDS* as a body a great deal, including his participation in the October 23 Paris rally. In Marmande's absence, he signaled some warming to the *CDS* by his decision to publish his memoirs with *La Bataille Syndicaliste*, the one leftist publication with which it retained close ties—despite what he said was a much higher offer from *Le Matin*.[24] In addition, he accepted the services of the *CDS*'s Eugène Péronnet in preparing them.

But the factors that really served to corrode Rousset's relationship with Marmande were more personal than political. One was Rousset's deepening suspicion that Marmande was indeed involved in financial chicanery—and with Rousset's own finances. Specifically, there was a sharp disagreement

FEUILLETON DU 3 NOVEMBRE 1912

— 6 —

Mes Mémoires

PAR

Emile Rousset

Dessins de Raieter.

Je dirai tout

Le lendemain des obsèques de notre camarade je n'y tins plus : j'écrivis aux parents d'Aernoult pour leur apprendre comment était mort leur fils. J'écrivis également à mon frère Louis, de Lyon, à ce sujet.

J'avais le désir ardent de dire, de crier la vérité. Pendant les heures de repos, quand je fermais les yeux, je voyais défiler devant moi de longues théories de suppliciés. C'étaient les victimes des chaouchs. Ils me montraient leurs poignets, où la pression des chaînes avait fait naître de gros bourrelets sanguinolents, et leurs torses zébrés de longues plaies d'où s'écoulait un sang noirâtre.

Je revoyais aussi le cimetière de Beni-Ounif, avec ses croix de bois sur lesquelles des noms de disciplinaires étaient gravés au canif.

Et puis des maisonnettes de paysans, des chambres d'ouvriers, des gens accablés qui pleuraient...

Il me sembla impossible de taire plus longtemps ce qui s'était passé dans la Cour des Miracles quelques jours auparavant. Je crus de mon devoir de dénoncer les atrocités qui se commettaient journellement à Djenan-ed-Dar.

Je ne voulus confier à personne le soin de mettre à la poste mes lettres révélatrices.

Un soir, après l'appel de neuf heures, m'étant couché tout habillé, je me levai sans bruit, et, franchissant la ligne des sentinelles, je fis à la course et sans arrêt les six kilomètres qui séparent Djenan-ed-Dar de la gare de Beni-Ounif.

Heureux du devoir accompli je pus réintégrer sans dommage notre redoute.

Jusqu'au 15 juillet aucun fait ne vint rompre la monotonie de notre existence.

Mais ce 15 juillet, on amena un convoi de disciplinaires ; parmi ceux-ci se trouvait un nommé Marcel Moreau.

Sans doute la forme du nez de Moreau déplut aux gradés ; ce fut la tête de Turc choisie.

Le 17 juillet, il transportait du sable dans une brouette ; exténué, il tomba.

Le sergent Casanova lui dit en ricanant :

— Moreau, je vais être obligé de faire cesser bientôt la petite comédie que vous jouez !

A ce moment, je résolus d'intervenir :

— Sergent, dis-je, ce que vous faites est honteux. Vous venez d'assassiner un de nos camarades et il vous faut déjà une autre victime !

Immédiatement, Casanova m'intima l'ordre de me rendre aux locaux pénitentiaires, et j'eus huit jours de cellule agrémentés d'une demande de soixante jours de prison pour avoir dit, en parlant des gradés, que c'étaient une « bande de v... ». Pourtant, je n'avais jamais tenu ce propos.

On craignait sans doute que je propageasse les idées de révolte qui fermentaient en moi, et l'on m'envoya travailler seul dans une carrière.

Sous la surveillance d'un tirailleur en

Rousset's memoirs were serialized in *La Bataille Syndicaliste*, 1912.

between the two men regarding the sum of 270 francs that Rousset claimed to have entrusted to Marmande after his release from prison to cover various near-term travel expenses. Rousset evidently expected those funds to cover his trip to Paris for the October 23 rally. But he and his entourage of friends and family members found themselves without lodgings upon arriving in Paris. Péronnet had to bail them out, and Rousset was furious.[25]

Marmande's side of the story was that Rousset actually owed that sum, and considerably more, to the Rousset Affair Committee for what it had already spent on clothes and cash disbursements to him.[26] By Marmande's reckoning, in fact Rousset owed *him*, personally, a great deal of money, since he himself was "the soul of the Rousset [Affair] Committee" financially and otherwise. He would publicly cite fellow Rousset Affair Committee members, who testified that "to help Marmande in his work we had only our good will and very little money. He went down there . . . not knowing how he would be able to live right up to the end of it, or how he would get back to France."[27] Indeed, Marmande would always avow that he had utterly bankrupted himself through his involvement in the Aernoult-Rousset Affair. Rousset's ingratitude, after all that Marmande had sacrificed, was as confusing as it was hurtful.

But Rousset was increasingly receptive to the unflattering portrait of Marmande painted by Thuillier and the *CDS* leadership. That portrait was now reinforced by *CGT* militants like Victor Griffuelhes, who claimed to be "99 percent certain that Marmande is an agent of the Government, whether he belongs to the *Sûreté Générale*, the *Préfecture de Police*, or is a free agent."[28] A police informant reported to his superiors that "despite serious investigations and patient research, the *CGT* and the *CDS* do not possess, at the moment, anything against Marmande but some suppositions, some hypotheses, which, however realistic they are, are hardly proofs."[29] But this didn't prevent Griffuelhes from describing Marmande as "a sad individual, a professional at indiscretions and swindles," or insisting to Rousset that Marmande's "whole attitude from the beginning of this business testified to his lively desire to arrange things so as to avoid all tumultuous demonstrations."[30]

The October 23 demonstration at the salle Wagram, however, was tumultuous enough. Accompanied by Thuillier, Rousset was passionately acclaimed by the crowd, which he earnestly thanked for having helped save him. Their cries of *Vive Rousset!* were welcome, he said, but perhaps not entirely appropriate—their thoughts should be focused not on his triumph but on the ordeal of Aernoult and the thousands of prisoners who, Rousset claimed, still languished in military prisons. For his own part, he had no intention of resting, despite his ill health. He was determined to fight military justice tooth and nail until one of them finally succumbed.[31]

But to René de Marmande, Émile Rousset was no longer Theseus. He was no longer heroic; he was no longer an intimate. He was, increasingly, just a painful memory.

The final break began with a letter that, according to Marmande, Rousset wrote him on November 7. Rousset had begun it with soothing words about extricating their relationship from the thicket of "boutique" political quarrels in which it was currently ensnared. He proceeded to explain that he had returned to his brother Louis's home in Lyons, but that a falling out with Louis and Marie necessitated his prompt departure. Fortunately, he confided, he had finally had a stroke of good luck. He had found a "little working girl" (*une petite ouvrière*), an employee at a box factory, who he knew could make him forget all that he had suffered. He intended to marry her and move to Paris. While pressing Steeg to lift the ban on Rousset's entry into the capital, would Marmande be so kind as to find and furnish a small apartment there for himself and his bride-to-be?

Wounded and exasperated, Marmande hadn't been entirely sure how to respond—until November 10, when Rousset sent him an inexplicably curt note demanding payment for 240 francs he claimed Marmande still owed him.[32] This, finally, was the last straw. It was time to strike back, and Marmande did so in a series of articles in *Les Temps Nouveaux* chronicling his entire involvement in the Aernoult-Rousset Affair.[33] Taken together, the articles really constituted one long howl of pain and rage—at Rousset; at the *CDS*, which had torn the two apart; at the entire militant world, which had rounded so viciously on him.

He stood accused of "adventurism." Yes, "adventurer" he certainly was. What other sort of person, if you please, dares "to venture madly, breaking with your career, with your relations, with your goods, with your normal life and the promises of the future, to throw yourself at full gallop into the social melee—on the side where there is hardly any future, any situation, little pleasure and a lot of pain?"[34] He had lived that life out of passion alone, a passion for justice he had once shared with the denizens of the *CDS*. Yet those men were now taking that life from him, leaving him nothing but memories. Well, those memories they could never efface, and he would share them now.

He had saved Émile Rousset because he believed in him and the justness of his cause. He still loved and would always love Émile Rousset—not the Rousset of today, sick, disturbed by his long ordeal, in thrall to demagogues—but the Rousset of yesterday, of Constantine, of the long struggle. He could recall some Algerian journalists jokingly promising, when he first took up Rousset's cause, not to laugh when the prisoner stole his purse. But in the end, Rousset had in fact stolen something far more valuable: "my illusions, and my pure memories." Someday the new darling of the *CDS* would realize the error he had made in spurning his savior: "Of baseness, I don't believe there is anything that surpasses this." Rousset would be sorry, Rousset would weep. But in the meantime the world should be alerted that those memoirs running in *La Bataille Syndicaliste*—the ones assembled under the guidance of Péronnet rather than Marmande—really couldn't be trusted.[35]

As for the *CDS*, it was led by liars and their allegations were just a pack of lies. Granted, he may have made some accounting mistakes. Was this so strange, in such a complex and arduous campaign? True, he had always been prone to losing things—receipts, records of various sorts. Yes, his correspondence with associates in Paris was perhaps less regular than it might have been. In fact, Marmande would go so far as to acknowledge openly that his life was "not exempt from faults, from imprudences, some of the errors that doubtless all men's lives contain." But there was no one more honest or more dedicated. He could still produce more than adequate documentation of expenses incurred during this great undertaking; he could demonstrate his probity to any reasonable person. The truth was, he had sold all his belongings, his books and the few items his mother had left him, to underwrite the struggle. And the charges of police connections were simply beneath contempt, possibly even a form of projection by the *CDS*. The police, in fact, had evinced special zeal in persecuting *him*, precisely because he had so often defeated their plots! It was the *CDS* that had played the police's game, the *CDS*'s own actions that had dissipated the energies that should have been galvanized by Rousset's liberation.[36] So direct and obvious was the correlation between the *CDS*'s divisiveness and Steeg's tactic that one could only wonder whether the former might not have acted deliberately.[37]

What could be stated with certainty, Marmande wrote, was that the *CDS* had treated the Rousset Affair Committee as a deadly rival and himself as a turncoat out of nothing more than a desire to maintain sole "ownership" of what *CDS* leaders called "*their* Dreyfus Affair" (Marmande's italics). Marmande was convinced that the access to important government officials provided by individuals on the Rousset Affair Committee—access the *CDS* itself had obviously never enjoyed—had been invaluable in saving Rousset. Examples abounded. The prisoner would never have been granted provisional liberty while awaiting his *non-lieu* without Havet. The prohibition against entry into Paris had been lifted in late October thanks to Painlevé's and Pressensé's personal relationships with Steeg. Indeed, much could be attributed to the attitude of Millerand himself, who, however horrid his politics in general, "had observed a perfect impartiality" in the Rousset Affair—an impartiality he could never have shown if Rousset's interests had been represented exclusively by militants.[38]

But the *CDS* had revealed its real nature, Marmande argued, by its actions regarding the publication of Rousset's judicial dossier. Their determination to keep it from him—to forestall publication in any journal less well disposed toward themselves than, perhaps, *La Bataille Syndicaliste*—revealed the depths to which, in their sectarian fever, they had sunk. They were actually willing to impede the liberation of Rousset if that liberation did not redound to their own benefit, and only their own. They, who claimed such tender feelings for Rousset, had actually exploited him in the most callous fashion. But then, what could be expected of people who—yes, he was sure it was one of them—could be so base as to write horrible anonymous letters to his mother ("Yes, to my mother! You read right. . . .") and even to send her a bag of ordure?[39]

In fact, by late 1912, wedges had been driven through a variety of once warm relationships within the antimilitarist movement. The estrangements between Marmande and Rousset as well as between Marmande and the *CDS* may have actually reflected a broader torsion the movement as a whole was undergoing, a shift in direction that some elements within it found difficult to countenance. Rifts were even appearing within the ranks of the *CDS* itself. As early as late July, on the eve of *La Bataille Syndicaliste*'s publication of the letters in which witnesses in Rousset's murder case recanted their testimony, an actual fistfight broke out at a meeting convened by the committee to discuss its next move. Jean Bonnafous, a particularly fiery orator, had accused the editors of the committee's *Bulletin* of deviation from a properly revolutionary position on the Berry-Millerand Law—whereupon one of those editors, Miguel Almereyda, had punched him in the face, and a general brawl ensued.[40] Almereyda would abruptly resign from the *CDS*, as would Eugène Merle and Émile Tissier—all prominent, dedicated militants. What was happening that could actually pit the *CDS* against itself?

Those defections from the *CDS*, along with a great many other matters, would be discussed in a general postmortem on the Aernoult-Rousset Affair published in *La Guerre Sociale* on October 9. Entitled "Why Rousset Didn't Come to Paris" and apparently written by resignees themselves, it began with an expression of respect for the "proven militants" of the *CDS*. But the authors then went on to note that "almost all libertarians or syndicalists, [those militants] are so violently, passionately anti-socialist that several among us, quite libertarian and syndicalist ourselves but partisans of understanding with the Socialist Party, left some months ago, we who were among the founders of the committee, as a form of protest against the politics of clique and division." It was indeed striking to find this sort of criticism of the *CDS* in *La Guerre Sociale*: the journal had been the committee's ideological *doppelgänger*, the official voice of precisely the sort of implacable militance the *CDS* represented in the field. Yet now it was accusing the committee of a counterproductive purism, attributing the failure of the Cirque de Paris demonstration to the *CDS*'s unwillingness to cooperate with other elements on the left. The authors went so far as to suggest that, but for the mediating role assumed by *La Guerre Sociale* itself, the committee's antisocialist virulence would have destroyed the fragile coalition that had secured victory in the Aernoult-Rousset Affair. On October 15 *L'Humanité* had chimed in as well, essentially reinforcing *La Guerre Sociale*'s critique of the *CDS*—especially the point that the committee, unlike the Socialist Party or various labor organizations, had no real mandate from the working classes.

The *CDS*, for its part, replied with an angry denunciation of the treachery of *La Guerre Sociale* ("whose editors and administrators of the first plan were, until the last few days, counted among the most esteemed members of the committee") and denial that the journal had ever "imposed accord" between itself and the Socialists. The resignees themselves epitomized that treachery. They had become pariahs within the *CDS*, the broadside proposed, because they had been complicit in Marmande's semi-theft of Rousset's judicial dossier from the committee (which, *CDS* leaders claimed, had been entrusted by attorney Toretta to Merle, who had kept it to himself until he was finished pillaging it for the benefit of other organizations). "These are the men," sniffed the *CDS*, "who have commercialized everything, joy as much as pain, who now accuse us of raising boutique quarrels."[41] Above all, the *CDS* had decried the arch-traitor Marmande, listing the charges to which he would respond in detail in *Les Temps Nouveaux*.

Marmande had begun his engagement in the affair as a member in good standing of the *CDS*. He had also held an editorial position at *La Guerre Sociale*. In 1910, this hardly suggested divided loyalties. But things were different in 1912. As far as the *CDS* was concerned, *La Guerre Sociale* had gone over to the enemy camp; like all leftist journals except *La Bataille Syndicaliste*, it was now a mere "nursery for candidates."[42] In fact, the *CDS*'s growing suspicion of Marmande tracked its growing suspicion of *La Guerre Sociale* because something important, and to *CDS* militants entirely unwelcome, was happening there. It was happening to Gustave Hervé, the journal's founder, and through him to French antimilitarism as a whole.

It was a shift to the right: a shift toward *rapprochement* with Socialists and, in fact, toward *rapprochement* with the government. It was, indeed, a shift toward nationalism. To most members of the *CDS*, that was simply unconscionable.

Scholars have dated the onset of a "nationalist revival" in France from as early as 1905.[43] In the public life of the nation, the signs were many: the growing prominence of nationalist tropes in the language of moderate and even center-left parties, where it had been largely absent; the persistence of nationalist leagues founded around the time of the Dreyfus Affair; the demonstrable appeal of nationalist Maurice Barrès to educated French youth, as both novelist and politician; and more. Certainly, rising levels of concern about German intentions lent force to public calls for Frenchmen to rally to flag and country—the stern visage Poincaré turned toward Germany upon assuming the presidency in 1912 was nothing less than the nation seemed, in the main, to want. It was not accidental that Poincaré could now succeed where others had failed, in establishing a national holiday honoring Joan of Arc, warrior redemptress of the nation. Nor was it surprising that Millerand would succeed in reestablishing the weekly military parades that had been banned in Paris since the Dreyfus Affair. These were symbolic gestures but, as such, significant ones.

The deepening nationalist mood clearly augured well for the army, simultaneously facilitating measures thought to enhance military strength and discouraging further expressions of antimilitarist sentiment. The ease of passage of the Berry-Millerand Law in 1912 reflected the spirit of the times, as would legislation the following year increasing the term of active service from two to three years. Antimilitarists were particularly alarmed by that new "three-year" law. Not only did it suggest governmental acceptance of the inevitability of conflict with Germany, it also represented a definitive rejection of Jaurèsian Socialists' calls for greater reliance on reserve forces—a substantial defeat for antimilitarists' vision of "the nation in arms" by proponents of military professionalization. But what was most disheartening was that resistance to the three-year law, while intense in some quarters, was so sporadic, so uncoordinated overall. This indicated weakening discipline and loosening bonds within the antimilitarist world.

Something of what was happening was suggested by the experience of Georges Yvetot, antimilitarist firebrand and longtime associate of Hervé. Nearly arrested in Germany in July 1911 for participating in a peace demonstration, upon his return to France he published an enthusiastic "Salute to My Country" in, of all places, *La Bataille Syndicaliste*. Yvetot had learned that German Socialists, even syndicalists, would be neither able nor necessarily even willing to impede Germany's war effort if the long-dreaded conflict should actually break out.[44] They lacked the freedom of association and expression their French counterparts enjoyed under the Third Republic; indeed, all too few of them shared the intensity of their French counterparts' internationalist and pacifist commitments. Yvetot was prepared to reconsider the counsel he and other antimilitarists had once offered French conscripts: resistance, including desertion and even sabotage, in the event of war. If

French leftists succeeded in obstructing their country's war effort while German leftists failed to disrupt theirs, the results could be catastrophic—especially for the working classes. The Third Republic, whatever its faults, was infinitely preferable to the German Empire.

This perception was shared by no less than the high priest of antimilitarism, Gustave Hervé himself. In fact, Hervé was engaged in a top-to-bottom reconsideration of his entire worldview. His awareness of the political weakness of the insurrectionist left had deepened, as had his appreciation of the successes of its reformist element. He watched developments in Germany with great interest and was increasingly persuaded that the best way to safeguard peace was to gift the French government with a united front *vis-à-vis* relations with the empire. He found himself attracted as well to the idea that at least a portion of the army was either endowed with, or could be converted to, sympathy for the working-class cause. By 1911 Hervé had concluded that he had been wrong in his conception of the struggle against militarism as the real key to working-class emancipation. He was also wrong, he now felt, to consider anti-patriotism a viable political strategy. By 1914 the *Sans-Patrie* of old was an unabashed nationalist. Indeed, with the announcement of general mobilization on August 2, the forty-three-year-old Hervé would publicly importune the war minister to "place me in the first regiment leaving for the front."[45] It was one of the most astonishing ideological transformations in the history of the French left, one that in the end would lead Hervé all the way to General Pétain and the Vichy regime.

This was the setting in which the *CDS*'s attack on Marmande, and his counterattack on them, occurred. From the committee's point of view, Hervé had initiated nothing less than a massive act of class treason, which reached into their own inner circle. One of the prime vehicles of this treason, obviously, was his once esteemed journal *La Guerre Sociale*. Its mealy-mouthed, Jaurèsian calls for "social peace" and "the appeasement of class hatreds" directly reflected the hideous transmogrification of its manager. And from this increasingly despicable journal, now little more than a "nursery for candidates," René de Marmande had launched himself into the Aernoult-Rousset Affair.[46] How could the *CDS* continue to trust him as, over the three-year course of the agitation, his journal and its opportunistic master moved ever farther rightward? His invitation to the bourgeoisie to take control of the movement (i.e., his formation of the Rousset Affair Committee) was, to the *CDS*'s inner circle, all but inevitable. It was, really, only a symptom of the far larger betrayal rending the movement.

This little implosion within antimilitarist ranks helps explain one of the oddest features of the Aernoult-Rousset Affair as a historical phenomenon—its apparent lack, or at least dearth, of direct, demonstrable consequences. Apart, perhaps, from the relocation of penal camps to metropolitan France, the basic institutions of military justice were not significantly affected by the whole affair. *Conseil de guerre* procedures, the investigative practices of military *parquets*, the content of the *Code de Justice Militaire*: when the dust of this three-year agitation settled, all would function much as they had previously. This is striking, in that the revelations occasioned by the Aernoult and Rousset cases were arguably more damaging to the jurisdiction than those of the Dreyfus case (simply because the Aernoult-Rousset agitation stayed focused on military justice, while the Dreyfus controversy had spilled beyond those confines to the broader question of anti-Semitism in French society). In truth, antimilitarists might have been hard-pressed to convert their victory in the Aernoult-Rousset Affair into real traction for their movement even without their own internal divisions, given the increasingly nationalistic climate of the times. But whatever momentum there was had simply dissipated, thanks to that internal disarray—a disarray finally distilled into the Marmande/*CDS* imbroglio.

Thus was the military jurisdiction reprieved, yet again. Divisions among its political enemies and the strengthened position of its political friends meant that the system remained substantially unreformed on the eve of World War I. The Aernoult-Rousset Affair had done more than raise grave questions about the procedures of French military justice. It had revealed that those procedures *could*, in fact, be undone by determined, sustained political action; that the structural arrangements designed to preclude political interventions, daunting as they were, could be overcome; that military justice could be rendered accountable. Yet nearly nothing was substantially changed. France's military jurisdiction emerged from this challenge structurally intact, despite the weaknesses its antagonists had revealed—just as it had from the Dreyfus Affair, and from the twenty-one reform efforts launched in the wake of that controversy. The paradoxical outcome of the Aernoult-Rousset Affair was that the minotaur's overall strength had been confirmed, or even enhanced, even while its particular vulnerabilities had been revealed.

Afterword

Theseus Unbound

If at this point we return to the central theme of the entire Aernoult-Rousset Affair, the contest between insularity and accountability with respect to military justice, then the multiple ironies of the situation simply clamor for attention. In fact, as we step back and survey the entirety of this story, those ironies practically define it.

To the champions of the military jurisdiction, "politics" was the enemy of discipline and must be kept as far from the daily operations of the jurisdiction as possible. They had acted on that conviction in aborting the many reform projects brought before the legislature. But, far from securing the ramparts, their obstructionism had galvanized antimilitarist passions and triggered the Aernoult-Rousset Affair—by which those ramparts were actually breached in myriad ways. In defending themselves from the toxic force of "politics," then, supporters of military justice called forth a political firestorm. And most of the damage was suffered by the jurisdiction.

Yet this damage was healed and forgotten, and the political insularity so prized by the system's defenders restored and even reinforced by—perversely—"politics," or a shift in the political winds. A nationalist sirocco was now scorching and dividing the enemies of military justice, while comfortably warming its friends. This, and only this, spared French military justice the need to narrow the gulf between its practices and those of the civilian legal world. The jurisdiction's defenders had long feared exposure to political currents. But *these* currents were celebrated. "Politics," so loudly decried as a mortal threat to military justice, had in fact saved it—from itself.

Yet it will not do to conclude this study with a simple inventory of ironies. There remains the matter of judgment. Was the outcome of the Aernoult-Rousset Affair a good thing for the military jurisdiction? Was it a good thing for the nation? Was justice served in any way? The answers are no, no, and maybe.

It is important to recognize at the outset a simple truth, one that defenders of the military jurisdiction, in their anti-political zeal, could not see. "Politics" comes in many shapes and sizes. The relatively orderly process of parliamentary reform is one thing. The volatile, unpredictable dynamic unleashed by the Aernoult and Rousset cases was something else entirely. It is quite fair to say that the public agitation over those cases owed far more to passion—and barely governable ones, at that—than to reason. The Aernoult-Rousset Affair was largely driven by unseen, intra-leftist rivalries; indeed, its precise trajectory was shaped by unknowable personal intimacies and antipathies. Those churning, combustible energies were granted far more political space than anyone could have expected—certainly far more than defenders of the military jurisdiction did—simply because of unanticipated governmental preoccupation with larger questions. Exposure to these latter varieties of politics ("street" politics, and international *realpolitik*) were infinitely more damaging to military justice than the politics of parliamentary reform precisely because they were not predictable or in any way subject to the control of the jurisdiction's spokesmen. Parliamentary reform, on the other hand, had proceeded with due deference to military interests, for the simple reason that its defenders could not be denied their role in the deliberations—however much the authors of reform may have wished they could.

Appearances to the contrary notwithstanding, the outcome of the Aernoult-Rousset Affair did represent a significant loss of control for the military jurisdiction. It had managed to elude its foes and avoid any real penalty for the structural shortcomings that had been revealed. But it had escaped that reckoning through luck, not design; the jurisdiction was "rescued" by a change in the nation's political mood, not by the wisdom or fortitude of its own personnel or supporters. In fact, the political change that so benefited the jurisdiction owed more to decisions taken in Berlin than to any taken in France. Sophisticated defenders of the jurisdiction, like General Bourelly, could hardly have been pleased at the thought that the Kaiser had served as a sort of *deus ex machina* whose interventions created the climate in which French military justice could be shielded from its enemies. There was no honor in this, or in the fact that the "victory" of military justice at the conclusion of the Affair reflected the fact that it had essentially lost—or, rather, eschewed—real control of its own destiny.

Furthermore, the outcome of the Aernoult-Rousset Affair (i.e., the failure of the reform impulse) would turn out to be a bad thing for France. The case for this revolves around the actual performance of French military justice during World War I—albeit not in the way that might initially be assumed.

The actions of the jurisdiction during that hideous ordeal remain an understudied subject despite recent scholarly contributions.[1] It must be acknowledged, however, that much of what we do know actually compels respect for the jurisdiction's performance in the field. The discipline it enforced was certainly essential to final victory; and if its courts were hard on soldiers (some six hundred were executed over the course of the war), they were not mindlessly brutal. Most of those executions occurred during the first months of the war, when the unexpected horrors of combat led to desertions, acts of cowardice, and assaults on officers on an unanticipated scale. During those desperate times, the jurisdiction had recourse to special bodies, the *conseils spéciaux de guerre,* which consisted of three-man panels that rendered immediate judgment on soldiers openly caught committing military offenses. These bodies, duly authorized by the Chamber of Deputies in March 1915, were indeed harsh, harsher even than the regular tribunals. But they were also effective; and they were formally revoked by the legislature in December 1916, as soon as the worst phase of the emergency was deemed to have passed. The general work of the jurisdiction in combat theaters over the duration of the war merits much closer study. It should be noted, however, that the most notorious instance of collective indiscipline during the entire conflict, the mutiny of 1917, was met not with a return to the most punitive measures but, wisely, with gentler ones.

But there is more to the story. During the war years, French military justice did fulfill the most dire predictions of, for instance, Georges Lhermitte and other critics who were alarmed by what they had long described as the jurisdiction's inherent tendency to encroach on and suborn aspects of the civilian legal order. On August 2, 1914, at the moment of general mobilization, the government invoked a peculiar (and still valid) French legal principle that can be traced back to the revolutionary era: the *état de siège* (state of siege), a kind of "statutory institutionalization of the crisis mode of government" by means of which the civilian government, faced with invasion or a similar grave national emergency, willingly confers many of its own functions on military authorities for the duration of the crisis.[2] Through this act, military courts were granted jurisdictional authority—throughout all of France, not just combat zones—over all offenses against "order, security, and public safety," as well as the power to determine which offenses were to be categorized as such.[3] Civilian courts continued to function alongside military ones, but the official subordination of the former to the latter was unchallengeable. A great many French civilians, along with foreign nationals unfortunate enough to find themselves in France at the outbreak of hostilities, would learn for themselves what the military jurisdiction's prioritization of "celerity" and "exemplarity" really entailed. For many it was not a happy experience. In their determination to suppress espionage, trafficking with the enemy, and speech harmful to morale, military courts gave French and other civilians a taste of the draconian punishments they had long inflicted on soldiers, with the same minimal concern for suspects' procedural rights. They did not shrink even from the establishment of concentration camps, where both French and foreign "undesirables" could be sequestered for the duration of the conflict.[4] If the American poet e.e. cummings's account is at all accurate, these were singularly charmless places.[5] It is hardly surprising that at the conclusion of the war hostility to French military justice was no longer confined to the political left (although the jurisdiction's defenders would manage to stave off structural reforms for another ten years, until 1928).

France herself—civilian France—did pay a price for reformers' failures to remake military justice prior to 1914. Of course, none of the reform efforts advanced between the Dreyfus and Aernoult-Rousset Affairs would have tempered the jurisdiction's operations during World War I even if they had been implemented. Most of those efforts addressed the jurisdiction's peacetime organization and allowed, however grudgingly, for a harder and crueler system in wartime (and, in fact, the "state of siege" could have been invoked even if they hadn't). But the failure of some fifteen years of reform efforts is significant nonetheless. For if they had succeeded, they would have denied the jurisdiction what its supporters most wanted in 1914. They would have drained meaning from the essential postulates of the system—that the chasm dividing military from civilian justice was both morally legitimate and a practical necessity, and that all efforts to bridge this chasm were futile. On August 2, 1914, the power of that idea remained uppermost in the minds of most French people, outside leftist quarters. Had it not, a great many of those peoples' lives might have played out very differently.

But if the Aernoult-Rousset Affair had not permanently altered the structure or functioning of the military jurisdiction, it nevertheless had achieved something. It had secured freedom and a kind of exoneration for Émile Rousset. This may seem a small thing in light of the larger questions involved. It wasn't. In fact, it entails the very largest question of all—the question of justice. For what Rousset's liberation represented, of course, was a particular *kind* of justice, an explicitly politicized kind. It was justice manufactured in a political crucible, justice as the direct outcome of explicitly political pressures. It is, perhaps, worth considering whether this "politicized" brand of justice was the real thing. Here our conclusions must necessarily be more provisional and our approach more elliptical.

Ideally, justice rests on clear truths. But those are denied us here. This is actually not so much because we can never know what really transpired in the Court of Miracles in Djennan-ed-Dar, or in that dimly lit corridor in Médéa. The real problem is what we feel certain we *do* know—for certainty all too easily shades into complacency in cases like these, and complacency is not helpful in considering the type of justice at issue here. What we can say for certain is that the sort of investigations that officers like Lieutenant Pan-Lacroix conducted and the sort of tribunals over which officers like Colonel Ungerer presided were incompatible with procedural fairness as presently understood. This, however, does not necessarily mean that the *results* of those investigations and trials were wrong—or that their reversal through *political* interventions yielded "justice." It is all too tempting to endorse alternative renderings of those events, based simply on dislike for the "official" renderings of them. For instance, we may conclude that Sabatier was guilty and Rousset innocent simply because we are so appalled at the way the military jurisdiction treated each. But this would be an elementary logical and moral error. Émile Rousset may indeed have been convicted of Brancoli's murder based on coerced or manipulated testimony. This does not mean he was innocent or that the release his supporters finally won for him represented a just outcome.

In fact, disquieting questions remain regarding Rousset's murder case. Certainly, in legalistic terms the case against him was fatally flawed. Yet we can also recognize that his own defense was hardly airtight. It relied on implausibilities (e.g., his explanation of how his knife had gotten to the place where it was discovered) and unproven claims (e.g., his insistence that Bordessoulle was half mad and fully capable of killing with no apparent motive). The retractions of prosecution testimony that finally terminated the case against him are not entirely reassuring, in light of the abruptness of those retractions and lingering questions about the methods by which the CDS had secured them. We can say that Rousset's prosecutors failed to bring genuinely compelling evidence against him; we can say that they failed to meet our own procedural standards. But we cannot say more about whether justice was done through the politicization of Rousset's case.

Or can we? Actually, we may be able to say something more, something about the fundamental postulate from which the treatment of Rousset—and of all the Roussets within the military jurisdiction—had always proceeded. We can offer a small and qualified observation that, for all its modesty, may yet be worth something, as we try to puzzle out the merits of the politicized justice that was finally secured in at least this case. For in the end, the essence of that justice was a politically generated and enforced rejection of the basic assumption that had always governed the treatment of men like Rousset. That was, quite simply, their incorrigibility.

The operating principle within the military jurisdiction was that these men must never be granted the benefit of the doubt. Certainly neither Finot nor Alix nor Pan-Lacroix nor Godiot nor Guillaud nor any other representative of military justice ever granted it to Rousset. Men like him had long ago forfeited that privilege, by their own actions. The entire system—its harshness, its indifference toward the rights of the accused—presumed them in the main irredeemable. This, in the eyes of the system's defenders, was precisely what the "politicians" who sought to intrude on the jurisdiction's affairs didn't understand or wouldn't accept. This was precisely why the "politicized" justice they advanced must be resisted. It represented a willful blindness to generations of accumulated wisdom regarding the nature of certain kinds of men.

How reliable was that accumulated wisdom in individual cases? How reliable was it in Rousset's case? It might be interesting to look at how he lived his life after the end of the Affair. We do have at least some scraps of information pertaining to the two decades after his release from military prison, because his decision to remain involved in the antimilitarist movement meant that the police would continue monitoring his activities.[6]

He was enraged when the army tried to reactivate him for reserve duty in the summer of 1913. At an antimilitarist meeting held by the Committee of Young Syndicalists that September, he began his remarks by boldly identifying the police agent in the room and vowing to speak his mind no matter what was recorded. He then defiantly announced that he had managed to get his reactivation suspended for another year on the basis of continued ill health. Finally, he expressed the hope that by the summer of 1914 social revolution would have arrived and suppressed military service entirely.[7]

Of course, something very different happened in the summer of 1914. But some of Rousset's other ambitions were realized. He did abandon the criminal life he had been leading prior to his induction into the army, just as he had promised Marmande he would. He did come to Paris, where he "lived conjugally" with a twenty-year-old woman named Jeanne Beury, who by December 1913 was "in an advanced state of pregnancy."[8] He became a "real" worker, securing regular employment as a mechanic in a precision-instruments factory.

He could not avoid reactivation when war finally broke out in August 1914 and served in the Seventy-fifth Regiment of Colonial Infantry. He was stationed in Tunisia—certainly an uncomfortable posting, given his history, despite its remove from the main front. But Rousset had no further encounters with military justice. In fact, he was mustered out of the army in March 1919 with the rank of sergeant. He lived in various sites in and around Paris for some years, finally acquiring a small house of his own in 1923. By then he had a daughter and was supplementing his income by selling perfumes and other items, including old copies of his memoirs.

After the war Rousset retained his affiliation with the CDS. Marmande would have regretted his continuing closeness to that particular group, but Rousset was, in fact, fulfilling another promise he had made to his former champion and intimate: to continue the fight, to pay back the debt he owed the antimilitarist movement by dedicating a portion of his considerable energies to it. He was surprisingly temperate in his views of the men who actually staffed the military jurisdiction. He was very critical of Albert Londres's reportage on military prisons, for instance, because he felt that Londres had heaped disproportionate blame for conditions on the *sous-offs* and underlings of the camps. What Rousset had derived from his own life experiences was the conviction that "all men are basically good, but it's society that makes them bad, and at 'Biribi,' as elsewhere, there are some honest people."[9]

But if he could be equitable in judgments of individuals, he never lost his loathing for the army as an institution, or for all things military. To Émile Rousset the army was one big prison, and he retained a burning hatred for all prisons everywhere. He identified strongly with the mutineers of 1917 and threw himself into the movement to amnesty them. At a meeting held at the salle Wagram on February 13, 1920, he exhorted the crowd to "demolish the Ministry of War."[10] At a meeting of Young Socialists held on October 8 of that year, he announced that "dying for your country is cowardice. If a new war breaks out, I hope that young people won't be cowardly enough to respond to the order of mobilization."[11]

Over time, the plight of individuals he identified as "political prisoners" emerged as the cause that carried the most personal meaning for Rousset. He interested himself in a wide array of specific cases he determined to be "political" in nature, from Spanish syndicalists to French Communists; and the efforts he made on behalf of defendants were substantial. He collected evidence for their trials, visited them in prison, and raised funds for them at meetings and demonstrations. In 1930 he abandoned the anarchist and syndicalist groupings with which he had previously aligned himself and joined the Communist Party, perhaps out of regard for its attention to the treatment of political prisoners.

He eventually married a certain Marie-Louise Mollion, and his domestic life was apparently unexceptional. Several police reports note that "privately, he gives no grounds for any unfavorable remark."[12] There were, however, occasional flashes of the old, violent Rousset. At a meeting held on October 3, 1920, an attendee claimed to recognize him as a sergeant in a North African disciplinary battalion during the war. Rousset had to be dragged from the man.[13] When a writer for the journal *La Rumeur* accused him of having fleeced a former convict, Rousset and some friends paid the man a personal visit, where, it seems, more than pleasantries were exchanged.[14]

Yet, all in all, it appears that Émile Rousset, at least in these decades, lived in such a way as to more or less confirm the image Marmande and other supporters had formed of him during the long struggle. He seems to have transformed himself—to have developed a passion for justice, and a willingness to fight for it. Considering the man he had been, that was no small thing.

It is, perhaps, something we might at least factor into our own consideration of what "politics" had really wrought, when he was finally released from his last military prison and returned to the world.

Appendix A
Judicial Dossier of Émile Rousset

The *Service Historique de la Défense* (*SHD*), the archival service of the French Ministry of Defense, holds Émile Rousset's judicial dossier (*côté* 12J 1247) at its research facility in Vincennes, outside Paris. In accordance with Statute no. 79 018 of January 3, 1979, judicial dossiers held at Vincennes are classified for one hundred years based on the date of the last official document therein. Prior consultation requires a formal derogation of that law, conferred by the Ministry of Defense. I am deeply grateful to M. Jean-Paul Bodin, Archival Director of the Ministry of Defense, for granting me that derogation in 2004. With some exceptions, the materials in Rousset's judicial dossier were what enabled me to reconstruct the operations of military justice in these cases, especially Rousset's.

The Rousset dossier is quite large, containing official documentation of the several proceedings in which Rousset was involved between 1909 and 1912. Most of these documents (*pièces*) are transcripts of depositions, investigators' reports, official correspondence, and the like. Most (but not all) are numbered, titled, and dated.

One set of materials in *SHD* 12J 1247 relates to Rousset's trial before the military court of Oran on January 19, 1910 (*procès d'Oran*) for refusal to obey and "outrage" toward a superior. There are also voluminous official materials pertaining to Rousset's murder case. These fall under two subdivisions.

There is one set of documents collected in preparation for his December 8, 1911, trial in Algiers (*procès d'Algers*). There is a second set, collected when Rousset's conviction by the Algiers tribunal was quashed and the case reinvestigated under the aegis of the Constantine *parquet* (*procès de Constantine*). The anticipated retrial, of course, never occurred.

In addition, Rousset's judicial dossier contains a couple of loose-leaf folders (*suppléments)* containing miscellaneous materials on the other investigations (into Aernoult's death, and the actions of the officers implicated in it) in which Rousset's testimony figured prominently. Many of the pièces in these dossiers are untitled and apparently unofficial. Most are contained in a supplément bearing the heading "*à insérer dans le dossier Sabatier et consorts sans l'indiquer sur la chemise*" ("to be inserted into the record on Sabatier and associates without so indicating on the folder").

Appendix B
General Rabier's Report

General Rabier's report on the circumstances surrounding Aernoult's death was commissioned by and delivered to the war minister around December 1910. Technically, it should be described as part of the military record of the case; but there is no copy of it in Rousset's judicial dossier, nor could one be located in the archive at Vincennes. The version that was published in *La Bataille Syndicaliste* on September 27, 1912, may have been redacted, although this cannot be ascertained without a copy of the original.

It should be noted that the Rabier report diverges in important respects from the testimony of officers, preserved in SHD 12J 1247, who dealt with Aernoult on his final day. Fairness demands that each account be considered.

Rabier concluded that Aernoult had done his punishment without trouble for the first couple of hours; while Sergeant Casanova said he was resistant from the beginning. Rabier concluded that, subsequently, Aernoult was physically incapable of further exertion; while Casanova insisted that he didn't want to work. Rabier concluded that Aernoult had made a deliberate decision to get himself brought before a *conseil de guerre*, while Lieutenant Sabatier represented him as emotionally out of control (the lieutenant claimed that he himself intervened only when the prisoner hurled a bucket of ordure against a wall, since "it wasn't possible not to address this act of indiscipline"). Rabier concluded that Aernoult, while certainly verbally threatening, had never represented a physical menace to anyone; while Sabatier insisted that he did. Rabier submitted that, even if the officers' judgments on that point were correct, they should have briefly restrained him on the spot rather than returning him to his cell and restraining him there.

Rabier did defer to officers' accounts, or at least maintain neutrality, in some respects. He was noncommittal on Rousset's claim that Sabatier struck Aernoult with his cane. He was also unpersuaded by other prisoners' claims that Beignier had either beaten Aernoult during sieste or had native auxiliaries beat him.

Rabier also argued that the gravity of Aernoult's physical condition should have been obvious, meriting greater solicitude from Beignier, Casanova, and Sabatier. He also concluded that Aernoult probably was beaten severely later in the afternoon, including after his collapse, when officers mistook his worsening physical condition for deliberate shamming. Rabier also found "disquieting" Sabatier's decision to place Aernoult in an isolated cell when he was returned from the punishment ground for the last time, in the early evening (although he was willing to accept the officers' accounts of what transpired for the next few hours). Finally, Rabier determined that Aernoult almost certainly had not dashed his head against the wall of his cell in his death throes (no blood was found there, and his head wounds were not consistent with that action), or inflicted any but his more minor wounds on himself.

Above all, Rabaer concluded that the real cause of the tragedy was the officers' conviction that Aernoult must not be permitted to "flank" them by getting before a *conseil de guerre*, plus their decision to force him physically to obey their orders. He also criticized Captain Finot's failure to order an immediate autopsy and to provide Aernoult the proper burial obsequies—both omissions occasioned, in Rabier's view, by officers' concern to minimize the complications of Aernoult's death for themselves and the camp.

Finally, Rabier criticized the conduct of earlier inquiries into the matter. He criticized the inconclusiveness of Doctor Dorange's original medical report, which in Rabier's view contained "only one clear affirmation," namely, that "Aernoult died of a stroke; the rest is nothing but hypotheses." Captain Finot, Rabier felt, should not have accepted, or represented, that report as definitive. Furthermore, Rabier felt that the *parquet*'s initial investigations of Aernoult's death—where officers had simply been asked to provide their own accounts of what had happened—was inadequate. Those accounts, Rabier argued, had not been rigorously challenged or cross-referenced, while prisoners' and dissenting auxiliaries' accounts had been dismissed or undervalued.

Appendix C
Lieutenant Pan-Lacroix's Report

Lieutenant Pan-Lacroix's original report on the murder of Augustin Brancoli, delivered to Captain Giacomoni on August 31, 1911, is missing from Rousset's judicial dossier at Vincennes, where it was originally filed as pièce #3 of the procès d'Algers materials. A version of that report did appear in *Les Temps Nouveaux* on February 8, 1912 (see Appendix D), as part of the entire "*Dossier de l'Affaire Rousset*" published by that journal on that date. This version of Pan-Lacroix's report also appears as an annotated appendix in René de Marmande's *Émile Rousset et l'enquête du lieutenant Pan-Lacroix* (Paris: Librairie Schleicher Frères, 1912).

Lieutenant Pan-Lacroix was often described as the police judicial officer on the Rousset murder case. Technically this was inaccurate since Captain Giacomoni of the Médéa garrison held that function. But the error was understandable, based on the prominent role Pan-Lacroix played in the investigations conducted by both the Algiers and Constantine *parquets*.

There is no copy of Captain Giacomoni's own, independent report in SHD 12J 1247; nor was a copy of one printed in *Les Temps Nouveaux* on February 8, 1912. It may have been retained by General Oudard, or by the public minister of the military *parquet* of Algiers. However, references to it in other sources make clear that Giacomoni accepted Pan-Lacrox's findings (and, apparently, much of the wording of his report). Giacomoni's willingness to essentially approve and pass on Pan-Lacroix's report helps explain the common misperception that the latter's report was the official submission of the police judicial officer.

Subsequently, while Captain Godiot was conducting the officially authorized, investigation of the Algiers *parquet*, Pan-Lacroix apparently took statements from witnesses both he and Giacomoni had already interviewed (e.g., Bordessoulle, Bintein, Leprêtre, Despax, and Sappa), as well as other individuals, who he said had agreed to come forward with new information. Since Pan-Lacroix was neither police judicial officer nor *rapporteur* in the investigation, he was not formally authorized to take depositions; those statements carried no official juridical weight and are not contained in SHD 12J 1247 at Vincennes. Captain Godiot, however, evidently found them helpful; he went on to depose the same individuals formally, sometimes for a second time. The statements Pan-Lacroix collected were included in "*Le Dossier de l'Affaire Rousset*" published by *Les Temps Nouveaux* on February 8, 1912 (see Appendix D).

Rousset's defenders would harshly criticize not only the conclusions Pan-Lacroix submitted but also the methods by which he arrived at them. Those criticisms, of course, would prove important in the ultimate resolution of the case. Pan-Lacroix provided his own account of how he proceeded, in his depositions to both Captain Godiot (SHD 12J 1247, procès d'Algers, pièce #32) and Captain Guillaud (SHD 12J 1247, procès de Constantine, pièce #24). In addition, there is the extensive confrontation with Rousset that Pan-Lacroix was required to undergo during the Constantine investigation (SHD 12J 1247, procès de Constantine, pièce #180), in which the lieutenant also described his investigative methods.

The account I have provided of Pan-Lacroix's procedures is drawn from those sources. He and his critics would disagree vehemently on the appropriateness of those procedures. But the basic account here of what he actually did—as well as when and even why—would not, I think, have been disputed by either side.

Appendix D

Les Temps Nouveaux

"Le Dossier de l'Affaire Rousset," February 8, 1912

Exactly who divulged to *Les Temps Nouveaux* the dossier that Captain Godiot of the Algiers *parquet* had compiled on the Rousset murder case is not clear. But "*Le Dossier de l'Affaire Rousset*" that appeared on February 8, 1912, in the special issue of that journal does constitute a part of the military record on the case—especially valuable since it presents some pièces that are missing from Rousset's judicial dossier at Vincennes.

These include pièce #3, Lieutenant Pan-Lacroix's initial report (see Appendix C). There is no reason to believe that the transcript appearing in *Les Temps Nouveaux* did not represent what Pan-Lacroix actually wrote; but it may not reproduce it in its entirety. Some of the depositions printed in *Les Temps Nouveaux* are shortened versions of the originals contained in SHD 12J 1247 at Vincennes, raising the possibility that Pan-Lacroix's report may also have been edited prior to publication (possibly for reasons having to do with the economics of publishing so massive a volume of material in a special edition of the journal). In addition to Pan-Lacroix's report, *Les Temps Nouveaux* presented pièces #4–#10 from the procès d'Algers compilation,which were also missing from Rousset's judicial dossier at Vincennes.

Notes

Introduction

1. Gustave Rouanet, "Juges militaires," *L'Humanité,* 4 février 1907, p. 1.

2. In France, where both the philosophy and history of law have undergone something of a scholarly renaissance over the last generation, the subject formed the basis of a particularly provocative issue of the journal *Archives de la Philosophie du Droit* (16, 1971) entitled "Le Droit investi par le politique" (Paris: Sirey, 1971). See, especially, Henri Batiffol's introductory essay "Problèmes et frontières: Droit et politique." That journal was founded in part by Michel Villey, one of the key figures in the reinvigoration of these inquiries.

3. Judith Shklar's *Legalism: Law, Morals, and Political Trials* (Cambridge, Mass.: Harvard University Press, 1986) remains extremely valuable for its challenging, eloquent defense of at least occasional admixtures of political calculations into juridical procedures.

1—"L'Armée, c'est la Nation"

1. Général Jules Bourelly, "L'Armée est-elle, doit-elle être la nation?" *Le Correspondant de Paris,* 25 avril 1902, pp. 193–220; and Général Jules Bourelly, "L'Armée française au commencement de 1904," *Le Correspondant de Paris,* 10, 25 février 1904, pp. 402–27, 686–714.

2. Général Jules Bourelly, *Souvenirs de la campagne de 1859 en Italie* (Paris: Combet, 1904); and *La Guerre de 1870–1871 et la traité de Francfort d'après les derniers documents* (Paris: Perrin, 1912).

3. Commandant Jules Bourelly, *Le Maréchal de Fabert (1599–1662): Étude historique d'après ses lettres et des pièces inédites,* 2 vols. (Paris: Didier et Cie, 1879–1881); Lt.-Col. Jules Bourelly, *Cromwell et Mazarin: Deux campagnes de Turenne en Flandre, la bataille des Dunes* (Paris: Perrin, 1886); Général Jules Bourelly, *Questions de défense nationale dans les Alpes-Maritimes* (Paris: R. Chapelot, 1902).

4. Bourelly, "L'Armée est-elle, doit-elle être la nation?" p. 193.

5. Ibid., p. 211.

6. Ibid., p. 209.

7. Quoted in François Bederida, "L'Armée et la république," *Revue Historique* (septembre 1964), p. 159.

8. Quoted in Raoul Girardet, *La Société militaire dans la France contemporaine, 1815–1939* (Paris: Librairie Plon, 1953), p. 179.

9. Gaetan Moisand, *Faut-il supprimer les conseils de guerre?* (Paris: A. Perdone, 1908), pp. 5–6.

10. Bourelly, "L'Armée est-elle, doit-elle être la nation?" p. 210.

11. Ibid., p. 209.

12. Arpad F. Kovacs, "French Military Legislation in the Third Republic, 1871–1940," *Military Affairs* 13, no. 1 (Spring 1949): 1.

13. Quoted in Kovacs, "French Military Legislation," p. 3.

14. Bourelly, "L'Armée est-elle, doit-elle être la nation?" pp. 197–98. See also David B. Ralston's discussion of the 1872 legislation in *The Army of the Republic: The Place of the Military in the Political Evolution of France, 1871–1914* (Cambridge, Mass.: MIT Press, 1967), pp. 29–63.

15. Bourelly, "L'Armée est-elle, doit-elle être la nation?" p. 198.

16. The question of just how deeply antirepublican the French army really was at the time has attracted a great deal of scholarly attention. See, for instance, Girardet, *La Société militaire dans la France contemporaine*; Paul-Marie de La Gorce, *La France et son armée* (Paris: Fayard, 1963); Bederida, "L'Armée et la république." In the anglophone literature, see Ralston, *Army of the Republic*, and Alistair Horne, *The French Army and Politics, 1870–1970* (New York: Harper and Row, 1984).

17. Bourelly, "L'Armée française au commencement de 1904," p. 402.

18. Ibid., pp. 402–3.

19. For a good discussion of this subject see Richard D. Challener's study *The French Theory of the Nation in Arms, 1866–1939* (New York: Russell and Russell, 1965).

20. Bourelly, "L'Armée est-elle, doit-elle être la nation?" p. 198. See also Colonel Frédéric-Léopold Bidault, *L'Armée française et le service de deux ans* (Paris: Charles-Lavauzelle, 1898).

21. Bourelly, "L'Armée est-elle, doit-elle être la nation?" p. 212.

22. See Ralston, *Army of the Republic*, pp. 46–90 (quote on p. 78).

23. Bourelly, "L'Armée est-elle, doit-elle être la nation?" p. 210; italics in original.

24. Ibid., p. 215. Earlier, Bourelly had published in *Le Correspondant de Paris* an extended consideration of military justice entitled "De la réforme de la justice militaire en temps de paix." It appeared in two parts: the first on May 10, 1899 (pp. 563–79), the second on May 25 of that year (pp. 759–91).

25. Bourelly, "De la réforme de la justice militaire en temps de paix," 10 mai 1899, p. 572.

26. Moisand, *Faut-il supprimer les conseils de guerre?* p. 6.

27. Bourelly, "De la réforme de la justice militaire en temps de paix," 10 mai 1899, p. 572.

28. Ibid., p. 571.

29. Ibid., p. 572.

30. Lieutenant F.M. Alix, *Le Vol militaire et sa répression* (Nancy: Imprimerie Berger-Levrault, 1906), p. 85.

31. Bourelly, "De la réforme de la justice militaire en temps de paix," 10 mai 1899, p. 578. He was quoting the report of the commission that had successfully brought forward in 1857 a proposal for a new, unified Code de Justice Militaire (CJM).

32. See Philip Nord's study entitled *The Republican Moment: Struggles for Democracy in Nineteenth-Century France* (Cambridge, Mass.: Harvard University Press, 1995).

33. Bourelly, "De la réforme de la justice militaire en temps de paix," 10 mai 1899, p. 579.

34. Constitutionally, the Third Republic was built on the principle of legislative supremacy, which extended to the judicial as well as the executive branch of government.

The judiciary was theoretically independent but, denied the power of judicial review, hardly sovereign. Alex Sweet Stone provides a particularly good discussion of the period's juridical thought and the history behind it in his study *The Birth of Judicial Politics in France: The Constitutional Council in Comparative Perspective* (New York: Oxford University Press, 1992).

2—The Theory and Practice of French Military Justice

1. Waldemar Fontaine, *De l'application du droit commun en matière de délits commis par les militaires de l'armée de terre* (Lille: Université de Lille, Faculté de Droit, 1909), pp. 125–30. See also Francis de Pressensé's preface to Georges Lhermitte's study *Le Sabre et la loi* (Paris: P.-V. Stock, 1900), pp. v–xi.

2. General Jules Bourelly, "De la réforme de la justice militaire en temps de paix," *Le Correspondant de Paris,* 10 mai 1899, p. 567.

3. For overviews of military justice under the ancien régime, see Fontaine, *De l'application du droit commun*; Pierre Hugueney, *Traité théorique et pratique de droit pénal et de procédure pénale militaire* (Paris: Librairie du Recueil Sirey, 1933), pp. 6–9; and Marc Letort, *Réforme de la justice militaire: Historique de la justice militaire en France* (Algiers: E. Pfister, 1928), p. 9. For a description of past disciplinary sanctions, see also Gaston Dubois-Desaulle, *Camisards, Peaux de lapins et Cocos: Corps disciplinaires de l'armée française* (Paris: Éditions de la *Revue Blanche*, 1901), p. 9.

4. Bourelly, "De la réforme de la justice militaire en temps de paix," *Le Correspondant de Paris,* 10 mai 1899, p. 571.

5. Samuel F. Scott, "Problems of Law and Order during 1790, the 'Peaceful' Year of the French Revolution," *American Historical Review* 80, no. 4 (1975): 866–88.

6. Charles H. Hammond, Jr., "The French Revolution and the Enlightening of Military Justice," *Proceedings of the Western Society for French History* 34 (2006): 136.

7. Ibid., p. 137.

8. Letort, *Réforme de la justice militaire,* p. 13.

9. Quoted in ibid., p. 11.

10. Hammond, "The French Revolution and the Enlightening of Military Justice," p. 139.

11. Hugueney, *Traité théorique et pratique de droit pénal,* p. 10.

12. Letort, *Réforme de la justice militaire,* pp. 15–16.

13. Hammond, "The French Revolution and the Enlightening of Military Justice," p. 141.

14. Quoted in Letort, *Réforme de la justice militaire,* p. 16.

15. Bourelly, "De la réforme de la justice militaire en temps de paix," *Le Correspondant de Paris,* 10 mai 1899, p. 568. Letort calls the penalties the Directory established both "pitiless" and "indispensable" (*Réforme de la justice militaire,* p. 17).

16. Letort, *Réforme de la justice militaire,* p. 18.

17. Cited in ibid., pp. 16–17.

18. Ibid., p. 16.

19. Hugueney, *Traité théorique et pratique de droit pénal,* p. 11.

20. See Letort, *Réforme de la justice militaire,* p. 17.

21. Ibid., pp. 22, 27.

22. See Letort's general discussion of the Directory's legislation on military justice, ibid., pp. 21–29. For a specific discussion of the law of 13 *brumaire de l'an* V (November 3,

1796), see Hugueney, *Traité théorique et pratique de droit pénal*, p. 12.

23. Hugueney states flatly that "the jury did not survive the reaction of 9 thermidor" (ibid., p. 11), while Letort observes that "the jury the Constituent [Assembly] had created and the Convention had maintained was suppressed, as well as the civil judges who composed the tribunal" (*Réforme de la justice militaire*, p. 25).

24. Letort, *Réforme de la justice militaire*, p. 26.

25. Hugueney, *Traité théorique et pratique de droit pénal*, p. 12.

26. Letort, *Réforme de la justice militaire*, pp. 29–30.

27. Hugueney, *Traité théorique et pratique de droit pénal*, p. 13.

28. This long record of futile attempts to reconsider and reconfigure military justice is summarized by Bourelly, "De la réforme de la justice militaire en temps de paix," pp. 569–71, and by Letort, *Réforme de la justice militaire*, pp. 29–31.

29. See L. Tripier, *Code de Justice Militaire pour l'armée de terre, expliqué par l'exposé des motifs, le rapport, et la discussion au Corps legislatif; 2 éd. augmentée d'un supplément et mise en rapport avec la législation actuelle par A. Champoudry* (Paris: Mme Mayer-Odin/L. Larose, 1857–1879).

30. The 1857 code generated surprisingly little analysis by legal scholars until the entire question of military justice assumed public salience in the decades before World War I. Among the few earlier commentaries are the following: Victor Foucher, *Commentaire sur le Code de Justice Militaire pour l'armée de terre, promulguée le 4 août 1857* (Paris: Firmin-Didot, 1858); and Paul-Louis Ernst Pradier-Fodéré and Amédée Le Faure, *Commentaire sur le Code de Justice Militaire, précédée d'une introduction historique* (Paris: J. Dumaine, 1873). Among the most important figures in the study of military law were Colonel Joseph Augier and Gustave le Poittevin, whose *Traité théorique et pratique de droit pénal et de procédure criminelle militaire* (Paris: Librairie de la Société du Recueil Sirey, 1918); and *Traité des recours en révision contre les jugements des conseils de guerre en temps de guerre* (Paris: L. Tenin, 1915–1916) are still very valuable.

31. Hugueney, *Traité théorique et pratique de droit pénal*, pp. 277–78.

32. Quoted by Lhermitte in *Le Sabre et la loi*, p. 6.

33. Ibid., p. 5.

34. *Code de Justice Militaire: Dispositions diverses, supplément arrêté à la date du 31 décembre 1912* (Paris: Henri Charles-Lavauzelle, Éditeur Militaire, 1912), p. 7.

35. Commandant Caille, *Des Pouvoirs judiciaires du général commandant le Corps d'Armée* (Paris: Jouve et Cie, Éditeurs, 1921), p. 10.

36. Lieutenant François Bassieux, *La Justice militaire* (Caen: Chez M. Brunet, 1907), p. 7.

37. Caille, *Des Pouvoirs judiciaires du Général commandant*, pp. 11–12.

38. A. J. Ambrosini, *Petit Dictionnaire de jurisprudence criminelle militaire: Contenant toutes les décisions des Conseils de révsion de Paris et d'Algers* (Paris: Librairie Militaire de L. Baudoin, 1893), p. 7.

39. L. Herpin, *De la réforme de la compétence et de la composition des conseils de guerre: Discours prononcé à la séance solennelle de réouverture de la conférence des avocats stagiaires, barreau de Poitiers* (Poitiers: Imprimerie Blais et Roy, 1909), p. 9.

40. Xavier Dufay, *Les Garanties accordées à la défense devant les tribunaux militaires* (Besançon: Imprimerie Cariage, 1913).

41. Caille, *Des Pouvoirs judiciaires du Général commandant*, p. 11.

42. Henri Barboux, "Projets de réforme de la juridiction militaire," *Revue Politique et Parlementaire (*octobre 1899): 9–10.

3—The View from the Left

1. See, e.g., Ralston, *Army of the Republic*. See also the first two chapters of Douglas Porch's *The March to the Marne: The French Army, 1871–1914* (London: Cambridge University Press, 1981).

2. For the theoretical underpinnings of French socialism, see Frank Manuel's *The Prophets of Paris* (Cambridge, Mass.: Harvard University Press, 1962). For the intellectual and institutional distinctions between the socialist and anarchist strains of the French left, see Jeremy Jennings's excellent *Syndicalism in France: A Study of Ideas* (London: Macmillan, 1990). For an illustration of insurrectionist practice in those decades, see Jill Harsin's *Barricades: The War of the Streets in Revolutionary Paris, 1830–1848* (New York: Palgrave Macmillan, 2002).

3. On the Boulanger Affair, see especially, William D. Irvine's *The Boulanger Affair Reconsidered: Royalism, Boulangism, and the Origins of the Radical Right in France* (New York: Oxford University Press, 1989); and Frederick Seager's *The Boulanger Affair: Political Crossroad of France, 1886–1889* (Ithaca, N.Y.: Cornell University Press, 1969).

4. Barrès, an important figure in configuring this "new right," has been the subject of numerous studies, including Zeev Sternhell's *Maurice Barrès et le nationalisme français* (Paris: A. Colin, 1972); Robert Soucy's *Fascism in France: The Case of Maurice Barrès* (Berkeley and Los Angeles: University of California Press, 1972); and C. Stewart Doty's *From Cultural Rebellion to Counterrevolution: The Politics of Maurice Barrès* (Athens: Ohio University Press, 1976). The "masculinist" dimension of the new right in France has been explored in more recent studies. See especially Christopher Forth's *The Dreyfus Affair and the Crisis of French Manhood* (Baltimore, Md.: Johns Hopkins University Press, 2004).

5. For an excellent study of French antimilitarism during these years, see Paul Miller's *From Revolutionaries to Citizens: Antimilitarism in France, 1870–1914* (Durham, N.C.: Duke University Press, 2002).

6. See Edward Shorter's *Strikes in France, 1830–1968* (London: Cambridge University Press, 1974).

7. Dubois-Desaulle, *Camisards, Peaux de lapins et Cocos*, pp. 18–21.

8. Georges Lhermitte, *Le Sabre et la loi*; and *Le Code rouge: À bas la justice militaire!* (Paris: Librairie de "la Raison," 1904).

9. Lhermitte, *Le Code rouge*, pp. 50–51; *Le Sabre et la loi*, pp. 98–100.

10. Lhermitte, *Le Code rouge*, pp. 64–69.

11. Lhermitte, *Le Sabre et la loi*, pp. 171–216.

12. Lhermitte, *Le Code rouge*, pp. 56–58.

13. Lhermitte, *Le Sabre et la loi*, p. 170; Lhermitte, *Le Code rouge*, pp. 105–10.

14. Lhermitte, *Le Sabre et la loi*, pp. 87–94.

15. Quoted in ibid., p. 45.

16. Ibid., pp. 52–56.

17. Ibid., pp. 54–56.

18. Ibid., pp. 8–33.

19. De Pressensé, preface, in ibid., pp. v–xi.

20. Lhermitte, *Le Sabre et la loi*, pp. 41–42.

21. Jean Eric Lundy, *Le Traitement pénal dans l'armée française sous la 3ième République* (Paris: Université René Descartes, 1987).

22. Ibid., p 12.

23. Francis Delaisi, *Contre la loi Millerand* (Paris: "Les Temps Nouveaux," 1912).

24. Anthony Clayton, *France, Soldiers, and Africa* (London: Brassey's Defence Publishers, 1988), p. 212.

25. Ibid., pp. 212–16.

26. See Jacques Dhur's reportage on these units in *Le Journal*, 7–8 mars 1907, and in *La Guerre Sociale*, 6–12 juillet 1910. See also Charles Vallier, *Les Conseils de guerre et la justice militaire* (Paris: Éditions de la *Revue Blanche*, 1902).

27. See Dominique Kalifa's excellent *Biribi: Les Bagnes coloniaux de l'armée française* (Paris: Perrin, 2009) for a comprehensive overview of this subject. Kalifa, it should be noted, draws no essential distinction between the Bats d'Af themselves, and more specialized penal units (the various types of *compagnies de discipline*) as components of Biribi. In his account, the term refers to a set of camps where felons and undesirables could be quarantined and, in effect, punished again for offenses already punished or punishable in the civilian system; and both the Bats d'Af and the more specialized units served that purpose.

28. Auriant, preface to George Darien's *Biribi* (1890; reprint, Paris: Jérôme Martineau Éditeur, 1966), p. xiv.

29. Dubois-Desaulle, *Camisards, Peaux de lapins et Cocos*, pp. 45–65.

30. Ibid., p. 58.

31. Quoted in ibid., p. 43.

32. Ibid., pp. 43–45.

33. Ibid., p. 72.

34. Lundy, *Le Traitement pénal dans l'armée française*, p. 4.

35. Darien, *Biribi*, p. 31.

36. Ibid., pp. 52, 53–54.

37. Ibid., pp. 63, 67.

38. Ibid., pp. 71–75.

39. Ibid., pp. 89–90.

40. Ibid., pp. 95–96.

41. Ibid., pp. 112–13.

42. Ibid., pp. 247–49.

43. Ibid., pp. 237–39.

44. Ibid., pp. 275–77.

45. Ibid., pp. 104–5.

4—The Dreyfus Affair and the Debate over Military Justice

1. Bernard H. Moss, *The Origins of the French Labor Movement, 1830–1914* (Berkeley and Los Angeles: University of California Press, 1976), p. 107.

2. Primary source documents articulating these and other socialist positions on political action can be found at www.marxists.org/archive/guests/1899/12/speech.htm (consulted Oct. 27, 2008).

3. Harvey Goldberg, *The Life of Jean Jaurès* (Madison: University of Wisconsin Press, 1962).

4. In 1910 a series of articles Jaurès had written earlier on military organization was published as *L'Armée nouvelle*. The most recent reprinting was in 1992, with a preface by Jean-Noël Jeanneney (Paris: Imprimerie Nationale Éditions).

5. *Documents Parlementaires*, Chambre des Députés, 8 février 1894, Sess. Ord. #357, p. 135.

6. For a good treatment of Hervé's ideas, career, and general role in the socialist movement, see the third chapter of Miller's *From Revolutionaries to Citizens.*

7. Ibid., pp. 73–74.

8. Ibid., chaps. 1–3.

9. Christopher Ansell, *Schism and Solidarity in Social Movements: The Politics of Labor in the French Third Republic* (Cambridge: Cambridge University Press, 2001), pp. 189–90.

10. Humbert Ricolfi, *Le Code de Justice Militaire du 9 mars 1928. Historique, discussion devant le Parlement, principes de la réforme, commentaires, texte de la loi* (Paris: Charles-Lavauzelle, 1928), p. 18.

11. Recent anglophone entries in the voluminous literature on the Dreyfus Affair include Louis Begley's *Why the Dreyfus Affair Matters* (New Haven, Conn.: Yale University Press, 2009) and George Whyte's *The Dreyfus Affair: A Chronological History* (New York: Palgrave Macmillan, 2005). My own discussion of the affair relies heavily on Jean-Denis Bredin's *The Affair: The Case of Alfred Dreyfus* (New York: George Braziller, 1986); and two excellent anthologies, *L'Affaire Dreyfus de A à Z*, ed. Michel Drouin (Paris: Flammarion, 1994), and *L'Affaire Dreyfus*, ed. Michel Winock (Paris: Éditions de Seuil, 1998).

I am particularly indebted, however, to Benjamin Martin's excellent essay "The Dreyfus Affair and the Corruption of French Justice," in Norman L. Kleeblatt, ed., *The Dreyfus Affair: Art, Truth, and Justice* (Berkeley and Los Angeles: University of California Press, 1987).

12. Girardet, *La Société militaire dans la France contemporaine,* quoted in Ralston, *Army of the Republic*, p. 249.

13. See Maurice Vaïsse and Jean-François Boulanger, "La Conspiration des militaires," in Drouin, *L'Affaire Dreyfus de A* à *Z*, pp. 51–66.

14. Bredin, *The Affair*, pp. 118–19.

15. Ibid., p. 96.

16. See Pierre Guiral's essay "Georges Clemenceau" in *L'Affaire Dreyfus de A à Z*, pp. 156–60.

17. Quoted by Martin, "The Dreyfus Affair and the Corruption of French Justice," p. 43.

18. Albéric Nazair-Blanc, *La Justice militaire et maritime et des réformes qui y ont été apportées durant ces dernières années* (Toulouse: Librairie des Étudiants, 1913), p. 70, ff #2.

19. Martin, "The Dreyfus Affair and the Corruption of French Justice," p. 42.

20. Ibid., p. 44.

21. For an insightful treatment of the *Cour de Cassation*'s role in the Dreyfus Affair and the peril posed to basic rule of law by the political tumult, see Vincent Duclert's essay "La Cour de cassation" in *L'Affaire Dreyfus de A à Z*, pp. 361–72.

22. Clemenceau, "Pour la révision avec renvoi," in *Justice militaire* (Paris: P.-V. Stock, 1901), p. 43.

23. *Documents Parlementaires*, Chambre des Députés, 25 octobre 1898, Sess. extra. ann. #288, p. 97.

24. *Documents Parlementaires*, Chambre des Députés, 7 décembre 1893, #123, p. 151.

25. Ibid., 4 novembre 1898, Sess. extra. ann. #311, p. 147.

26. Émile Duclaux, *Propos d'un solitaire II. Les Conseils de guerre* (Paris: Au Siège de la Ligue Française pour la Défense des Droits de l'Homme, 1899), p. 21.

27. See the *Code de Justice Militaire pour l'armée de terre: Annexes, formules, modèles et dispositions diverses*, 7th ed. (Paris: Henri Charles-Lavauzelle, Éditeur Militaire, 1912), pp. 187–202.

28. For a good discussion of these initiatives, see Odile Roynette's excellent article "Les Conseils de guerre en temps de paix entre réforme et suppression, 1898–1928," *Vingtième Siècle, Revue d'Histoire* 73 (janvier–mars 2002): 52.

29. Quoted by Henri Barboux in "Projets de réforme de la juridiction militaire," p. 12.

30. Ibid., p. 7.

31. Bourelly, "De la réforme de la justice militaire en temps de paix," *Le Correspondant de Paris*, 10 mai 1899, 25 mai 1899.

32. Ibid., 25 mai 1899, pp. 765–72.

33. Ibid., 10 mai 1899, p. 574.

34. Ibid., 25 mai 1899, pp. 785–91.

35. Barboux, "Projets de réforme de la juridiction militaire," pp. 12–13.

36. Ibid., p. 14.

37. Ibid., p. 15.

38. Ibid., p. 9.

39. Ibid., pp. 17–19.

40. Ibid., p. 18.

41. Ibid.

42. See, e.g., Henri Pernot, *Des Conseils de guerre et des réformes dont ils seraient susceptibles* (Paris: A. Chevalier-Maresco et Cie, Éditeurs, 1901), pp. 220–22; and Nazair-Blanc, *La Justice militaire et maritime et des réformes*, p. 17. See also Roynette, "Les Conseils de guerre," p. 55.

5—"Can the Judge of Liberty Be the Judge of Obedience?"

1. Simon Robert, "La Suppression des conseils de guerre," *Revue Politique et Parlementaire* 155 (mai 1907): 262–63.

2. Lhermitte, *Le Sabre et la loi*, pp. 126–27.

3. Ibid., p. 130.

4. Ibid., p. 91.

5. Georges Clemenceau, preface to *Justice militaire* (Paris: P.-V. Stock, 1901), p. v.

6. See the retrospective analysis of the 1902 Massé proposal in the report on the proposed reform of military justice advanced by the government in 1907, prepared by the Commission on Judicial Reform and Civil Legislation *(Documents Parlementaires*, Chambre des Députés, 7 mai 1907, Sess. ord. ann. #920, p. 335).

7. See chapter 6 of Ralston, *Army of the Republic*, and chapters 5 and 6 of Douglas Porch's *The March to the Marne*. See also Kovacs's "French Military Legislation."

8. Quoted in Ralston, *Army of the Republic*, p. 183.

9. Ibid, pp. 266–68.

10. *Le Temps*, 19 janvier 1902; quoted in ibid., p. 268.

11. Bourelly, "L'Armée française au commencement de 1904," p. 425.

12. Ibid.

13. Ibid., note 2.

14. See William D. Irvine's discussion of the *affaire des fiches* in "The Politics of

Human Rights: A Dilemma for the League for the Defense of the Rights of Man," Historical Reflections/*Réflexions Historiques* 20, no. 1 (Winter 1994): 5–28. For a briefer discussion see his *Between Justice and Politics: The Ligue des droits de l'homme, 1898–1945* (Stanford, Calif.: Stanford University Press, 2007), pp. 30–31. See also the discussion in chapter 6 of Porch, *The March to the Marne*.

15. Quoted in Challener, *The French Theory of the Nation in Arms*, p. 63.

16. Porch, *The March to the Marne*, p. 86. Porch goes so far as to suggest that "Radicals looked to make service to the republic a purgatory, forcing officers to conform or resign."

17. Duclaux, *Propos d'un solitaire*, p. 19.

18. Lhermitte, *Le Code rouge*, pp. 19–30.

19. Rouanet, "Jugês militaires," *L'Humanité*, 4 février 1907, p. 1.

20. As Benjamin Martin puts it, by the court's reckoning "no one had been a traitor in 1894—not Dreyfus, not Esterhazy, not anyone else." Martin describes the 1906 ruling as a triumph of expediency over both fact and law, "as surely an example of *raison d'état* as the first conviction of Dreyfus had been." Martin, "The Dreyfus Affair and the Corruption of the French Legal System," in Norman Kleeblatt, ed., *The Dreyfus Affair: Art, Truth, and Justice* (Berkeley and Los Angeles: University of California Press, 1987), p. 47. On the other hand, Vincent Duclert insists that the *Cour de Cassation* acted within a defensible understanding of Article 445 of the Code of Criminal Investigation, which stipulated that no further judicial proceeding was necessitated if, with the quashing of a prior verdict, no further grounds remained on which to base suspicion of a criminal act by the individual whose case was at issue. Duclert, "La Cour de Cassation," in *L'Affaire Dreyfus de A à Z*, p. 369.

21. Geoffrey Brun, *Clemenceau* (Cambridge, Mass.: Harvard University Press, 1943), pp. 76, 80.

22. Robert, "La Suppression des conseils de guerre," p. 263.

23. Gustave Bouniols, *À Propos des conseils de guerre* (Paris: A. Pedone, 1907), cited in ibid., p. 262.

24. Bassieux, *La Justice militaire*, p. 17.

25. *Documents Parlementaires*, Chambre des Députés, 7 mai 1907, p. 334.

26. Ibid., 21 janvier 1907, p. 63.

27. Among the most thorough and thoughtful discussions of the 1907 legislation are two articles by Simon Robert, military correspondent for the *Revue Politique et Parlementaire*: "Revue des questions militaires," no. 153 (mars 1907): 625–35, and especially "La Suppression des conseils de guerre," pp. 262–78.

28. *Documents Parlementaires*, Chambre des Députés, 7 mai 1907, p. 403.

29. Rouanet, "Juges militaires," p. 1.

30. Robert, "La Suppression des conseils de guerre," pp. 271–73.

31. The degree to which Dreyfusards and other critics of military justice idolized Picquart is evident in Francis de Pressensé's *Un Héros: le colonel Picquart* (Paris: P.-V. Stock, 1899).

32. See the treatment of the "revolt of the 17th" in Miller's *From Revolutionaries to Citizens*, pp. 122–32.

33. Quoted by Letort in *La Réforme de la justice militaire*, pp. 54–55.

34. *L'Humanité* covered the debate on March 24, 31, April 2, May 15, 28, and June 4, 5, 9, 1909.

35. *L'Humanité*, 15 mai 1909, p. 2.

36. *Débats Parlementaires*, Sénat, 17 juin 1909, p. 450; 19 juin 1909, p. 543; 19 octobre 1909, p. 823.

37. See Simon Robert's discussion in his article "Revue des questions militaires," in *Revue Politique et Parlementaire* 181 (juillet 1909): 171–74. See also the discussion by Albéric Nazair-Blanc in *La Justice militaire et maritime et des réformes qui y ont été apportées durant ces dernières années*, pp. 159–63.

38. See Dominique Kalifa's "Magistrature et crise de répression à la veille de la grande guerre, 1911–1912," *Vingtième Siècle, Revue d'Histoire* 67 (juillet–septembre 2000): 43–59.

39. Lt. Paul Maire, *Discipline, criminalité, et justice militaire: Notes et aperçus historiques* (Paris: Henri Charles Lavauzelle, 1909), p. 90. Additional statistics on the subject are cited by Paul Chassagnade-Belmin in *Délits militaires et délits du droit commun commis à l'armée en temps de paix* (Paris: A. Pedone, 1910), pp. 241, 250. For a more modern discussion of the problem, see Roynette, "Les Conseils de guerre," p. 160.

40. Maire, *Discipline, criminalité, et justice militaire*, p. 6.

41. Ibid.

42. Bourelly, "L'Armée française au commencement de 1904," 10 février 1904, p. 407.

6—Djennan-ed-Dar, 1909

1. *New York Times*, June 1, 3, 9, 1903.

2. Dhur's reportage first appeared in *Le Journal* (7–8 mars 1907). Much of it was recapitulated in *La Guerre Sociale* under the title "L'Enfer militaire" (6–12 juillet 1910).

3. "Dans les bagnes d'Afrique: Djennan-ed-Dar," *La Bataille Syndicaliste*, 7 octobre 1912.

4. *Societé Historique de la Défense*, Vincennes (*SHD*) 12J 1247, supplément ("à insérer dans le dossier Sabatier et consorts sans l'indiquer sur la chemise"), pièce #78 (procès-verbal, capitaine Finot interrogé par capitaine Alix, 27 janvier 1911).

5. See, e.g., the biography of Aernoult by René de Marmande entitled "Histoire d'Aernoult, de Rousset et des bagnes militaires" in *La Guerre Sociale*, 30 mars 1910. See also the article "La Mort d'Aernoult" in *L'Humanité*, 11 juillet 1910.

6. *Archives Nationales* (*AN*), F/7/12909 (rapport, Commissaire de Police, Bordeaux, 11 février 1912).

7. The recruiter's identity is not clear. In subsequent descriptions of this episode he was sometimes identified as a councilor at the *Cour de Cassation* named Voisin; sometimes simply as a "civilian magistrate"; sometimes (as in Marmande's account, 1910) as "a decorated officer." Dominique Kalifa, in his treatment of the Aernoult-Rousset Affair, reports that Aernoult was simply conscripted after leaving prison, as the law required (*Biribi*, p. 40).

8. *SHD* 12J 1247, supplement, pièce #77 (capitaine Finot interrogé par capitaine Alix, 24 janvier 1911).

9. "La Mort d'Aernoult," *L'Humanité*, 11 juillet 1910.

10. *SHD* 12J 1247, supplément, pièce #77.

11. "L'Assassinat d'Aernoult: Rapport du général Rabier," *La Bataille Syndicaliste*, 27 septembre 1912.

12. *SHD* 12J 1247, supplément, pièce #77.

13. *AN* F/7/12909 (rapport, "Renseignements sur Émile Rousset et sur les membres de sa famille," Paris, 5 février 1912).

14. Émile Rousset, "Mes Mémoires," *La Bataille Syndicaliste*, 28 octobre 1912.

Rousset's memoirs were serialized in this journal from October 28 to December 7, 1912.

15. *SHD* 12J 1247, procès d'Oran, pièce #5 (Relevé des punitions). See also René de Marmande, *Émile Rousset et l'enquête du lieutenant Pan-Lacroix* (Paris: Librairie Schleicher Frères, 1912), pp. viii–x.

16. Marmande, *Émile Rousset*, p. 12.

17. *SHD* 12J 1247, procès d'Oran, pièce #25 (autopsie, [illegible], juillet 1909); pièce #27 (lettre à M. le Chef de bataillon Bonnelet, 29 août 1909).

18. "Comment Aernoult est mort," *L'Humanité*, 4 juillet 1910.

19. Rousset, "Mes Mémoires," *La Bataille Syndicaliste*, 3 novembre 1912.

20. Émile Rousset, *Du fond de l'abîme . . . Lettres d'Émile Rousset* (Paris: Au Bureau du "Temps Nouveaux," 1912), p. 6.

21. *SHD*, 12J 1247, procès d'Oran, pièce #39 (rapport sur l'affaire du soldat Rousset, Émile Étienne, par Rapporteur du 2 Conseil de Guerre d'Oran, 27 décembre 1909).

22. Rousset, "Mes Mémoires," *La Bataille Syndicaliste,* 3 novembre 1912.

23. *SHD*, 12J 1247, procès d'Oran, pièce #39.

24. Ibid.

25. Ibid., pièces #8 and #9.

26. Ibid., pièce #3.

27. Ibid., pièce #2.

28. Ibid., pièce #12 (procès-verbal de la première comparution de Rousset, 6 août 1909).

29. Ibid., pièce #12.

30. Ibid., pièce #19 (Émile Rousset, lettre au Commissaire du gouvernement).

31. Ibid., pièce #18 (lettre au Commissaire du gouvernement).

32. Ibid., pièce #13 (Bulletin de renseignements, 21 septembre 1909).

33. Ibid., pièces #15 (Beignier), #16 (Casanova), #17 (Sabatier).

34. Ibid., pièce #17 (Sabatier).

35. Ibid., pièce #39.

36. Ibid., pièces #7 (Finot, 20 juillet 1909), #34 (Finestre, 11 novembre 1909).

37. Ibid., pièce #20.

38. Ibid., pièces #40, #41.

39. Ibid., pièce #39.

40. Ibid., pièces #35, #37.

41. See, e.g., Rousset's memoirs in *La Bataille Syndicaliste* (5 novembre 1912); Camille Pelletan's concluding article on the Aernoult-Rousset Affair in *Le Matin,* 19 juillet 1912; and René de Marmande's article "À Oran" in *La Guerre Sociale,* 15 juin 1910.

42. Marmande, "À Oran."

43. *Bulletin Officiel de la Ligue des Droits de l'Homme,* no. 8, 30 avril 1910, p. 500.

44. *SHD* 12J 1247, procès d'Oran, pièce #24.

45. Ibid.

46. *SHD* 12J 1247, procès d'Oran, pièce #39.

47. Marmande, *Émile Rousset*, pp. 12–16.

48. Ibid., p. 16.

49. Marmande, "À Oran."

50. *SHD* 12J 1247, procès d'Oran, [unn.], "Bulletin de jugement du 2 Conseil de Guerre de la Division d'Oran, délibérant à huis clos."

51. *AN* F/7/13323 (préfecture de police, "L'Affaire Aernoult-Rousset," 9M/4991, Paris, 8 décembre 1910).

7—The Aernoult-Rousset Affair

1. Goldberg, *The Life of Jean Jaurès*, pp. 404–7.

2. See, e.g., Hervé's *My Country, Right or Wrong* (London: Jonathan Cape, 1910).

3. *AN* F/7/12909 (unidentified clipping, probably from *Bulletin* #7 of the Comité de la Défense Sociale, octobre 1912).

4. René de Marmande, "Mes Mémoires," *Les Temps Nouveaux* (n.d. [1912]).

5. Préfecture de la Police de Paris (PP), B/A 882 ("*CDS*," clippings from *Le Journal*, *Écho de Paris*, *Gil Blas*, janvier 1911).

6. *AN* F/7/13331 (rapport, M/4302, 26 mai 1910).

7. Jean-Jacques Becker, *Le Carnet B: Les Pouvoirs publics et l'antimilitarisme avant la guerre de 1914* (Paris: Klincksieck, 1973).

8. See *L'Humanité*, 29 novembre 1910, which reprints a letter Aernoult père sent to the interior minister at that time, in which these earlier exchanges were referenced.

9. *AN* F/7/13323 (préfecture de police, "L'Affaire Aernoult-Rousset," M/4991, Paris, 8 décembre 1910); and F/712908 (préfecture de police, M/1775/U, Paris, 23 mars 1910).

10. Ibid., 8 décembre 1910, 23 mars 1910.

11. Avner Ben-Amos, *Funerals, Politics, and Memory in Modern France, 1789–1996* (Oxford: Oxford University Press, 2000).

12. *Bulletin Officiel de la Ligue Française pour la Défense des Droits de l'Homme et du Citoyen*, no. 8, 30 avril 1910, pp. 501–3.

13. *La Guerre Sociale*, 1 juin 1910.

14. See Herpin, *De la réforme de la compétence et de la composition des conseils de guerre*, pp. 6–8. See also Francis de Pressensé, "'L'Affaire Rousset, l'Affaire Bach-Hamba,' discours de M. Francis de Pressensé au Congrès de la Ligue pour la Défense des Droits de l'Homme (Le Havre, 25 mai 1912)," in *Bulletin Officiel de la Ligue Française pour la Défense des Droits de l'Homme et du Citoyen*, no. 12, 30 juin 1912, p. 639.

15. *AN* F/7/12908 (préfecture de police, 5 mars 1910).

16. Quoted in Miller, *From Revolutionaries to Citizens*, p. 163.

17. Ibid., p. 68.

18. Venita Datta, *Birth of a National Icon: The Literary Avant-Garde and the Rise of the Intellectual in France* (Albany, N.Y.: SUNY Press, 1999), pp. 141–43.

19. Miller, *From Revolutionaries to Citizens*, pp. 76–78.

20. *AN* F/7/13331 (*rapport, réunion de CDS*, M/4302, Paris, 26 mai 1910).

21. Kalifa, *Biribi*, p. 45.

22. *AN* F/7/12908 (préfecture de police, 20 avril 1910).

23. Candace Faulk et al., eds., *Emma Goldman: A Documentary History of the American Years*, vol. 2: *Making Speech Free* (Berkeley and Los Angeles: University of California Press, 2003), p. 235.

24. *AN* F/7/12909 (Rapport du Commissaire Spécial, Marseille, au Ministère de l'Intérieur, 2 octobre 1912).

25. Émile Rousset, "Mes Mémoires," *La Bataille Syndicaliste* (6, 7, 8, 11 novembre 1912).

26. Marmande, *Émile Rousset*, p. 19.

27. Marmande, "Une visite au vaillant Rousset," *La Guerre Sociale*, 24 mai 1910.

28. Rousset, *Du fond de l'abîme*.

29. Marmande, *Émile Rousset*, p. 20.

30. *L'Humanité*, 18 janvier 1911.

31. *AN* F/7/12908 (préfecture de police de Paris, 4 juin 1910).

32. Ibid. (police report, unsigned, 10 décembre 1910).

33. Ibid. (telegram, 18 juin 1910, 11 heures, from Kurz in Beni-Ounif to Renaudel at office of *L'Humanité* in Paris).

34. Ibid. (police report, unsigned, 10 décembre 1910).

35. Ibid. (telegram, 18 juin 1910).

36. See, e.g., Eugène Péronnet's article "Le Jésuitisme de Briand," and A. Jobert's "Jésuites et fripouilles" in *La Bataille Syndicaliste*, 22, 28 février 1912, resp.

37. *AN* F/7/12908 (préfecture de police, Paris, 14, 15 juin 1910).

38. Ibid. (préfecture de police, M/1853/U, Paris, 16 juin 1910).

39. Ibid.

8—Triumph of the Political

1. The "Down with Biribi!" trial of July 4–5, 1910, was covered extensively in *L'Humanité* and *La Guerre Sociale*. *La Gazette des Tribunaux* also provided an overview of the proceedings, which were described in more detail by attorney Joseph Hild in his work *À Propos de Biribi, une affaire antimilitariste: Provocation à l'indiscipline et au meurtre* (Rodez: Imprimerie Forveille, 1913). Paris's major, general-readership journals provided only light reportage of the trial. The latter's official stenographic record has not been located.

2. "Biribi Condamné," *La Guerre Sociale*, 6–12 juillet 1910.

3. *AN*, F/7/12909 (Eugène Péronnet, *L'Affaire Rousset*, undated pamphlet, p. 2).

4. "Le Procès de Biribi," *La Guerre Sociale*, 6–12 juillet 1910.

5. Hild, *À Propos de Biribi, une affaire antimilitariste*, p. 8.

6. Portions of Dorange's report were finally published by *L'Humanité* on the first day of the trial: "Comment Aernoult est mort," 4 juillet 1910.

7. "Il faut libérer Rousset," *L'Humanité*, 6 juillet 1910.

8. Hild, *À Propos de Biribi, une affaire antimilitariste*, p. 35.

9. Ibid., p. 20.

10. Ibid., p. 9.

11. "Acquittés!" *La Guerre Sociale*, 6–12 juillet 1910.

12. *L'Humanité*, 17 mars 1911.

13. *AN* F/7/13331 (préfecture de police de *CDS*, M/4696, 1 décembre 1910).

14. *AN* F/7/13331 (rapport, M/4963, 1 décembre 1910); *AN* F/7/12908 (rapport, M/3267, 9 mars 1911).

15. *AN* F/712908 (rapport, M/4689, Paris, 26 septembre 1910).

16. Ibid. (rapports, 10 et 15 novembre 1915).

17. Ibid. (rapports, 28 septembre 1910, 2, 9, 10, 16 novembre 1910).

18. *L'Humanité* reprinted the letters, 24 juillet 1910.

19. See Bonzon's call to end the insularity of the military jurisdiction in *La Liberté d'Opinion* (septembre–octobre 1910).

20. "Ce que fut la première enquête?" *L'Humanité*, 29 septembre 1910.

21. "L'Affaire Rousset: Respect à la 'chose jugée'!" *L'Humanité*, 25 septembre 1910.

22. See, e.g., Captain Finot's angry protest, expressed later when he was deposed by Captain Alix as part of the investigation of Lieutenant Sabatier and Sergeants Beignier and Casanova. *SHD* 12J 1247, supplément, "à insérer dans le dossier Sabatier et consorts sans l'indiquer sur la chemise," pièce #77, 24 janvier 1911.

23. On November 29 *L'Humanité* published another letter from Aernoult's parents, this time to the interior minister, in which they reiterated the results of their various petitions for this purpose.

24. Significant portions of the Rabier report were published in *La Bataille Syndicaliste*, 27 septembre 1912 (see Appendix B).

25. *La Guerre Sociale*, 13–19 juillet, 10 août 1910.

26. *Bulletin Officiel de la Ligue Française pour la Défense des Droits de l'Homme et du Citoyen*, no. 6, 31 mars 1911, pp. 414–15.

27. The general's decision was reported in the *Journal Officiel* (*Documents Parlementaires*, 14 décembre 1910) as part of a response to a written request for information on the return of Aernoult's body that Deputy Veber had submitted to the war minister.

28. "Vers la justice! La grâce de Rousset," *L'Humanité*, 17 mars 1911.

29. Marmande, *Émile Rousset*, p. 23.

30. *SHD* 12J 1247, procès de Constantine, pièce #173, 30 août 1912.

31. *AN* F/7/12908 (rapport, préfecture du Rhône, 3 avril 1911).

32. Reprinted in Rousset, *Du fond de l'abîme*.

33. Émile Rousset, "Mes Mémoires," *La Bataille Syndicaliste*, 12 novembre 1912.

34. Rousset cited this circular in letters of complaint reprinted in *La Guerre Sociale* on May 10, 1911, and in *L'Humanité* on May 6, 1911. See also Marmande, *Émile Rousset*, p. 24.

35. That circular was dated 24 juillet 1908. *Code de Justice Militaire: Dispositions diverses, supplément arrêté à la date du 31 décembre 1912* (Paris: Henri-Charles Lauvauzelle, 1912), pp. 19–20.

36. Caille, *Des pouvoirs judiciaires du général commandant*, pp. 11–12.

37. "Prenez garde," *L'Humanité*, 6 mai 1911. War Minister Berteaux was assassinated by a Croatian nationalist during a state ceremony on May 21. François Goiran succeeded him briefly (May 27–June 27); then Adolphe Messimy held the position until January 14, 1912. It then passed to Alexandre Millerand, who held it until January 12, 1913.

38. "L'Affaire Aernoult," *L'Humanité*, 28 april 1911.

39. *L'Humanité*, 11 janvier 1911.

40. Notes and letters exchanged among the war minister, General Alix, the Solicitor-General, and the Justice Minister (*garde des sceaux*) can be found both in *AN* BB/18 (2460 786 A/11) and in *SHD* 12J 1247, supplément, "à insérer dans le dossier Sabatier et consorts sans l'indiquer sur la chemise."

41. General Alix's dispatch of the dossiers to the justice minister on May 24, 1911, is referenced in the minister's response dated June 29 (*SHD* 12J 1247, supplément, "à insérer dans le dossier Sabatier et consorts"). The general's opinion of Captain Alix is referenced in the Solicitor-General's letter to the *garde des sceaux* of 15 juin 1911 (*SHD* 12J 1247, supplément, "à insérer dans le dossier Sabatier et consorts").

42. The Solicitor-General added that "even if Article 24 . . . were applicable, it would entail the removal of the captain-reporter who knew the Rousset affair but hardly the *parquet* of Oran." Procurator-General à *Garde des Sceaux*, 15 juin 1911 (*SHD* 12J 1247,

supplément, "à insérer dans le dossier Sabatier et consorts").

43. Ibid. The Solicitor-General's position was also outlined in a handwritten note on stationery of the justice ministry (Division of Criminal Affairs and Pardons) of June 14, 1911 (*AN* BB/18 2460 786 A/11).

44. "Les Témoins devant le conseil de guerre: Odieuse machination contre Rousset," *L'Humanité*, 17 août 1911.

45. "Un Verdict scandaleux," *La Bataille Syndicaliste*, 18 août 1911.

9—The Rousset Murder Case

1. Bourelly, "L'Armée est-elle, doit-elle être la nation?" pp. 193–220.

2. *SHD* GR 7 N 9.

3. E.g., see coverage in *Le Journal* ("Plus d'apaches dans l'armée") 10 février 1910; and in *La Petite République* ("L'Épuration de l'armée"), 10 février 1912. See also the discussion of these and other attempts to "reform" the *compagnies de discipline* in Kalifa, *Biribi*, pp. 143–58.

4. Bassieux, *La Justice militaire*, p. 23.

5. *SHD* GR 7 N 11. On January 8, 1903, War Minister André wrote a lengthy letter to the commanding officer of the Nineteenth Corps of the Tunisian occupation force detailing the pros and cons of entirely replacing corporals with sergeants, "as much to maintain discipline better as to avoid frequent *conseil de guerre* cases."

6. Émile Rousset, "Mes Mémoires," *La Bataille Syndicaliste*, 24 novembre 1912.

7. *Code de Justice Militaire: Dispositions diverses, supplément arrêté à la date du 31 décembre 1912* (Paris, Henri Charles-Lavauzelle, 1912), p. 7.

8. Rousset, "Mes Mémoires," *La Bataille Syndicaliste*, 28 octobre 1912.

9. Despax's statement was one of sixteen independently collected by Pan-Lacroix and delivered to Captain Giacomoni, for eventual use in the investigation of *capitaine-rapporteur* Godiot of the Algiers *parquet* (see Appendix C). These were published, along with the rest of the dossier Captain Godiot had assembled, by *Les Temps Nouveaux* in a special edition of February 8, 1912 (see Appendix D).

10. *SHD* 12J 1247, procès d'Algers, pièce #61 (letter, octobre 7 1911), pièce #77 (procès-verbal, 18 octobre 1911).

11. Rousset recounted his own thoughts and actions at that time in the interviews Captain Godiot conducted with him on September 23 and October 7, 1911. *SHD* 12J 1247, procès d'Algiers, pièce #31.

12. "Le Rapport du Lieutenant Pan-Lacroix, Médéa [pièce #3, le 31 août 1911]" in "Le Dossier de l'Affaire Rousset," *Les Temps Nouveaux*, 8 février 1912.

13. Ibid.

14. Captain Giacomoni officially recorded the testimony of Deliat-Besson and Lelarge. See *SHD* 12J 1247, procès d'Algers, pièces #11, #12.

15. Pièces #4–#10 of the Algiers investigation are missing from *SHD* 12J 1247 but were published in a special issue of *Les Temps Nouveaux* dated 8 février 1912 (see Appendixes C and D). Those early interviews with Sauval, Bordessoulle, and Bintein appear there as pièces #8, #9, and #10. The interviews with Deliat-Besson, Lelarge, and Sappa remain in *SHD* 12J 1247, procès d'Algers, pièces #11, #12, and #13.

16. *SHD* 12J 1247, procès d'Algers, pièce #7.

17. Ibid., pièce #14.

18. "Une Lettre de Rousset," *L'Humanité,* 9 septembre 1911.

19. Pressensé, "L'Affaire Rousset, l'Affaire Bach-Hamba," p. 642.

20. "Au Conseil de Guerre d'Oran: L'Affaire Aernoult," *L'Humanité,* 8 septembre 1911.

21. Ibid. See also Rousset, "Mes Mémoires," *La Bataille Syndicaliste,* 21 et 22 novembre 1912.

22. "Trois acquittements scandaleux," *L'Humanité,* 13 septembre 1911.

23. *L'Humanité,* 11, 13 septembre 1911.

24. Ibid.

25. *L'Humanité,* 4 décembre 1911, 3 janvier 1912.

26. "Des Témoignages très accablants: Un Réquisitoire trop partial," *L'Humanité,* 12 septembre 1911.

27. Rousset, "Mes Mémoires," *La Bataille Syndicaliste,* 21 et 22 novembre 1912.

28. *L'Humanité,* 12 septembre 1911.

29. "Une lettre de Rousset," *L'Humanité,* 9 septembre 1911.

30. "Les Témoins devant le Conseil de guerre: Odieuse machination contre Rousset," *L'Humanité,* 9 septembre 1911.

31. *L'Humanité,* 11 septembre 1911.

32. *La Bataille Syndicaliste* reported these press accounts on October 12, 1911. They are also discussed in Eugène Péronnet's pamphlet *L'Affaire Rousset* (*AN* F/7/12909), and referenced in *L'Humanité*'s coverage of the Sabatier/Beignier/Casanova trial.

33. Pan-Lacroix personally took a deposition from Blé on September 16, 1911. Godiot's own September 23 interview with Blé is in *SHD* 12J 1247, procès d'Algers, pièce #38.

34. *SHD* 12J 1247, procès d'Algers, pièce #33.

35. Pierlot spoke to Pan-Lacroix on September 15. His interview with Godiot was held September 29–30 (*SHD* 12J 1247, procès d'Algers, pièce #34). He would render the same account in a personal confrontation with Rousset arranged by Captain Godiot during his October 7 interview with the latter (ibid., pièce #31).

36. Vigoroux spoke to Pan-Lacroix on September 16. His interview with Godiot is in *SHD* 12J 1247, procès d'Algers, pièce #114.

37. See, e.g., ibid., pièces #33 (Bordessoulle, 28 septembre), #45 (Bintein, 5 octobre), and #46 (Sauval, 26 septembre).

38. Two of the letters from Chabot to Rousset are in *SHD* 12J 1247, procès d'Algers (pièces #58, #65). They are only partially legible but do seem to confirm that Chabot and Rousset were close and that Chabot was aggrieved by an accusation Sauval had leveled at him.

39. Ibid., pièce #40, 30 septembre 1911.

40. Ibid., pièce #23, 16 septembre.

41. On September 22 Godiot took depositions from orderlies Feignon, Janicot, and Zerapha (ibid., procès d'Algers, pièces #27, #28, #29).

42. Ibid., pièce #32.

43. "Une Lettre de Rousset," *L'Humanité,* 9 septembre 1911.

44. *SHD* 12J 12347, procès d'Algers, pièce #31, 23 septembre 1911.

45. Ibid., pièce #31, 14 octobre 1911.

46. Ibid., pièce #31, 21 octobre 1911.

47. Ibid., pièce #44, pièce #85.

48. Ibid., pièce #68, 9 octobre 1911.

49. During the Algiers investigation, Godiot would arrange confrontations between

Rousset and Pierlot on October 7; between Rousset and Bordessoulle on October 14; and between Rousset and Bintein on November 16 (all included in pièce #31).

50. *SHD* 12J 1247, procès d'Algers, pièce #31, 26 novembre 1911.

51. Ibid., pièce #102, 6 novembre 1911.

10—Breaking Codes

1. *SHD* 12J 1247, procès d'Algers, pièce #116.

2. Delaisi, *Contre la loi Millerand*, p. 7.

3. See, e.g., the consideration of the Rousset murder case offered by Georges Montorgueil in the conservative journal *L'Éclair*, 2 février 1912.

4. See Pierre Renaudel's introduction to the stenographic record of Rousset's December 1911 trial, published by *L'Humanité* on 10 février 1912.

5. *AN*, F/7/12908 (préfecture de police, 13 décembre 1911).

6. *AN* F/7/12908 (rapport, M/1494, 15 décembre 1911).

7. *L'Humanité*, 20 septembre 1911.

8. *AN* F/7/12909 (préfecture de police, 3 octobre 1912).

9. Ibid.

10. *Les Temps Nouveaux*, 24 août 1912, pp. 2–3.

11. Ibid., p. 3.

12. Ibid., pp. 7–9.

13. Marmande, *Émile Rousset*, p. 20.

14. Ibid., p. 31.

15. Ibid., pp. 34–36.

16. Rousset, "Mes Mémoires," *La Bataille Syndicaliste*, 18 novembre 1912.

17. Marmande, *Émile Rousset*, p. 44.

18. Marmande, "Ma Réponse." This lengthy article provides Marmande's own perspective on the entire Aernoult-Rousset Affair and his involvement in it. It was submitted in response to what he felt were misrepresentations emanating from the *CDS* and other radical organizations. He followed "Ma Réponse" with another self-exculpatory piece in the same journal entitled "Rapport du Secrétaire du Comité de l'Affaire Rousset" (16 décembre 1912). Both are preserved in *AN* F/7/12909.

19. "La Sténographie du procès Rousset," *L'Humanité*, 10 février 1912.

20. See Eugène Péronnet's *L'Affaire Rousset* (*CDS*).

21. "La Sténographie du Procès Rousset."

22. Ibid.

23. Péronnet, *L'Affaire Rousset* (*CDS*), p. 14.

24. "La Sténographie du procès Rousset."

25. Letter dated 28 décembre 1911; reprinted in Rousset, *Du fond de l'abîme*, p. 19.

26. *AN* F/7/12908 (préfecture de police, Paris, 12 décembre 1911).

27. *AN* F/7/12331 (rapport, M/3075/U, Paris, 20 décembre 1911).

28. *AN* F/7/12908 (rapport, M/1494, Paris, 14 décembre 1911).

29. *AN* F/7/13331 (rapports, M/3075/U et M/34074/U, Paris, 20 décembre 1911).

30. Ibid. (extrait d'un rapport de la préfecture de police, Paris, 20 décembre 1911).

31. "Pour les obsèques d'Aernoult," *L'Humanité*, 6 février 1912.

32. See the first two chapters in William D. Irvine's *Between Justice and Politics: The*

Ligue des Droits de l'Homme, 1898–1945 (Stanford, Calif.: Stanford University Press, 2007).

33. *Les Temps Nouveaux* published an extended time line of the entire Aernoult-Rousset Affair on August 24, 1912, noting both the League's January 7 letter to the High Court of Appeal and the formation of the new Rousset Committee on February 5.

34. *L'Humanité*, 9 janvier, 8 février 1912.

35. Marmande, "Ma Réponse."

36. *Archives de la Préfecture de Police* (*PP*), Paris, B/A 882 (rapport, 11 septembre 1911).

37. Marmande, "Ma Réponse."

38. Ibid.

39. *AN* F/7/12909 (rapport, Bordeaux, 12 janvier 1912).

40. *PP*, Paris, B/A/882, Paris, 18 janvier 1912.

41. "L'Affaire Rousset," *La Libertaire*, 27 janvier 1912.

42. Marmande, "Ma Réponse," and "Rapport du secrétaire du Comité de l'Affaire Rousset."

43. Letter from Pressensé to War Minister Brun, Oct. 9, 1910; reprinted in *Bulletin Officiel de la Ligue Française pour la Défense des Droits de l'Homme et du Citoyen*, no. 6, 31 mars 1911, pp. 414–15.

44. In the winter of 1913 the *CDS* would release a long statement of grievances it felt it had endured as an organization throughout the Aernoult-Rousset Affair. The statement, which may have first appeared in the committee's own *Bulletin* (probably #7), can be found in *AN* F/7/12909.

45. See Grave's brief postscript to Marmande's "Mes Réponses."

46. *PP*, Paris, B/A 927 (rapport, 8 décembre 1911).

47. Ibid. (rapport, 9 novembre 1911).

48. *AN* F/7/12908 (rapport, M/6449, 9 février 1912).

49. *PP*, Paris, B/A/927 (rapport, 17 janvier 1912).

11—"Glory to Rousset"

1. *AN* F/7/12909 (rapports, 8–11 février 1912).

2. *AN* F/7/12908 (rapport, 12 février 1912). See also *La Bataille Syndicaliste*, 12 février 1912.

3. *L'Humanité*, 12 et 13 février 1912.

4. *AN* F/7/12908 (rapport supplémentaire, Préfet de Police, 11 février 1912).

5. See, e.g., *Le Journal* and *Le Petit Parisien*, both 12 février 1912.

6. *Le Temps*, 12 février 1912.

7. See, e.g., *La Bataille Syndicaliste*, 12 février 1912.

8. Porch, *The March to the Marne*, p. 171.

9. Ibid., p. 173. See also Ralston, *Army of the Republic*, p. 339.

10. "Les Lois scélérates dans l'armée," *L'Humanité*, 31 mai 1912.

11. *SHD* 12J 1247, procès d'Algers, pièce #3, 22 février 1912.

12. *AN* F/7/1290 (rapport, 1 mars 1912).

13. "Un Nouveau Crime se prépare," *L'Humanité*, 28 février 1912. See also Marmande's conclusion to *Émile Rousset*.

14. *L'Humanité*, 22 février 1912.

15. *La Guerre Sociale,* 11 février 1912.
16. *AN* F/7/12909.
17. Ibid. (rapport, 5 mars 1912).
18. *SHD* 12J 1247, procès de Constantine, pièce #26.
19. Ibid., pièce #24, 3 avril 1912.
20. Ibid., pièce #114.
21. Ibid., pièces #50, #50 ter.
22. "Quels sont les motifs de la réforme de Sauval?" *L'Humanité,* 14 février 1912.
23. *SHD* 12J 1247, procès de Constantine, pièce #7.
24. Ibid., pièce #114.
25. Ibid., procès d'Algers, pièce #31.
26. Ibid., procès de Constantine pièce #113.
27. Ibid., pièce #79.
28. Ibid., pièce #95.
29. Ibid., pièce #114.
30. *Les Temps Nouveaux,* 24 août 1912 (time line).
31. These requests are referenced in the war minister's subsequent correspondence with the ministers of justice and the interior, portions of which can be found, along with some of the Solicitor-General's commentary, at *AN* BB 18 2460 786/A/11.
32. *AN* BB 18 2460 786/A/11 (lettre, 13 juin 1912).
33. Ibid. (lettre, 12 juin 1912).
34. Ibid. (lettre, 24 juin, 1912).
35. *AN* F/7/12909 (rapport de commissariat spécial de la gare de Saint-Étienne, 1 juin 1912).
36. *AN* BB 18 2460 786/A/11 (lettres, 6, 13 juin 1912).
37. Ibid. (lettre, 12 juin 1912).
38. *Les Temps Nouveaux,* 24 août 1912 (time line).
39. *SHD* 12J 1247, procès de Constantine, pièce #125 [bis #1, #2].
40. Ibid., procès d'Algers, pièce #55.
41. Ibid., procès de Constantine, pièce #125 [bis #5].
42. Ibid., pièce #125 [bis #3]
43. Ibid., pièce #125 [bis #4].
44. Ibid., pièce #1225 [bis #11-#14].
45. Ibid., pièce #125 [bis #14].
46. Ibid., pièce #125 [bis #13].
47. Ibid., pièce #3.
48. Ibid., pièce #125 [bis #12].
49. Ibid., pièce #127.
50. Ibid., pièce #131.
51. Ibid., pièce #129, #130.
52. Ibid., pièce #180.

12—Marmande Agonistes

1. *AN* F/7/12908 (rapport, "L'Affaire Aernoult-Rousset à la Chambre," 16 mars 1911).
2. Marmande, *Émile Rousset*; Rousset, *Du fond de l'abîme*; Péronnet, *L'Affaire Rousset.*

See also *AN* F/7/12909 (rapport, préfecture de police, 3 octobre 1912).

3. Delaisi, *Contre la loi Millerand,* p. 3.

4. *AN* F/7/12909 (Marmande, "Ma Réponse").

5. Ibid.

6. In "Ma Réponse" Marmande referred to charges he said the *CDS* aired in its *Bulletin* #7. An untitled, undated document setting forth the *CDS*'s general perspective of the entire Aernoult-Rousset Affair, including its dealings with Marmande, exists in *AN* F/7/12909. It bears all the hallmarks of that *Bulletin* and will henceforth be referenced as such. Like Marmande's own "Ma Réponse" in *Les Temps Nouveaux,* it would have appeared in November or December 1912. See also *AN* F/7/12909 (rapport, préfecture de police, Paris, 2 octobre 1912).

7. René de Marmande, "Rapport du Secrétaire du Comité de l'Affaire Rousset," *Les Temps Nouveaux,* 16 décembre 1912.

8. *AN* F/712909 (*CDS, Bulletin* #7; rapport, préfecture de police, Paris, 2 octobre 1912).

9. *AN* F/7/12909 (rapport, commissaire spécial près de la préfecture de police, Marseilles, 30 septembre 1912).

10. *AN* F/7/12909 (rapport, commissaire spécial, Marseilles, 1 et 2 octobre, 1912).

11. *AN* F/7/12909 (rapport, commissaire spécial, Marseilles, 2 octobre 1912; rapport, préfecture de police, Paris, 2 octobre 1912).

12. *AN* F/7/12909 (rapport, commissaire spécial, Marseilles, 2 octobre 1912).

13. *La Bataille Syndicaliste,* 1 octobre 1912.

14. Ibid.

15. *AN* F/7/12909 (rapport, préfecture de police, Paris, 28 septembre 1912).

16. Marmande, "Ma Réponse."

17. *AN* F/7/12909 (*CDS, Bulletin* #7).

18. Marmande, "Ma Réponse."

19. Ibid.

20. See reportage in *La Guerre Sociale* (9 octobre 1912) and *L'Humanité* (15 octobre 1912). Both journals would claim that the *CDS* had refused to advertise the demonstration in their pages in a self-defeating attempt to minimize participation by their respective readerships. Coverage in *La Bataille Syndicaliste,* on the other hand, was considerably more positive.

21. *AN* F/7/12909 (rapport, Préfet du Rhône à M. le Ministre de l'Intérieur, 5 octobre 1912).

22. *AN* F/7/12909 (rapport, 3 octobre 1912).

23. Ibid.

24. *AN* F/7/12909 (rapport, préfecture de police, Paris, 3 octobre 1912).

25. *AN* F/7/12909 (rapport, préfecture de police, Paris, 27 octobre 1912).

26. Marmande would offer that accounting in a November 12 note he sent Rousset, in response to Rousset's own November 10 note demanding payment. He quoted both notes in "Ma Réponse."

27. Marmande, "Ma Réponse."

28. *AN* F/7/12909 (rapport, préfecture de police, 24 octobre 1912).

29. Ibid.

30. *AN* F/7/12909 (rapports, préfecture de police, Paris, 2 et 24 octobre 1912).

31. Ibid., 24 octobre 1912.

32. Marmande, "Ma Réponse."

33. Along with his lengthy "Ma Réponse" and his "Rapport du secrétaire du Comité de l'Affaire Rousset" (16 décembre 1912), Marmande published in *Les Temps Nouveaux* an article entitled "Souvenirs sans remords" and another, untitled but also dated 16 décembre 1912.

34. Marmande, "Ma Réponse."

35. Ibid.

36. Ibid.

37. Ibid.

38. Ibid.

39. Marmande, "Ma Réponse" and "Rapport du secrétaire du Comité de l'Affaire Rousset."

40. *AN* F/7/12909 (rapport, préfecture de police, Paris, 28 juillet 1912).

41. *AN* F/7/12909 (*CDS, Bulletin* #7). According to the *CDS*'s account, attorney Toretta had given Merle a copy of the dossier to be delivered to the committee. But Merle had not delivered it when expected, and from him it had passed through various hands until Berthon finally handed it to Marmande. Berthon had been severely chastised by the *CDS* for this breach of faith and subsequently participated actively in the *CDS*'s effort to separate Rousset from Marmande.

42. *AN* F/7/12909 (*CDS, Bulletin #7).*

43. Eugen Weber, *The Nationalist Revival in France, 1905–1914* (Berkeley and Los Angeles: University of California Press, 1968).

44. Miller, *From Revolutionaries to Citizens*, p. 181.

45. Ibid., pp. 190–94.

46. *AN* F/7/12909 *(CDS, Bulletin* #7*)*. Indeed, the *CDS*'s preferred organ, *La Bataille Syndicaliste*, had been founded in 1911 in part to counter Hervé's turn rightward (Miller, *From Revolutionaries to Citizens*, p. 192).

Afterword

1. See chapter 3 in Peter Judson Richards's *Extraordinary Justice: Military Tribunals in Historical and International Context* (New York: New York University Press, 2007), entitled "France and the *Conseils de Guerre* of the First World War." Odile Roynette also addresses the subject at the conclusion of his article"Les Conseils de guerre en temps de paix entre réforme et suppressions, 1898–1928." Roynette, in turn, draws on the work of Nicolas Offenstadt, *Les Fusillés de la Grande Guerre et la mémoire collective, 1914–1999* (Paris: Éditions Odile Jacob, 1999); and Vincent Suard, "La Justice militaire française et la peine de mort au début de la première guerre mondiale," *Revue d'Histoire Moderne et Contemporaine* 41, no. 1 (janvier–mars 1994).

2. Richards, *Extraordinary Justices*, p. 71.

3. Ibid., pp. 76–77.

4. Ibid., pp. 82–83.

5. e.e. cummings, *The Enormous Room* (New York: The Modern Library, 1922).

6. Archives de la Préfecture de Police, Paris, B/A 927.

7. Ibid., rapport, 28 septembre 1913.

8. Ibid., rapport, 4 décembre 1913.

9. Ibid., rapport, 29 avril 1924.
10. Ibid., rapport, août 1933.
11. Ibid., rapport, 13 octobre 1920.
12. Ibid., rapports, 13 octobre 1920, août 1933.
13. Ibid., rapport, 7 octobre 1920.
14. Ibid., rapport, 3 octobre 1928.

Bibliography

Primary Sources

Archival Materials

Archives Nationales—Paris

F/7/12908, 12909, 13331: press clippings, police reports, miscellaneous materials on all aspects of the Aernoult-Rousset Affair

F/7/13330: on the Berry-Millerand Law

BB 18/2460/786—A 11 Ministère de la Justice: notes, letters regarding the prosecution of Aernoult's alleged killers; notes, letters regarding the Rousset murder investigation

Préfecture de Police de Paris—Paris

B/A 882: Committee for Social Defense

B/A 927: newspaper clippings related to Aernoult-Rousset Affair, police-agent reports on the Aernoult funeral demonstration, Committee for Social Defense, Rousset biography, etc.

Service Historique de la Défense—Vincennes

Côté 12J 1247 Dossier Judiciaire d'Émile Rousset: includes full records of Rousset's cases before the Oran, Algiers, and Constantine tribunals; plus ancillary material on the investigation into Aernoult's death and the trial of his alleged killers.

Côté GR 7 N 9 (N10, N11) Notes Ministérielles: include dispatches by war ministers Freycinet, Picquart, and André on the *Bataillons d'Infanterie Légère d'Afrique* and the *compagnies de discipline.*

Period Journals

La Bataille Syndicaliste

Débats Parlementaires (Sénate)

Documents Parlementaires (Chambre des Députés)

L'Écho de Paris

La Guerre Sociale

L'Humanité

Le Journal

La Petite République

Revue Politique et Parlementaire

Les Temps Nouveaux

Books and Journal Articles

Alix, Lieutentant F. M. *Le Vol militaire et sa répression.* Nancy: Imprimerie Berger-Levrault, 1906.

Ambrosini, A. J. *Petit Dictionnaire de jurisprudence criminelle militaire: Contenant toutes les décisions des Conseils de révision de Paris et d'Alger.* Paris: Librairie Militaire de L. Baudoin, 1893.

Augier, Joseph, and Gustave le Poittevin. *Traité des recours en révision contre les jugements des conseils de guerre en temp de guerre.* Paris: L. Tenin, 1915–1916.

———. *Traité théorique et pratique de droit pénal et de procédure criminelle militaire.* Paris: Librairie de la Société du Recueil Sirey, 1918.

Barboux, Henri. "Projets de réforme de la juridiction militaire." *Revue Politique et Parlementaire,* octobre 1899.

Bassieux, François. *La Justice militaire.* Caen: Chez M. Brunet, 1907.

Bidault, Colonel Frédéric-Léopold. *L'Armée française et le service de deux ans.* Paris: Charles-Lavauzelle, Éditeur Militaire, 1898.

Bouniols, Gustave. *À propos des conseils de guerre.* Paris: A. S. Pedone, Éditeur, 1907.

Bourelly, Général Jules. "L'Armée est-elle, doit-elle être la nation?" *Le Correspondant de Paris,* 25 avril 1902.

———. "L'Armée française au commencement du 1904 (L'oeuvre du Général André)." *Le Correspondant de Paris,* 10, 25 février 1904.

———. "De la réforme de la justice militaire en temps de paix." *Le Correspondant de Paris,* 10, 25 mai, 5 octobre 1899.

Caille, Commandant. *Des pouvoirs judiciaires du Général commandant le Corps de l'Armée.* Paris: Jouve et Cie, Éditeurs, 1921.

Chassagnade-Belmin, Paul. *Délits militaires et délits du droit commun commis à l'armée en temps de paix.* Paris: A. Pedone, Éditeur, 1910.

Clemenceau, Georges. *Justice militaire.* Paris: P.-V. Stock, 1901.

Code de Justice Militaire: Dispositions diverses, supplément Arrêté à la date du 31 décembre 1912 (Bulletin officiel du Ministère de la Guerre, no. 56 bis). Paris: Henri Charles-Lavauzelle, Éditeur Militaire, 1912.

Darien, Georges. *Biribi.* 1890. Rpt. Paris: Jérôme Martineau Éditeur, 1966.

Delaisi, Francis. *Contre le loi Millerand.* Publication des "*Temps Nouveaux.*" Paris: La Productive, septembre 1912.

Desbons, Georges. *L'Agonie de la justice militaire.* Paris: Librairie des Sciences Politiques et Sociales, 1913.

Dubois-Desaulle, Gaston. *Camisards, Peaux de lapins et Cocos: Corps disciplinaires de l'armée française.* Paris: Éditions de *La Revue Blanche*, 1901.

Duclaux, Émile. *Propos d'un solitaire II. Les Conseils de guerre.* Paris: Au Siège de la Ligue Française pour la Défense des Droits de l'Homme, 1899.

Dufay, Xavier. *Les Garanties accordées à la défense devant les tribunaux militaires.* Besançon: Imprimerie Cariage, 1913.

Duguit, Léon. "The Law and the State." *Harvard Law Review* 31 no. 1 (November 1917).

———. "Theory of Objective Law Anterior to the State." In *Modern French Legal Philosophy,* ed. A. Fouillée et al., trans. Franklin Scott and Joseph P. Chamberlain. New York: Macmillan, 1921.

Fontaine, Waldemar. *De l'application du droit commun en matière de délits commis par les militaires de l'armée de terre*. Université de Lille, Faculté de Droit, 1909.

Foucher, Victor. *Commentaire sur le Code de justice militaire pour l'armée de terre, promulguée le 4 août 1857*. Paris: J. Dumaine, 1873.

Herpin, L. *De la réforme de la compétence et de la composition des conseils de guerre: Discours prononcé à la séance solennelle de réouverture de la conférence des avocats stagiaires barreau de Poitiers*. Poitiers: Imprimerie Blais et Roy, 1909.

Hervé, Gustave. *My Country, Right or Wrong*. London: Jonathan Cape, 1910.

Hild, Joseph. *À propos de Biribi, une affaire antimilitariste: Provocation à l'indiscipline et au meurtre*. Rodez: Imprimerie Forveille, 1913.

Jaurès, Jean. *L'Armée nouvelle* (préface de Jean-Noël Jeanneney). Paris: Imprimerie Nationale Éditions, 1992.

Larnaude, F. "Notre Programme." *Revue de Droit Public et de la Science Politique en France et à l'Étranger* 1 (1884).

Le Faure, Amédée, and Paul-Louis Ernst Pradier-Fodéré. *Commentaire sur le Code de Justice Militaire, précédée d'une introduction historique*. Paris: J. Dumaine, 1873.

Lhermitte, Georges. *Le Sabre et la loi*. Paris: P.-V. Stock, 1900.

———. *Le Code rouge: À bas la justice militaire!* Paris: Librairie de "la Raison," 1904.

Maire, Lt. Paul. *Discipline, criminalité et justice militaire: Notes et aperçus historiques*. Paris: Henri Charles-Lavauzelle, Éditeur Militaire, 1909.

Marmande, René de. *Émile Rousset et l'enquête du lieutenant Pan-Lacroix: Étude d'après la correspondance d'Émile Rousset*. Paris: Librairie Schleicher Frères, 1912.

Moisand, Gaetan. *Faut-il supprimer les conseils de guerre?* Paris: A. Pedone, 1908.

Nazair-Blanc, Albéric. *La Justice militaire et maritime et des réformes qui y ont été apportées durant les dernières années*. Toulouse: Librairie des Étudiants, 1913.

Pedoya, Général. *La Réforme des conseils de guerre*. Paris: Charles-Lavauzelle, Éditeur Militaire, 1906.

Pernot, Henri. *Des Conseils de guerre et des réformes dont ils seraient susceptibles*. Paris: A. Chevalier-Maresco et Cie, Éditeurs, 1901.

Péronnet, Eugène. *L'Affaire Rousset*. La Comité de Défense Sociale, 1912.

Pressensé, Francis de. "L'Affaire Aernoult-Rousset, l'Affaire Bach-Hamba." *Bulletin Officiel de la Ligue Française pour la Défense des Droits de l'Homme et du Citoyen*, no. 2, 30 juin 1912.

———. *Un héros: Le colonel Picquart*. Paris: P.-V. Stock,1899.

———. *Le Parti socialiste et la loi des tres ans: Discours prononcé par le citoyen Francis de Pressensé au Congrès du Parti Socialiste à Brest le 24 mars 1913*. Paris, 1913.

Rabier, Général. "Rapport." *La Bataille Syndicaliste*, 27 septembre 1912.

Ricolfi, Humbert. *La Code de justice militaire du 9 mars 1928. Historique, discussion devant le Parlement, principes de la réforme, commentaires, texte de la loi*. Paris: Charles-Lavauzelle, Éditeur Militaire, 1928.

Robert, Simon. "Revue des questions militaires." *Revue Politique et Parlementaire*, mars 1907.

———. "Revue des questions militaires." *Revue Politique et Parlementaire*, juillet 1909.

———. "La Suppression des conseils de guerre." *Revue Politique et Parlementaire*, avril 1907.

Rousset, Émile. *Du fond de l'abîme . . . Lettres d'Émile Rousset*. Paris: Au Bureau du *Temps Nouveaux*, 1912.

———. "Mes Mémoires." *La Bataille Syndicaliste* du 28 octobre au 7 décembre 1912.

Tripier, Louis. *Code de justice militaire pour l'armée de terre, expliqué par l'exposé des motifs, le rapport, et la discussion au Corps legislative; 2nd éd. augmentée d'un supplément et mise en rapport avec la législation actuelle par A. Champoudry*. Paris: Mme. Mayer-Odin, L. Larose, 1857–1879.

Vallier, Charles. *Les Conseils de guerre et la justice militaire*. Paris: Éditions de *La Revue Blanche*, 1902.

Secondary Sources

Ansell, Christopher. *Schism and Solidarity in Social Movements: The Politics of Labor in the French Third Republic*. Cambridge: Cambridge University Press, 2001.

Bates, David. "Political Unity and the Spirit of Law: Juridical Concepts of the State in the Late Third Republic." *French Historical Studies* 28, no. 1 (Winter 2005).

Battifol, Henri. "Problèmes et frontières: Droit et politique." *Archives de Philosophie du Droit* 16, special issue: "Le Droit investi par la politique" (1971).

Becker, Jean-Jacques. *Le Carnet B: Les Pouvoirs publics et l'antimilitarisme avant la guerre de 1914*. Paris: Klincksieck, 1973.

Bederida, François. "L'Armée et la République." *Revue Historique*, septembre 1964.

Begley, Louis. *Why the Dreyfus Affair Matters*. New Haven, Conn.: Yale University Press, 2009.

Ben-Amos, Avner. *Funerals, Politics, and Memory in Modern France, 1789–1996*. Oxford: Oxford University Press, 2000.

Bredin, Jean-Denis. *The Affair: The Case of Alfred Dreyfus*. New York: George Braziller, 1986.

Brissaud, Jean. *A History of French Public Law*. Translated by James W. Garner. Boston: Little, Brown, 1915.

Brun, Geoffre. *Clemenceau*. Cambridge, Mass.: Harvard University Press, 1943.

Challener, Richard D. *The French Theory of the Nation in Arms, 1866–1939*. New York: Russell and Russell, 1965.

Clayton, Anthony. *France, Soldiers, and Africa*. London: Brassey's Defence Publishers, 1988.

Datta, Venita. *Birth of a National Icon: The Literary Avant-Garde and the Rise of the Intellectual in France*. Albany: SUNY Press, 1999.

Doty, C. Stewart. *From Cultural Rebellion to Counterrevolution: The Politics of Maurice Barrès*. Athens: Ohio University Press, 1976.

Duclert, Vincent. "La Cour de cassation." In *L'Affaire Dreyfus de A à Z*, ed. Michel Drouin. Paris. Flammarion, 1994.

Faulk, Candace, et al. *Emma Goldman: A Documentary History of the American Years*. Vol. 2: *Making Speech Free*. Berkeley and Los Angeles: University of California Press, 2003.

Forth, Christopher. *The Dreyfus Affair and the Crisis of French Manhood*. Baltimore: Johns Hopkins University Press, 2004.

Gaynor, Lt. Col. James J. "The French Code of Military Justice." *George Washington Law Review* 33, no. 3 (January 1954).

Girardet, Raoul. *La Société militaire dans la France contemporaine, 1815–1939*. Paris: Librairie Plon, 1953.

Goldberg, Harvey. *The Life of Jean Jaurès*. Madison: University of Wisconsin Press, 1962.

Gorce, Paul-Marie de la. *La France et son armée*. Paris: Fayard, 1963.

Guiral, Pierre. "Georges Clemenceau." In *L'Affaire Dreyfus de A à Z*, ed. Michel Drouin. Paris: Flammarion, 1994.

Haines, Charles Grove. *The Revival of Natural Law Concepts*. New York: Russell and Russell, 1965.

Hammond, Charles H., Jr. "The French Revolution and the Enlightening of Military Justice." *Proceedings of the Western Society for French History* 34 (2006).

Harsin, Jill. *Barricades: The War of the Streets in Revolutionary Paris, 1830–1848*. New York: Palgrave Macmillan, 2002.

Horne, Alistair. *The French Army and Politics, 1870–1970*. New York: Harper and Row, 1984.

Hugueney, Pierre. *Traité théorique et pratique de droit pénal et de procédure pénale militaire*. Paris: Librairie du Recueil Sirey, 1933.

Huntington, Samuel. *The Soldier and the State: The Theory and Politics of Civil-Military Relations*. Cambridge, Mass.: Harvard University Press, Belknap Press, 1957.

Irvine, William D. *Between Justice and Politics: The Ligue des Droits de l'Homme, 1898–1945*. Stanford, Calif.: Stanford University Press, 2007.

———. *The Boulanger Affair Reconsidered: Royalism, Boulangism, and the Origins of the Radical Right in France*. New York: Oxford University Press, 1989.

Jennings, Jeremy. *Syndicalism in France: A Study in Ideas*. London: Macmillan, 1990.

Jèze, Gaston. "La Contrôle juridictionnel des lois." *Revue du Droit Public et de la Science Politique en France et à l'Étranger* 40 (1924).

Kalifa, Dominique. *Biribi: Les Bagnes coloniaux de l'armée française*. Paris: Perrin Press, 2009.

———. "Magistrature et crise de la répression à la veille de la grande guerre (1911–1912)." *Vingtième Siècle, Revue d'Histoire* 67 (juillet–septembre 2000).

Kleeblatt, Norman, ed. *Crime and Criminal Justice under the Third Republic: The Shame Marianne*. Baton Rouge: Louisiana State University Press, 1990.

Kovacs, Arpad F. "French Military Legislation in the Third Republic, 1871–1940." *Military Affairs* 13, no. 1 (Spring 1949).

LeTort, Marc. *La Réforme de la justice militaire*. Alger: E. Pfister, 1928.

Lundy, Jean Eriuc. "Le Traitement pénal dans l'armée française sous la 3ème république." Université René Descartes, Mémoire pour l'obtention du Certificat de l'Université de Criminologie appliquée à l'expertise mentale, 1987.

Manuel, Frank. *The Prophets of Paris*. Cambridge, Mass.: Harvard University Press, 1962.

Martin, Benjamin. "The Dreyfus Affair and the Corruption of the French Legal System." In *The Dreyfus Affair: Art, Truth, and Justice*, ed. Norman Kleeblatt. Berkeley and Los Angeles: University of California Press, 1987.

Miller, Paul. "De la révolution à la citoyenneté: La Gauche antimilitariste dans l'Affaire Aernoult-Rousset." Colloque Adiamos-89, "Plutôt l'insurrection que la guerre!" L'Antimilitarisme dans l'Yonne avant, 1914.

———. *From Revolutionaries to Citizens: Antimilitarism in France, 1870–1914*. Durham, N.C.: Duke University Press, 2002.

Moss, Bernard. *The Origins of the French Labor Movement, 1830–1914*. Berkeley and Los Angeles: University of California Press, 1976.

Nord, Philip. *The Republican Moment: Struggles for Democracy in Nineteenth-Century France*. Cambridge, Mass.: Harvard University Press, 1995.

Porch, Douglas. *The March to the Marne: The French Army, 1871–1914*. London: Cambridge University Press, 1981.

Propes, Charlotte. "'Patriotism Is Found in Us': Antimilitarist Arguments in Pre–World War I France." Ph.D. diss., University of Mississippi, 2003.

Ralston, David. *The Army of the Republic: The Place of the Military in the Political Evolution of France, 1871–1914.* Cambridge, Mass.: MIT Press,1967.

René, David. *French Law: Its Structure, Sources, and Methodology.* Baton Rouge: Louisiana State University Press, 1972.

Richards, Peter Judson. *Extraordinary Justice: Military Tribunals in Historical and International Context.* New York: New York University Press, 2007.

Roynette, Odile. "Les Conseils de guerre en temps de paix entre réforme et suppression, 1898–1928." *Vingtième Siècle, Revue d'Histoire* 73 (janvier–mars 2002).

Scott, Samuel. "Problems of Law and Order during 1790, the 'Peaceful' Year of the French Revolution." *American Historical Review* 80, no. 4 (1975).

Seager, Frederick. *The Boulanger Affair: Political Crossroad of France.* Ithaca, N.Y.: Cornell University Press, 1969.

Sherrill, Robert. *Military Justice Is to Justice as Military Music Is to Music.* New York: Harper and Row, 1969.

Shklar, Judith. *Legalism: Law, Morals, and Political Trials.* Cambridge, Mass.: Harvard University Press, 1986.

Shorter, Edward. *Strikes in France.* London: Cambridge University Press, 1974.

Soucy, Robert. *Fascism in France: The Case of Maurice Barrès.* Berkeley and Los Angeles: University of California Press, 1972.

Sternhell, Zeev. *Maurice Barrès et le nationalisme français.* Paris: A. Colin, 1972.

Stone, Alex Sweet. *The Birth of Judicial Politics in France: The Constitutional Council in Comparative Perspective.* New York: Oxford University Press, 1992.

Teitel, Ruti. *Transitional Justice.* New York: Oxford University Press, 2000.

Vaïsse, Maurice, and Jean-François Boulanger. "La Conspiration des militaires." In *L'Affaire Dreyfus,* ed. Michel Winock. Paris: Éditions de Seuil, 1998.

Weber, Eugen. *France Fin de Siècle.* Cambridge, Mass.: Harvard University Press, Belknap Press, 1986.

———. *The Nationalist Revival in France, 1905–1914.* Berkeley and Los Angeles: University of California Press, 1968.

Wesseling, H. L. *Soldier and Warrior: French Attitudes toward the Army and War on the Eve of the First World War.* Translated by A. Pomerans. London: Greenwood Press, 2000.

Whyte, George. *The Dreyfus Affair: A Chronological History.* New York: Palgrave Macmillan, 2005.

Wright, Gordon. *France in Modern Times.* Chicago: Rand-McNally, 1960.

Index

www.ingramcontent.com/pod-product-compliance
Lightning Source LLC
LaVergne TN
LVHW091525200926
848483LV00002B/312
9780875804330